Imprints 12

Imprints 12

VOLUME II

Essays
Media
Drama

Kathy Evans
Janet Hannaford
Stuart Poyntz

CONSULTANT
Ann Manson

EDITORIAL TEAM
Joe Banel
Sandra McTavish
Diane Robitaille
Cathy Zerbst

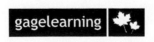
gagelearning

Permissions Editor: Elizabeth Long
Photo Research: Patricia Buckley
Design, Art Direction, & Electronic Assembly: Wycliffe Smith Design, Inc.
Cover Image: J.L. Stanfield/National Geographic/Firstlight.ca

National Library of Canada cataloguing in publication data

Main entry under title:

Imprints 12

For use in grade 12.
Issued also in 1 hardcover vol.
Contents: Essays, media and drama complied by Janet Hannaford, Stuart Poyntz
ISBN 0-7715-0949-9

1. Readers (Secondary). I. Farren, Lori.

PE1121.I537 2002a   428.6   C2001-903083-5

We acknowledge the financial support of the Government of Canada through
the Book Publishing Industry Development Program for our publishing activities.

ISBN-13: 978-0-7715-0949-0
ISBN-10: 0-7715-0949-9

6 7 8 9   16 15 14 13
Printed and bound in Canada

The selections collected in *Imprints* are drawn from a wide variety of sources. To respect
the integrity of these sources, Gage has preserved the original spelling, grammar, and
punctuation used by each author. Gage editorial style, however, is used throughout for
activities and other text generated by Gage writers.

Nelson Education Ltd.
1120 Birchmount Road,
Toronto, Ontario M1K 5G4.
Or you can visit our Internet site at www.nelson.com

Table of Contents

Essays and Other Non-Fiction

Media

Alternate Table of Contents

Essays
and Other Non-Fiction

Essays are how we speak to one another in print...
a kind of public letter.

Edward Hoagland

What I've Learned From Writing

Speech by Shauna Singh Baldwin

When I was in school—in India in the '70s—my teachers were quite confident that "literature" was written outside the boundaries of the subcontinent, and that anything written in India was "only writing." I have learned from writing that the distinction is irrelevant. Writers don't write because some of us live outside India where writing is magically elevated to the status of "literature." Writers, whether we use narrative or not, write because it helps us make sense of the world, contribute to it, rail at it with a non-violent socially-acceptable weapon —language.

You would not attend writer's conferences if you did not believe in the power of the written word to transform your life, to raise your thoughts above the mundane tasks of working and cooking, sleeping, washing, cleaning, to offer some explanation, some semblance of meaning to the rhythm of each day. We writers begin as readers. At writer's conferences, we come to study the craft, we come to ask one another how we can pry open the door between our conscious and our subconscious, we come for reassurance that all our solitude and our word-wrestling is worthwhile.

I wanted to "be a writer" when I was eleven years old. But to be a writer, I thought I must have some experience to express, something I wanted to say that no one else had said. I wish I had known then, there is no original thought, because all we humans think and feel has been thought and felt so many times before, by so many generations. There is only original perspective, there are only permutations of scenarios. As

Note: "What I've Learned From Writing" was a keynote speech delivered at the Great Lakes Writer's Conference held June 1998 at Alverno College, Wisconsin.

I grew older, the cacophony of the world grew ever louder and soon it seemed all the things that needed to be said were being said by others, all the interesting stories had already been told, told so much better than I could tell them. I now know from other writers that even my experience in this is not unique. But at the time, I fell silent like a child who stops singing because the singers on the radio are so much better.

The challenge of the adult writer is to recover that child who was so confident, ask it what it still needs to say, and find out what shape to give its thoughts that will hold a reader's attention.

There is an old saying I've heard attributed to many famous writers, "Writing is when you sit before the typewriter and bleed." It is the cheapest form of therapy, but no one tells you this: you perform it on yourself, unattended, alone, and you suffer the consequences alone. I'd like to start a campaign to put warning labels on pens, pads, word processing software, and especially post-it notes!

When the urge to scribble turns coherent, it's really difficult to know where to begin. I kept a writer's journal sporadically through my teens converting personal angst, pain and fun times to text; I'm glad it was something no one read but I. But the habit was a good one and today I am never without my writer's journal. A writer's journal is different from a diary, because you fill it with description, not merely with events, but with thoughts, with the texture of the present. It becomes a treasury of moments when words sang.

I wrote poetry—who doesn't?—through school and college, and it wasn't till I was thirty that I attempted my first (non-fiction) book: *A Foreign Visitor's Survival Guide to America*. I wrote it with a co-author, who gave it balance in perspective and gave me confidence. When we began, it was from an artless confidence that we had something to say, that there was a gap in the universe where this book should be, and that we were the ones who had both the lived experience and the research capability to do it.

By the time we'd finished, we were amazed at how much the book had taught us: about ourselves; about our friendship; about our values; and view of the world; about the need for accuracy in word choice. When an editor challenged our ideas we had to agree upon and stand behind each word in that book. By the end of the process when we had internalized the *Chicago Manual of Style*, we knew we would never have written that book if we'd known how arduous the process would be.

So, what did I learn?

Begin with the desire to speak into silence, begin from passion.

My next book, *English Lessons and Other Stories*, is about Indian women in my three countries, India, Canada and the U.S.A. I began it in 1992 and it came to publication in 1996. In it, I began to move past my lived experience and personal problems to enter the earliest form of role-playing game, the virtual reality game that predates computers: the world of fiction. In doing so, a new question rose. No longer "what is writing," but "what makes writing memorable?"

To answer this I returned to dog-eared friends whose words were more likely to be highlighted than not, and I read and reread their wonderfully-scented yellowing pages to find the answer that worked for me: Writers we remember are those who set aside their egos, moved from the purely personal to address the human condition, writers who help us all with this daily business of living, to give us inspiration past entertainment, past culture, past their times.

I also had to find an acceptable answer to the question—for whom do you write? I'm a hybrid of three cultures, Indian, Canadian and American and I write from the perspective of all three. Today my answer is: I write for the people I love, a hybrid, global audience, for people interested in the process of becoming human, the ways in which we live, the influence of history, philosophy, culture, tradition and memory on our sense of self.

After my book of short stories, a novel came to me slowly. I call it *What the Body Remembers*. This novel moved into my life about two years ago and is still in residence in our home. It has to be fed in the morning and cleaned up in the evening. It began shyly, revealing itself in snatches: strange people were talking and I would write down what they said first and then ask myself, "which character is this?"

I now had to appreciate the distinction between a poem, a short story and a novel: Most poems without narrative are likely to be static, where the poet comments on a situation or presents a problem and solution but does not show change in setting, or events. In a short story, the writer's job is to open a window into a situation and let the reader be a voyeur of sorts. The reader's job is to find the significance, tie up loose ends—in short, the reader has the responsibility to imagine. A novel, on the other hand, allows a writer room to stretch, place to expound, philosophize, and here the worst sin the writer can commit is to lose sight of the story and the characters. The reader has far less responsibility to imagine in this form of writing. In the short story and in the novel, the writer is confined only by the first rule of drama: causality. In both short stories and novels there must be conflict, but for there to be drama, the reader must be able to see cause and effect—coincidence in narrative is not appreciated, it's too real. So in writing my novel, I found that it felt like coding a good piece of software, designing a system, building a house—in other words, it's like any other creative endeavor—every detail, every word, should be there for a reason.

Now I began to truly appreciate writers through the ages who wrote without word processors, all those writers who did their research without the Internet, the Milwaukee Public Library system and interlibrary loan, all the writers who travelled miles to interview their sources, instead of sending out an email or picking up the phone.

I hope you will not believe mine is the usual progression. Some writers are comfortable with novels immediately, some enjoy the short story form always, some stay with poems. There are pitfalls along the way: some people enjoy being writers more than they enjoy writing. Others prefer to have written than to write. Some of us get perfect manuscript syndrome. Some of us walk into bookstores and realise

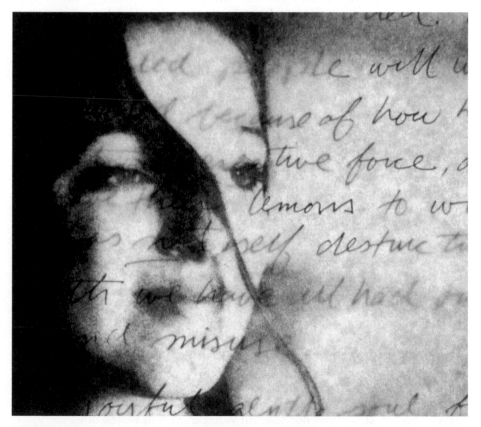

Woman and Handwritten Letter by Brandtner and Staedeli. Photo

Explain the impact this photo has on you and suggest reasons for including it with this essay.

we're competing for limited shelf space with every writer who has ever written and we go home and get writer's block for a month. But it's all part of the game—we write because we need to. And if it were really that easy, wouldn't everyone be doing it? We take from the world and give back, hopefully with beauty and philosophy or entertainment value and our own unique perspective added along the way.

Though we may all hear the same words at this writer's conference, we each learn something unique. I think that's because each of us is at a different stage of readiness to receive from and give to the world.

I'm still developing as a writer, letting the process teach me empathy as I venture deeper into the minds and hearts of selves I might have been if I wasn't me. I'm no longer quite as concerned about who will read my work, or even if anyone will. When it's published, my novel will sit on an overloaded bookshelf and invite some seeking soul to read it, and I hope he or she will find my characters good company. For myself, I hope I will have moved on by then to another book.

Shauna Singh Baldwin was born in Montréal, Canada, but was raised in India. She worked as an independent public radio producer from 1991–1994. In 1974, she won the national Shastri Award (Silver Medal) for English Prose and in 1995, the Writer's Union of Canada Award for Short Prose.

1. Response
a. This selection was the keynote speech given at a writer's conference. What advice from this selection do you think audience members would find most helpful? Explain why you think so.
b. Were you surprised by anything Shauna Singh Baldwin had to say about writing? If so, explain your surprise to a partner.
c. Reread two paragraphs from this speech aloud. What has the author done to make the speech effective? Consider techniques such as diction, rhythm, repetition, breaks or pauses in sentences, and parallel structure.

2. Literature Studies *Structure* With a partner, examine this speech and answer the following questions: How has this author structured her speech? What transition words does she use to connect each section of the speech? How is each section supported? Assess the effectiveness of the introduction and conclusion, the speech's overall structure, and its clarity, logical development, and supporting details.

What is the most important quality that a reader can possess? Read on to find out Virginia Woolf's opinion on the matter.

How Should One Read a Book?

Essay by Virginia Woolf

In the first place, I want to emphasise the note of interrogation at the end of my title. Even if I could answer the question for myself, the answer would apply only to me and not to you. The only advice, indeed, that one person can give another about reading is to take no advice, to follow your own instincts, to use your own reason, to come to your own conclusions. If this is agreed between us, then I feel at liberty to put forward a few ideas and suggestions because you will not allow them to fetter that independence which is the most important quality that a reader can possess. After all, what laws can be laid down about books? The battle of Waterloo was certainly fought on a certain day; but is *Hamlet* a better play than *Lear*? Nobody can say. Each must decide that question for himself. To admit authorities, however heavily furred and gowned, into our libraries and let them tell us how to read, what to read, what value to place upon what we read, is to destroy the spirit of freedom which is the breath of those sanctuaries. Everywhere else we may be bound by laws and conventions—there we have none.

But to enjoy freedom, if the platitude is pardonable, we have of course to control ourselves. We must not squander our powers, helplessly and ignorantly, squirting half the house in order to water a single rose-bush; we must train them, exactly and powerfully, here on the very spot. This, it may be, is one of the first difficulties that faces us in a library. What is "the very spot"? There may well seem to be nothing but a conglomeration and huddle of confusion. Poems and novels, histories and memoirs, dictionaries and blue-books; books written in all languages by men and women of all tempers, races, and ages jostle each other on the shelf. And outside the donkey brays, the women gossip at the pump, the colts gallop across the fields. Where are we to begin? How are we to bring order into this multitudinous chaos and so get the deepest and widest pleasure from what we read?

It is simple enough to say that since books have classes—fiction, biography, poetry—we should separate them and take from each what it is right that each should give us. Yet few people ask from books what books can give us. Most commonly we come to books with blurred and divided minds, asking of fiction that it shall be true, of poetry that it shall be false, of biography that it shall be flattering, of history that it shall enforce our own prejudices. If we could banish all such preconceptions when we read, that would be an admirable beginning. Do not dictate to your author; try to become him. Be his fellow-worker and accomplice. If you hang back, and reserve and criticise at first, you are preventing yourself from getting the fullest possible value from what you read. But if you open your mind as widely as possible, then signs and hints of almost imperceptible fineness, from the twist and turn of the first sentences, will bring you into the presence of a human being unlike any other. Steep yourself in this, acquaint yourself with this, and soon you will find that your author is giving you, or attempting to give you, something far more definite. The thirty-two chapters of a novel—if we consider how to read a novel first—are an attempt to make something as formed and controlled as a building: but the words are more impalpable than bricks; reading is a longer and more complicated process than seeing. Perhaps the quickest way to understand the elements of what a novelist is doing is not to read, but to write; to make your own experiment with the dangers and difficulties of words. Recall, then, some event that has left a distinct impression on you—how at the corner of the street, perhaps, you passed two people talking. A tree shook; an electric light danced; the tone of the talk was comic, but also tragic; a whole vision, an entire conception, seemed contained in that moment.

But when you attempt to reconstruct it in words, you will find that it breaks into a thousand conflicting impressions. Some must be subdued; others emphasised; in the process you will lose, probably, all grasp upon the emotion itself. Then turn from your blurred and littered pages to the opening pages of some great novelist—Defoe, Jane Austen, Hardy. Now you will be better able to appreciate their mastery. It is not merely that we are in the presence of a different person—Defoe, Jane Austen, or Thomas Hardy—but that we are living in a different world. Here, in *Robinson Crusoe*, we are trudging a plain high road; one thing happens after another; the fact and the order of the fact is enough. But if the open air and adventure mean everything to Defoe they mean nothing to Jane Austen. Hers is the drawing-room, and people talking, and by the many mirrors of their talk revealing their characters. And if, when we have accustomed ourselves to the drawing-room and its reflections, we turn to Hardy, we are once more spun round. The moors are round us and the stars are above our heads. The other side of the mind is now exposed—the dark side that comes uppermost in solitude, not the light side that shows in company. Our relations are not toward people, but toward Nature and destiny. Yet different as these worlds are, each is consistent with itself. The maker of each is careful to observe the laws of his own perspective, and however great a strain they may put upon us they will never confuse us, as lesser writers so frequently do, by introducing two different kinds of reality into the same book. Thus to go from one great novelist to another—from Jane Austen to Hardy, from Peacock to Trollope, from Scott to Meredith—is to be wrenched and uprooted; to be thrown this way and then that. To read a novel is a difficult and complex art. You must be capable not only of great fineness of perception, but of great boldness of imagination if you are going to make use of all that the novelist—the great artist—gives you.

But a glance at the heterogeneous company on the shelf will show you that writers are very seldom "great artists"; far more often a book makes no claim to be a work of art at all. These biographies and autobiographies, for example, lives of great men, of men long dead and forgotten, that stand cheek by jowl with the novels and poems, are we to refuse to read them because they are not "art"? Or shall we read them, but read them in a different way, with a different aim? Shall we read them in the first place to satisfy that curiosity which possesses us sometimes when in the evening we linger in front of a house where the lights are lit and the blinds are not yet drawn, and each floor of the house shows us a different section of human life in being? Then we are consumed with curiosity about the lives of these people—the servants gossiping, the gentlemen dining, the girl dressing for a party, the old woman at the window with her knitting. Who are they, what are they, what are their names, their occupations, their thoughts, and adventures?

> ... writing is the enemy of forgetfulness, of thoughtlessness. For the writer there is no oblivion. Only endless memory.
>
> Anita Brookner

Biographies and memoirs answer such questions, light up innumerable such houses; they show us people going about their daily affairs, toiling, failing, succeeding, eating, hating, loving, until they die. And sometimes as we watch, the house fades and the iron railings vanish and we are out at sea; we are hunting, sailing, fighting; we are among savages and soldiers; we are taking part in great campaigns. Or if we like to stay here in England, in London, still the scene changes; the street narrows; the house becomes small, cramped, diamond-paned, and malodorous. We see a poet, Donne, driven from such a house because the walls were so thin that when the children cried their voices cut through them. We can follow him, through the paths that lie in the pages of books, to Twickenham;[1] to Lady Bedford's Park, a famous meeting-ground for nobles and poets; and then turn our steps to Wilton,[2] the great house under the downs, and hear Sidney[3] read the *Arcadia* to his sister; and ramble among the very marshes and see the very herons that figure in that famous romance; and then again travel north with that other Lady Pembroke,[4] Anne Clifford,[5] to her wild moors, or plunge into the city and control our merriment at the sight of Gabriel Harvey[6] in his black velvet suit arguing about poetry with Spenser. Nothing is more fascinating than to grope and stumble in the alternate darkness and splendour of Elizabethan London. But there is no staying there. The Temples[7] and the Swifts,[8] the Harleys[9] and the St. Johns[10] beckon us on; hour upon hour can be spent disentangling their quarrels and deciphering their character; and when we tire of them we can stroll on, past a lady in black wearing diamonds, to Samuel Johnson and Goldsmith[11] and Garrick,[12] or cross the channel, if we like, and meet Voltaire[13] and Diderot,[14] Madame du Deffand;[15] and so back to England and Twickenham—how certain places repeat themselves and certain names!—where Lady Bedford had her Park once and Pope lived later, to Walpole's home at Strawberry Hill. But Walpole[16] introduces us to such a swarm of new acquaintances, there are so many houses to visit and bells to ring that we may well hesitate for a moment, on the Miss Berrys'[17] doorstep, for example, when behold up comes Thackeray; he is the friend of the woman whom Walpole loved; so that merely by going from friend to friend, from garden to garden, from house to house, we have passed from one end of English literature to another and wake to find ourselves here again in the present, if we can so differentiate this moment from all that have gone before. This, then, is one of the ways in which we can read these lives and letters; we can make them light up the many windows of the past; we can watch the famous dead in their familiar habits and fancy sometimes that we are very close and can surprise their secrets, and sometimes we may pull out a play or a poem that they have written and see whether it reads differently in the presence of the author. But this again rouses other questions. How far, we must ask ourselves, is a book influenced by its writer's life—how far is it safe to let the man interpret the writer? How far shall we resist or give way to the sympathies and antipathies that the man himself rouses in us—so sensitive are words, so receptive of the character of the author? These are questions that press upon us when we read lives and letters, and we must answer them for ourselves, for nothing can be more fatal than to be guided by the preferences of others in a matter so personal.

But also we can read such books with another aim, not to throw light on literature, not to become familiar with famous people, but to refresh and exercise our own creative powers. Is there not an open window on the right hand of the bookcase? How delightful to stop reading and look out! How stimulating the scene is, in its unconsciousness, its irrelevance, its perpetual movement—the colts galloping round the field, the woman filling her pail at the well, the donkey throwing back his head and emitting his long, acrid moan. The greater part of any library is nothing but the record of such fleeting moments in the lives of men, women, and donkeys. Every literature, as it grows old, has its rubbish-heap, its record of vanished moments and forgotten lives told in faltering and feeble accents that have perished. But if you give yourself up to the delight of rubbish-reading you will be surprised, indeed you will be overcome, by the relics of human life that have been cast out to moulder. It may be one letter—but what a vision it gives! It may be a few sentences—but what vistas they suggest! Sometimes a whole story will come together with such beautiful humour and pathos and completeness that it seems as if a great novelist had been at work, yet it is only an old actor, Tate Wilkinson,[18] remembering the strange story of Captain Jones; it is only a young subaltern[19] serving under Arthur Wellesley[20] and falling in love with a pretty girl at Lisbon; it is only Maria Allen[21] letting fall her sewing in the empty drawing-room and sighing how she wishes she had taken Dr. Burney's good advice and had never eloped with her Rishy. None of this has any value; it is negligible in the extreme; yet how absorbing it is now and again to go through the rubbish-heaps and find rings and scissors and broken noses buried in the huge past and try to piece them together while the colt gallops round the field, the woman fills her pail at the well, and the donkey brays.

But we tire of rubbish-reading in the long run. We tire of searching for what is needed to complete the half-truth which is all that the Wilkinsons, the Bunburys, and the Maria Allens are able to offer us. They had not the artist's power of mastering and eliminating; they could not tell the whole truth even about their own lives; they have disfigured the story that might have been so shapely. Facts are all that they can offer us, and facts are a very inferior form of fiction. Thus the desire grows upon us to have done with half-statements and approximations; to cease from searching out the minute shades of human character; to enjoy the greater abstractness, the purer truth of fiction. Thus we create the mood, intense and generalised, unaware of detail, but stressed by some regular, recurrent beat, whose natural expression is poetry; and that is the time to read poetry when we are almost able to write it.

> Western wind, when wilt thou blow?
> The small rain down can rain.
> Christ, if my love were in my arms,
> And I in my bed again![22]

The impact of poetry is so hard and direct that for the moment there is no other sensation except that of the poem itself. What profound depths we visit then—how sudden and complete is our immersion! There is nothing here to catch hold of; nothing to stay us in our flight. The illusion of fiction is gradual; its effects are prepared; but who when they read these four lines stops to ask who wrote them, or conjures up the thought of Donne's house or Sidney's secretary; or enmeshes them in the intricacy of the past and the succession of generations? The poet is always our contemporary. Our being for the moment is centred and constricted, as in any violent shock of personal emotion. Afterwards, it is true, the sensation begins to spread in wider rings through our minds; remoter senses are reached; these begin to sound and to comment and we are aware of echoes and reflections. The intensity of poetry covers an immense range of emotion. We have only to compare the force and directness of

> I shall fall like a tree, and find my grave,
> Only remembering that I grieve,[23]

with the wavering modulation of

> Minutes are numbered by the fall of sands,
> As by an hour glass; the span of time
> Doth waste us to our graves, and we look on it;
> An age of pleasure, revelled out, comes home
> At last, and ends in sorrow; but the life,
> Weary of riot, numbers every sand,
> Wailing in sighs, until the last drop down,
> So to conclude calamity in rest,[24]

or place the meditative calm of

> whether we be young or old,
> Our destiny, our being's heart and home,
> Is with infinitude, and only there;
> With hope it is, hope that can never die,
> Effort, and expectation, and desire,
> And something evermore about to be,[25]

beside the complete and inexhaustible loveliness of

> The moving Moon went up the sky,
> And nowhere did abide:
> Softly she was going up,
> And a star or two beside—[26]

or the splendid fantasy of

> And the woodland haunter
> Shall not cease to saunter
>   When, far down some glade,
> Of the great world's burning
> One soft flame upturning
> Seems, to his discerning,
>   Crocus in the shade,[27]

to bethink us of the varied art of the poet; his power to make us at once actors and spectators; his power to run his hand into character as if it were a glove, and be Falstaff or Lear; his power to condense, to widen, to state, once and for ever.

"We have only to compare"—with those words the cat is out of the bag, and the true complexity of reading is admitted. The first process, to receive impressions with the utmost understanding, is only half the process of reading; it must be completed, if we are to get the whole pleasure from a book, by another. We must pass judgment upon these multitudinous impressions; we must make of these fleeting shapes one that is hard and lasting. But not directly. Wait for the dust of reading to settle; for the conflict and the questioning to die down; walk, talk, pull

> It is so unsatisfactory to read a noble passage and have no one you love at hand to share the happiness with you.
>
> Clara Clemens

the dead petals from a rose, or fall asleep. Then suddenly without our willing it, for it is thus that Nature undertakes these transitions, the book will return, but differently. It will float to the top of the mind as a whole. And the book as a whole is different from the book received currently in separate phrases. Details now fit themselves into their places. We see the shape from start to finish; it is a barn, a pig-sty, or a cathedral. Now then we can compare book with book as we compare building with building. But this act of comparison means that our attitude has changed; we are no longer the friends of the writer, but his judges; and just as we cannot be too sympathetic as friends, so as judges we cannot be too severe. Are they not criminals, books that have wasted our time and sympathy; are they not the most insidious enemies of society, corrupters, defilers, the writers of false books, faked books, books that fill the air with decay and disease? Let us then be severe in our judgments; let us compare each book with the greatest of its kind. There they hang in the mind, the shapes of the books we have read solidified by the judgments we have passed on them—*Robinson Crusoe, Emma, The Return of the Native*. Compare the novels with these—even the latest and least of novels has a right to be judged with the best. And so with poetry—when the intoxication of rhythm has died down and the splendour of words has faded, a visionary shape will return to us and this must be compared with *Lear*, with *Phedre*, with *The Prelude*; or if not with these, with whatever is the best or seems to us to be the best in its own kind. And we may be sure that the newness of new poetry and fiction is its most superficial quality and that we have only to alter slightly, not to recast, the standards by which we have judged the old.

It would be foolish, then, to pretend that the second part of reading, to judge, to compare, is as simple as the first—to open the mind wide to the fast flocking of innumerable impressions. To continue reading without the book before you, to hold one shadow-shape against another, to have read widely enough and with enough understanding to make such comparisons alive and illuminating—that is difficult; it is still more difficult to press further and to say, "Not only is the book of this sort, but it is of this value; here it fails; here it succeeds; this is bad; that is good." To carry out this part of a reader's duty needs such imagination, insight, and learning that it is hard to conceive any one mind sufficiently endowed; impossible for the most self-confident to find more than the seeds of such powers in himself. Would it not be wiser, then, to remit this part of reading and to allow the critics, the gowned and furred authorities of the library, to decide the question of the book's absolute value for us? Yet how impossible! We may stress the value of sympathy; we may try to sink our own identity as we read. But we know that we cannot sympathise wholly or immerse ourselves wholly; there is always a demon in us who whispers, "I hate, I love," and we cannot silence him. Indeed, it is precisely because we hate and we love that our relation with the poets and novelists is so intimate that we find the presence of another person intolerable. And even if the results are abhorrent and our judgments are wrong, still our taste, the nerve of sensation that sends shocks through us, is our chief illuminant; we learn through feeling; we cannot suppress our own idiosyncrasy without improvising it. But as time goes on perhaps we can train our taste; perhaps we can make it submit to some control. When it has fed greedily and lavishly upon books of all sort—poetry, fiction, history, biography—and has stopped reading and looked for long spaces upon the variety, the incongruity of the living word, we shall find that it is changing a little; it is not so greedy, it is more reflective. It will begin to bring us not merely judgments on particular books, but it will tell us that there is a quality common to certain books. Listen, it will say, what shall we call *this*? And it will read us perhaps *Lear* and then perhaps the *Agamemnon* in order to bring out that common quality. Thus, with our taste to guide us, we shall venture beyond the particular book in search of qualities that group books together; we shall give them names and thus frame a rule that brings order into our perceptions. We shall gain a further and a rarer pleasure from that discrimination. But as a rule only lives when it is perpetually broken by contact with the books themselves—nothing is easier and more stultifying than to make rules which exist out of touch with facts, in a vacuum—now at last, in order to steady ourselves in this difficult attempt, it may be well to turn to the very rare writers who are able to enlighten us upon literature as an art. Coleridge and Dryden and Johnson, in their considered criticism, the poets and novelists themselves in their unconsidered sayings, are often surprisingly relevant; they light up and solidify the vague ideas that have been tumbling in the misty depths of our minds. But they are only able to help us if we come to them laden with questions and suggestions won honestly in the course of our own reading. They can do nothing for us if we herd ourselves under their authority and lie down like sheep in the shade of a hedge. We can only understand their ruling when it comes in conflict with our own and vanquishes it.

If this is so, if to read a book as it should be read calls for the rarest qualities of imagination, insight, and judgment, you may perhaps conclude that literature is a very complex art and that it is unlikely that we shall be able, even after a lifetime of reading, to make any valuable contribution to its criticism. We must remain readers; we shall not put on the further glory that belongs to those rare beings who are also critics.

But still we have our responsibilities as readers and even our importance. The standards we raise and the judgment we pass steal into the air and become part of the atmosphere which writers breathe as they work. An influence is created which tells upon them even if it never finds its way into print. And that influence, if it were well instructed, vigorous and individual and sincere, might be of great value now when criticism is necessarily in abeyance; when books pass in review like the procession of animals in a shooting gallery, and the critic has only one second in which to load and aim and shoot and may well be pardoned if he mistakes rabbits for tigers, eagles for barndoor fowls, or misses altogether and wastes his shot upon some peaceful cow grazing in a further field. If behind the erratic gunfire of the press the author felt that there was another kind of criticism, the opinion of people reading for the love of reading, slowly and unprofessionally, and judging with great sympathy and yet with great severity, might this not improve the quality of his work? And if by our means books were to become stronger, richer, and more varied, that would be an end worth reaching.

Yet who reads to bring about an end, however desirable? Are there not some pursuits that we practise because they are good in themselves, and some pleasures that are final? And is not this among them? I have sometimes dreamt, at least, that when the Day of Judgment dawns and the great conquerors and lawyers and statesmen come to receive their rewards—their crowns, their laurels, their names carved indelibly upon imperishable marble—the Almighty will turn to Peter and will say, not without a certain envy when He sees us coming with our books under our arms, "Look, these need no reward. We have nothing to give them here. They have loved reading."

---

[1]**Twickenham:** city on the Thames, near London
[2]**Wilton:** town in England
[3]**Sidney:** Sir Philip Sidney (1554–1586), English poet, soldier, and statesman
[4]**Pembroke:** Sidney's sister was Mary, Countess of Pembroke, whose country house was at Wilton
[5]**Anne Clifford:** Anne Clifford Herbert, Countess of Pembroke (1590–1676); her diary was published in 1923
[6]**Gabriel Harvey:** English author (circa 1545–1630)
[7]**The Temples:** Sir William Temple (1628–1699), English author and statesman
[8]**the Swifts:** Jonathan Swift, *cf.* "A Modest Proposal" above
[9]**the Harleys:** Robert Harley, first Earl of Oxford (1661–1724), English statesman, left a valuable collection of manuscripts and pamphlets

[10]**the St. Johns:** Henry St. John, first Viscount Bolingbroke (1678–1751), English statesman and writer
[11]**Goldsmith:** Oliver Goldsmith (1728–1784), English poet, novelist, and dramatist
[12]**Garrick:** David Garrick (1717–1779), English actor
[13]**Voltaire:** born François Marie Arouet (1694–1778), French satirist, philosopher, and historian, known as Voltaire
[14]**Diderot:** Denis Diderot (1713–1784), French philosopher and encyclopedist
[15]**Madame du Deffand:** Marie de Vichy-Chamrond, Marquise du Deffand (1697–1780), witty and cynical Frenchwoman, leader in Parisian literary and philosophical circles
[16]**Walpole:** Horace Walpole, fourth Earl of Oxford (1717–1797), English author
[17]**the Miss Berrys:** Mary Berry (1763–1852), English authoress, and Agnes Berry (1764–1852), were both friends of Horace Walpole
[18]**Wilkinson:** English actor (1739–1803), fond of telling stories of real people, author of *Memoirs of His Own Life*; see V. Woolf's *Death of the Moth*
[19]**subaltern:** see *Memoirs and Literary Remains* of Lieutenant-General Sir Edward Henry Bunbury, bart. (1868)
[20]**Arthur Wellesley:** Duke of Wellington, English general and statesman (1769–1852)
[21]**Maria Allen:** see William S. Allen, *Memoirs of Mrs. Allen of Woodbread Hall, Staffordshire*, 1871; mentioned by V. Woolf in two essays in *Granite and Rainbow*. (With thanks to Professors James Hafley, Donald Weeks, and J. J. Wilson, for these and following identifications.)
[22]anonymous Renaissance lyric
[23]from John Ford's *Lovers' Melancholy*
[24]ibid.
[25]from Wordsworth's *Prelude*, Book VI
[26]from Coleridge's *Ancient Mariner*
[27]from Ebenezer Jones' *When the World Is Burning*

Virginia Woolf, British novelist, critic, and essayist, was born in 1882. She was a leader in the literary movement of modernism, and used a "stream of consciousness" technique in her writing, which revealed her characters' lives by representing the flow of their thoughts and perceptions. Her works include the novels *To the Lighthouse, Orlando,* and *Mrs. Dalloway*, and the essay, *"A Room of One's Own."*

1. Response
a. Using your own words, develop a short summary of Woolf's argument in this essay. Discuss your summary with a classmate.
b. Why does Woolf suggest that readers "try to become" the author they are reading? Do you agree with the point she is trying to make? Why or why not?
c. Find one analogy in the essay and explain to a partner why it is or is not effective.
d. What is Woolf's final answer to the question she raises in the title? Explain your own position on this question.

2. Making Connections Reread the fourth paragraph and consider what Woolf is saying about the different worlds a novelist creates. Do you agree or disagree with her point? Choose one novelist she mentions, or another classic novelist, and describe the world he/she creates for you. How do you respond to this world? Do you choose to read certain novels because of how much you enjoy the world they create? Explain.

3. Focus on Context In the fifth paragraph, Woolf refers to "These biographies and autobiographies, for example, lives of great men, of men long dead and forgotten ..." Why do you think she does not use the gender-neutral phrase "lives of great people"? Use Internet or print resources to research the life of this great woman—Virginia Woolf—and then write a report explaining her use of gender-biassed language.

4. Writing *Essay* Brainstorm some questions that you consider important or essential, like Woolf's question, "How should one read a book?" Develop an outline for an essay that explores possible answers to that question. Use your outline to help you write an essay. Your title could be the original question you posed.

Theme Connections

- *"Two Words," a story about the power of words, Vol. I, p. 51*
- *"Making Poetry Pay," an anecdote about the power of words, Vol. II, p. 40*
- *"What Will Your Verse Be?" a movie monologue about the importance of language, Vol. II, p. 270*

Art History

Speech by Doreen Jensen

In my language, there is no word for "Art." This is not because we are devoid of Art, but because Art is so powerfully integrated with all aspects of life, we are replete with it. For the sake of brevity and clarity, I will use the word "Art" tonight.

This exhibition and forum, "Indigena," asks us to reflect on the impact of European colonization on indigenous cultures. In my talk, I'd like to offer a different perspective. I would like to remind you of the Art that the Europeans found when they arrived in our country.

The Europeans found Art everywhere. In hundreds of flourishing, vital cultures, Art was fully integrated with daily life. They saw dwellings painted with abstract Art that was to inspire generations of European painters. Ceremonial robes were intricately woven Art that heralded the wearers' identity and privilege in the community. Utilitarian objects, including food vessels, storage containers, and clothing, were powerfully formed and decorated with the finest, most significant Art.

Each nation had its theatre, music, and choreography. The first Europeans found hundreds of languages in use—not dialects but languages. And in every language, our Artists created philosophical argument and sacred ceremony, political discourse, fiction, and poetry.

The Europeans saw Earth Art and large-scale environmental Art projects. From the East to the West Coast, what were later called petroglyphs and pictographs recorded our histories. My own earliest memories of Art are of the tall sculptures that told the long histories of my people. These tall sculptures are called "totem poles," like the ones you see here in the Great Hall of the Museum of Civilization.

When the Europeans arrived, they found Aboriginal Artists creating beauty, culture, and historical memory. Art built bridges between human life and the natural world. Art mediated between material and spiritual concerns. Art stimulated our individuality, making us alert and alive. It affirmed our cultural identities.

I say all this to honour our cultural accomplishments. As Aboriginal Artists, we need to reclaim our own identities, through our work, our heritage and our future. We don't need any longer to live within others' definitions of who and what we are. We need to put aside titles that have been imposed on our creativity—titles that serve the needs of other people. For too long our Art has been situated in the realm of anthropology by a discourse that validates only white Artists.

Today there are many Art forms of the First Nations which are still not being recognized. Think of the exquisite sea grass baskets from the West Coast of Vancouver Island, the quill work and moose hair tufting Arts of the people east of the Rockies, and ceremonial robes, woven and appliquéd, throughout North America. Not surprisingly, these exquisite works of Art are mainly done by women.

Art can be a universal language which helps us bridge the gaps between our different cultures. But attitudes towards Art reveal racism. The first Europeans called our Art "primitive" and "vulgar." Today, people of European origin call our Art "craft" and "artifact."

Our elders have nurtured the important cultural traditions against tremendous odds. It is time for us to sit still, and let these powerful, precious teachings come to us. Our elders bequeathed us a great legacy of communication through the Arts.

Art is essential, for all of us. Artists are our spiritual advisers. In another five hundred years, who is going to remember Prime-Minister-What's-His-Name or Millionaire-What's-His-Name? Our cultural life—our Art—is all we will be remembered by.

I believe that culture is the soul of the nation. Canada *is* the First Nations. Canada *is* the English and the French who have struggled to make a new world here. Canada *is* also the other cultures who come to make a new life. The culture of the Indigenous people is the fertile soil where these new cultures are flourishing.

Think of the important Iroquois symbol of the eagle with five feathers in its talons. Because it is such a powerful image, the American government appropriated it to use as its insignia and cultural identity. This is just one tiny example of the unacknowledged appropriation of Indian Art which has nourished North American culture for five centuries.

As we enter this new age that is being called "The Age of Information," I like to think it is the age when healing will take place. This is a good time to acknowledge our accomplishments. This is a good time to share. We need to learn from the wisdom of our ancestors. We need to recognize the hard work of our predecessors which has brought us to where we are today. We need to look to the future, and to where we can incorporate our own wisdom and vision in a healing culture for all peoples.

During the Oka crisis, Canada's mask slipped to reveal the ugly and treacherous face of racism. At last, people could see the many injustices that need to be changed in order for Canada to become a strong country. Some cultural institutions have opened their doors a crack, and begun to take initiatives to mend the cultural fabric of Canada. All cultural institutions need to begin dialogues with Aboriginal people, and develop frameworks within which we can work together on a just representation of Aboriginal cultures.

First Nations Artists have something vitally important to offer—a new (or ancient) aesthetic, a way of understanding Art and the world that can heal this country, and help us all to find a place in it.

For North West Coast Indian Artists, the act of creativity comes from the cosmos. That is what I have been told by the old people. When I'm making Art, I am one with the universe. You can see it in the work, if you look with your heart, as well as your mind. If you really pay attention, you can "get the message"—and make it your own, without diminishing it or appropriating it.

If we pay attention, First Nations Art will remind us of this basic rule for being a human being: When I diminish others' "belongingness" in the universe, my own "belongingness" becomes uncertain.

Canada is an image which hasn't emerged yet. Because this country hasn't recognized its First Nations, its whole foundation is shaky. If Canada is to emerge as a nation with cultural identity and purpose, we have to accept First Nations Art, and what it has to tell us about the spirit and the land.

Our Art is our cultural identity; it's our politics. The late George Manuel said, "This land is our culture." I add to that, "Our culture is this land." Whether you acknowledge it or ignore it, the land and the culture are one. Land claims have to be settled, before Canadians can look at themselves in the mirror and see an image they would be proud to see.

George Erasmus said, "What has happened in the last five hundred years is not important. What is important is what we do in the next five hundred years."

Everywhere it is a time for choices. There is still white water ahead. The choices we make today can alter our course forever, not only nationally but throughout the world.

Today is a time to share, a time to enjoy the glory of your achievements. I congratulate all of you who have made this exhibition possible: the curators, the writers, and the museum. Most importantly, I thank you, the Artists—who have shared your personal visions.

Grizzly Bear Headdress, work in progress by Doreen Jensen.

Photos by Vickie Jensen

Examine the above photos and write a description of the
artwork they depict. Include your personal response to this
work of art.

Doreen Jensen (originally Hahl Yee) is a graduate of the Kitanmax School of North West Coast Indian Art and has won many awards for her work. Her first language is Gitksan, and she describes herself as a "traditional Gitksan artist," working in the fields of sculpture, performance art, songs, dance, writing, and fabric art. Jensen actively promotes Aboriginal cultures and works toward getting contemporary Aboriginal art into Canada's major art museums.

1. *Response*
a. What is Doreen Jensen trying to get her audience to understand or accept? What are her main points?
b. Do you agree with Jensen's main points? Why or why not?
c. Consider the first sentence as an example of concise writing. What information is conveyed in just nine words?
d. Look up the words *indigenous* and *aboriginal* to find their roots, and to compare their meanings. Also look up *First Nations* and *Indian,* and find out more about their meanings and preferred usage.

2. *Oral Language* *Group Discussion* With three or four classmates, respond to the following questions: What various forms does "art" encompass? How important is art to you? To your community or culture? Do you agree that art is all we will be remembered by? If so, what form or what particular piece of art would you choose to represent you and your community or culture?

3. *Literature Studies* *Persuasive Writing* In persuasive writing, writers state a thesis and provide support or evidence for their opinion. They often use logical reasoning and appeal to readers' emotions. Sometimes, they also predict any opposing viewpoints and refute them. Using the above criteria, assess the effectiveness of this selection.

4. *Focus on Context* Jensen delivered this as a talk at the Museum of Civilization in Hull, Québec, in 1992, for the opening of the display called "Indigena: Perspectives of Indigenous Peoples on Five Hundred Years." What clues are there in the selection that it was written for a specific purpose, and that it was an oral presentation? How has her context affected her content?

The artist, Gu Xiong, grew up in China during the
Cultural Revolution. During that time, the art he was
exposed to consisted mainly of postcards produced by
unknown artists during that period, and the works of the
Group of Seven. In fact, the Group of Seven paintings
formed his impressions of Canada. Gu Xiong produced
the following art exhibit with Canadian artist and curator
Andrew Hunter, to juxtapose the different images of
China and Canada that influenced them and their work.

Images From the
Cultural
Revolution

from an Art Exhibit
compiled by
Gu Xiong
and
Andrew Hunter

Mountains and Lake, 1929 by Lawren S. Harris.

只有解放全人類
才能最後解放無產
階級自己。

Sunlight Tapestry, circa 1939, by A.Y. Jackson

White Pine, circa 1957, by A. J. Casson.

Essays

Gu Xiong was born in the Sichuan province of the People's Republic of China in 1953. He was forced to flee China after the Tiananmen Square demonstrations in 1989. He now lives in Vancouver.

I. *Response*
a. In your own words, explain why Gu Xiong and Andrew Hunter chose to display these Chinese postcards from the Cultural Revolution with works by the Group of Seven.

b. Choose one image—either a postcard or painting—and record your response to it. How does the image make you feel? What does it make you think of? What does it remind you of? Share your response with a classmate.

c. If the Group of Seven paintings were the only Canadian artwork Gu Xiong saw as a youngster, how do you think he would have felt about Canada?

2. *Research and Inquiry* Use the Internet or library resources to investigate one member of the Group of Seven or a Chinese artist of the Cultural Revolution. Find out what influenced the artist, and the effect his/her work has had on others. Develop a two-page report on the artist, including an assessment of one piece of his/her art.

3. *Visual Communication* *Art Exhibit* Create a visual essay that juxtaposes two major influences in your life. Write a fifty-word introduction to your essay explaining the images you have chosen.

4. *Film Study* Investigate the life of an artist as portrayed in movies by watching a movie like *My Left Foot, Frida, Pollock, Lust for Life, Artemesia,* or *Basquiat.* Investigate the artist's life further by examining some print texts as well, such as a biography or autobiography. In your opinion, what advantages and disadvantages does a movie have in offering a portrayal of the life of an artist?

Stone
Faces

from an Essay by Sharon Butala

"I am always trying to see this land as it must have been before farmers plowed it, before domesticated cattle came to graze it bare, before there were highways, towns, power poles, and rows of gleaming steel grain bins."

On a clear fall morning, I went to St. Victor Historic Petroglyphs Park south of Moose Jaw. I climbed and climbed in my borrowed car to the top of the Wood Mountain Uplands until I reached the park gate, stopped, got out, found the stairs, and began the long climb on foot to the top of the cliff where the glyphs are incised on the horizontal surface of the rock. I was the only person in the entire park, and, in the stillness and the clarity of that morning, I felt my solitude gravely and as a blessing.

At the top I stopped and looked around. The beautiful, treed village of St. Victor was lost in foliage below, and to the north and on an angle beyond it Montague Lake shone softly. I could see for miles in two directions where not a soul, a bird, a cow stirred. On the still air a noise came faintly from the direction of the lake a mile or more away; I listened hard, trying to identify it. At first I thought it was a farm dog barking, then it seemed there was more than one voice and I thought, oh, coyotes, but no, the sound came clearer and I realized it was geese, pausing for water and to search out wheat kernels in the nearby farmer's field that had been thrown over during combining, as sustenance to strengthen them for their journey south. All alone and with no pressing business, I took the time to gaze and gaze out across the landscape. Soon two mule deer broke out of the brush below where I stood, climbed a wooded ridge and disappeared over its crown.

Eventually I remembered to look at the glyphs, which were at my feet immediately on the other side of the railing I was leaning on.

It took a moment, after that dazzling, endless view, to bring my mind and my eyes into focus so I could pick them out. Then I saw a human face staring up at me, carved when, no one is sure, and by whom, no one knows. Something unexpected gripped me quickly, hard, deep in my abdomen, a chill, a *frisson* of the numinous, and then let go.

In that silence and stillness I became aware of the sun hanging huge and yellow just above the back of my head, the guardian, the Other, the powerful and constant presence at that place. Its angled rays brought the many glyphs, invisible in higher light, into existence; each morning and each evening its rays created them anew: human hand-prints, faces and footprints, grizzly bear claws, bison hoofprints leading over the edge of the high cliff.

That year I had time to go to only one more prehistoric rock art site before winter snows covered them. This one is on another high, gently rounded, long hill, this time above a creek, and overlooks the small city of Swift Current. Here, two bison, their bodies chipped out of the rock till they form small basins, sat enigmatically just where they'd been for as long as two or three thousand years.

"Why would they do it?" an archaeologist asked me rhetorically. "They aren't work; that is, they don't produce food or clothing, or make houses. Think how hard this must have been to do, how long it must have taken. Their people must have seen it as important, and it follows, then, that these must have had to do with their spiritual life."

I am always trying to see this land as it must have been before farmers plowed it, before domesticated cattle came to graze it bare, before there were highways, towns, power poles, and rows of gleaming steel grain bins. I try to imagine it as the prehistoric people who lived here must have seen it and, from that, to feel what they might have felt. Now I rose from kneeling in the grass beside the stone bison and looked out toward the city where once there had been only uncounted hills and grass. At that moment it seemed less real than the petroglyph I'd come a hundred miles to see.

As I'd driven out of the yard that morning on my way to the edge of this distant city, the sun on my right was only a faint yellow gleam below the horizon, and on my left a white, three-quarter moon was riding the serpentine hills. For miles as I drove the deserted highway I watched the sun rise. First a red glow, then a radiant ruby arc like molten metal dissolving to gold at the edges, then the sun was above the horizon and too bright to look at. I began to watch its light pouring across the fields that flanked the highway, and beyond them the near hills, and behind them the land, as it lifted chunkily in blue folds toward the sky.

To ask what a carving in stone of a turtle, paintings or carvings of other animals and humans on or in stone, or human or animal footprints *mean* is to be distracted by something that seems to me irrelevant and unimportant. What matters is that they were *done* by humans like you and me. In such beauty there can be no response but awe. It was not an accident that all these sites had stunning views across miles of land with a clear view of the setting sun (sometimes the rising sun, I'm told) . . . It was the act of a people who, whether living ten thousand or two hundred years ago, knew desire and hope, remembered long and well, felt respect and reverence, had a sense of grace—had souls as puny and as magnificent, as various as ours.

Sharon Butala was born in Saskatchewan, Canada, in 1940 and attended the University of Saskatchewan. Her first novel, *Country of the Heart*, was nominated for the Books in Canada Best First Novel Award.

1. *Response*
a. Have you ever seen a petroglyph? Describe or sketch it. How did your response to it compare with that of Butala?
b. Butala's essay combines elements of descriptive and narrative essay techniques. Identify an exemplary passage for each type of essay.
c. Find some photos or paintings of the Saskatchewan landscape. How do you relate to that landscape?

2. *Language Focus* Word Choices
Professional writers make careful word choices to create exactly the image or message they want to get across to the reader. For example, consider Butala's use of the verbs "a cow *stirred*" and "light *pouring*." Substitute "moved" and "shining," respectively. Why are those verbs less effective?

Choose a part of speech, such as a verb, adjective, adverb, or noun, and find examples in this essay of effective word choices for that part of speech. Try substituting other words to see how effective Butala's words are.

3. *Making Connections*
With a partner, discuss "Art History" and "Stone Faces." Write a letter in role, from one author to the other, in which you comment on the other's selection and on how your ideas and opinions compare. Your partner can respond to your letter in role as the other author.

Langston Hughes was a central figure in the Harlem Renaissance—
a time of rising expression of African-American culture in the 1920s
and '30s. During the '30s and '40s, Hughes often went on tour to read
his poetry. In this selection, he recounts details
from his public readings.

Making Poetry Pay

Personal Essay
by Langston Hughes

By midwinter I had worked out a public routine of reading my poetry that almost never failed to provoke, after each
poem, some sort of audible audience response—laughter,
applause, a grunt, a groan, a sigh, or an "Amen!" I began my
programs quite simply by telling where I was born in Missouri,
that I grew up in Kansas in the geographical heart of the country, and was therefore very American, that I belonged to a family that was always moving; and I told something of my early
travels about the Midwest and how, at fourteen, in Lincoln, Illi-
nois, I was elected Class Poet for the eighth-grade graduating
exercises, and from then on I kept writing poetry.

After this biographical introduction I would read to my
audiences the first of my poems, written in high school, and
show how my poetry had changed over the years. To start my
reading, I usually selected some verses written when I was
about fifteen:

> *I had my clothes cleaned*
> *Just like new.*
> *I put 'em on but*
> *I still feels blue.*
>
> *I bought a new hat,*
> *Sho is fine,*
> *But I wish I had back that*
> *Old gal o' mine*
>
> *I got new shoes,*
> *They don't hurt my feet,*
> *But I ain't got nobody*
> *To call me sweet.*

Then I would say, "That's a sad poem, isn't it?" Everybody would laugh. Then I would read some of my jazz poems so my listeners could laugh more. I wanted them to laugh a lot early in the program, so that later in the evening they would not laugh when I read poems like "Porter":

> *I must say,*
> *Yes, sir;*
> *To you all the time.*
> *Yes, sir!*
> *Yes, sir!*
>
> *All my days*
> *Climbing up a great big mountain*
> *Of yes, sirs!*
>
> *Rich old white man*
> *Owns the world.*
> *Gimme yo' shoes to shine.*
>
> *Yes, sir, boss!*
> *Yes, sir!*

By the time I reached this point in the program my nonliterary listeners would be ready to think in terms of their own problems. Then I read poems about women domestics, workers on the Florida roads, poor black students wanting to shatter the darkness of ignorance and prejudice, and one about the sharecroppers of the Mississippi:

Just a herd of Negroes
Driven to the field,
Plowing, planting, hoeing,
To make the cotton yield.

When the cotton's picked
And the work is done,
Boss man takes the money
And you get none.

Just a herd of Negroes
Driven to the field.
Plowing, planting, hoeing,
To make the cotton yield.

Many of my verses were documentary, journalistic and topical. All across the South that winter I read my poems about the plight of the Scottsboro boys[1]:

Justice is a blind goddess.
To this we blacks are wise:
Her bandage hides two festering sores
That once perhaps were eyes.

Usually people were deeply attentive. But if at some point in the program my audience became restless—as audiences sometimes will, no matter what a speaker is saying—or if I looked down from the plat-form and noticed someone about to go to sleep, I would pull out my ace in the hole, a poem called "Cross." This poem, delivered dramatically, I had learned, would make anybody, white or black, sit up and take notice. It is a poem about miscegenation—a very provocative subject in the South. The first line—intended to awaken all sleepers—I would read in a loud voice:

My old man's a white old man....

And this would usually arouse any one who dozed. Then I would pause before continuing in a more subdued tone:

My old mother's black.

---

[1] **Scottsboro boys:** In 1931, in Alabama, nine black teenage boys were falsely accused of raping two white girls. The struggle for justice in the case went on for years.

Then in a low, sad, thoughtful tragic vein:

> *But if ever I cursed my white old man*
> *I take my curses back.*
>
> *If ever I cursed my black old mother*
> *And wished she were in hell,*
> *I'm sorry for that evil wish*
> *And now I wish her well.*
>
> *My old man died in a fine big house,*
> *My ma died in a shack.*
> *I wonder where I'm gonna die,*
> *Being neither white nor black.*

Here I would let my voice trail off into a lonely silence. Then I would stand quite still for a long time, because I knew I had the complete attention of my listeners again.

Usually after a résumé of the racial situation in our country, with an optimistic listing of past achievements on the part of Negroes, and future possibilities, I would end the evening with:

> *I, too, sing America.*
>
> *I am the darker brother.*
> *They send me*
> *To eat in the kitchen*
> *When company comes,*
> *But I laugh,*
> *And eat well,*
> *And grow strong.*
>
> *Tomorrow*
> *I'll sit at the table*
> *When company comes.*
> *Nobody'll dare*
> *Say to me,*
> *"Eat in the kitchen,"*
> *Then.*
>
> *Besides,*
> *They'll see*
> *How beautiful I am*
> *And be ashamed.*
>
> *I, too, am America.*

Langston Hughes was born in Missouri in 1902. He wrote novels, short stories, poetry, and plays, and his work was influenced greatly by jazz and blues. His works include the non-fiction titles, *I Wonder as I Wander*, and *The Langston Hughes Reader*. He died in 1967.

I. *Response*

a. What would you say are some features of a personal essay? Why could this selection be considered a personal essay?

b. What is the range of social issues that Hughes deals with in his poetry?

c. What kind of reactions did Hughes seek in his public readings? What kind of reaction does he seek in this essay? How is the reader of the essay similar to the listener in the audience of his poetry reading? Do you think that he was successful in "making poetry pay"?

2. *Focus on Context*
With a partner, read the biography of Hughes included above, and consider where and when he lived. If necessary, research his life further. Discuss what life would have been like for him as an African-American during that time period. How was his work affected by when and where he lived? How might readers at the time have been affected by his work? How are present-day readers affected by his work? Explain your personal response to one of the poems included in this selection.

3. *Language Conventions* *Transitional Words*
In examining the pattern of the essay, you probably noted the use of words that marked a change in time, which helped you identify the chronology of events. Identify and list three of these words. Where do they appear in the paragraphs? How effective is their use? How effectively do you use transition words in your essay writing?

4. *Literature Studies* *Essay Organization*
One of the ways of organizing an essay is through *chronological order*, meaning the writer examines a situation or event in the order in which it occurred. Trace the time pattern of this essay as it follows the pattern of Hughes's public readings. Then, consider how the poems work in the essay—how does each poem function in supporting Hughes's purpose?

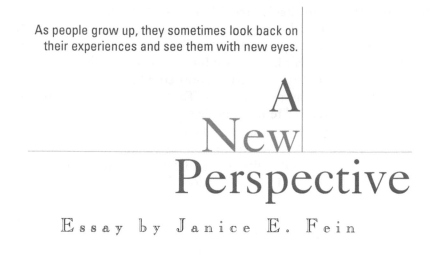

As people grow up, they sometimes look back on their experiences and see them with new eyes.

A New Perspective

Essay by Janice E. Fein

Our lives are shaped by the seemingly insignificant events of our youth. My childhood has become a series of mental snips of celluloid edited from the long playing film entitled "Cheated in Life."

My mother is walking me to kindergarten. I'm sure it must be kindergarten. In future years it would become vitally important for me to remember just exactly when it was. If it were first or second grade we would have been walking in the opposite direction but I can clearly see each familiar house as we pass by: Leedom's, Neiman's, Salem's, yes, it was definitely kindergarten. The film clip does not take us to our final destination, nor does it begin at home. It's a simple walk down a simple block in time. I can still feel my left fingers cradled in the smooth grip of her hand, one not much bigger than that of my own. I actually feel the warmth of the rising sun on my face as I look up at her each time she speaks. Aha! It was kindergarten! The sun always rose from behind that row of houses. If we had been walking anywhere else, the sun would have been in her face, not mine. She never walked me to elementary school. She only walked me to kindergarten, and very possibly, only that one time. Was it the first day of school? Or Parent's Day? It was unimportant. What became important, in later years, was my ability to woefully lament, "I only remember my mother walking one time in my life. She walked me to kindergarten."

Thereafter, all recollections of her were in her hospital bed, a massive ugly thing that took up a good portion of my parents' room. The debilitating effects of rheumatoid arthritis confined her to that bed. There were, however, what she referred to as "good days," days in which she was able to drag herself from her bed and onto a small kitchen chair with curved metal legs. She would then muster enough energy to force her hips in an awkward motion. Each painful hip movement would inch the chair laboriously forward, commanding it to perform the tasks that her frozen arthritic joints could not accomplish. My friends never came to my room to play. To do so they would have to pass by my parents' room. I remember that bed and that chair as embarrassing eyesores and how, once again, I had felt cheated.

Connie had the best playroom in the neighborhood. She was my very best friend and every day after school I would race home to change clothes and, in a heartbeat, I was at her door. Half of her basement was converted into a wonderful playhouse with panelling, carpets, and lace curtains to match. I was sure that every toy ever created was in that room. Despite the lure of all those treasures, what I remember most were the marvelous sounds and smells that drifted down to us from the kitchen above. Pots and pans clanging, water rushing through the pipes, and best of all, Connie's mother humming softly as she worked. One particular evening, the aroma was so compelling that I had to ask. Connie wrinkled her nose in disgust and said, "Lasagna ... again!" I pretended to have to use the bathroom so that I could pass through the kitchen and briefly glimpse what a lasagna looked like.

The oven timer was the saddest sound. When I heard it I knew what was coming next. "Connie, come wash up for supper," and I would have to leave. At a snail's pace, I would wander back to my own kitchen door. No wonderful aromas ever greeted me there. Sometimes there would be cold macaroni and cheese left over by one of my brothers or sisters. Most often I would prepare something on my own. Frozen hamburger patties, fish sticks, maybe I'll just have a can of soup. It never really mattered. It would never be lasagna. One evening, as I wander into my mother's room, bologna sandwich in hand, she shakes her head and says, "Is that the best you can find out there?" "I'm not very hungry," I lie. Only now can I see that the look in her eyes matched the despair in my heart, and yet, I felt cheated.

As childhood progressed, certain actions became innate. Handouts at school calling for volunteer room mothers and field trip chaperones were surreptitiously discarded along the nine-block journey home. I'll never forget those nine long blocks. In January and February they might just as well have been ninety! My classmates are piling into their mothers' warm waiting station wagons. I hunch my shoulders to my ears and silently watch as they disappear into the swirling gusts of snow. No steaming mug of hot cocoa is awaiting my arrival, just those sad eyes. Cheated.

I've rolled the film a thousand times. The scenes have never changed, only my perspective. It took the birth of my first child to truly see the whole picture. I've often tried to imagine what it would be like to see my son in pain and not be able to brush away a tear, mend a knee or simply hold him in my arms. I've seen the look in his eyes when he hit his first home run. I've "hugged him warm" on snowy days and "tickled him happy" when life was cruel. I've knelt with him to say his prayers and thanked God for my ability to do so. I may never understand why some of us are cheated in life. I only know, from this perspective, that I am not the one who was.

Janice E. Fein, born in 1948, graduated from the University of Akron in 1992. She works in the field of social services as a case worker for abused and neglected children.

I. *Response*
a. What were the predominant emotions felt by the author in her early school days?
b. What event determines the author's understanding of who was really "cheated" in life? Why do you think this particular event gives the author this insight?
c. As you were reading the essay, what was your feeling toward the author? Did your opinion change? How does the author guide her readers toward feeling that way? Explain.

2. *Literature Studies* *Essay Structure* The author of this essay follows a traditional essay structure; one that can be used in any type of essay (personal, analytic, persuasive, argumentative, narrative).

The *introduction*—(usually the first paragraph) clearly states the main idea or thesis.

The *body*—(a series of paragraphs after the introduction) develops ideas or arguments to support the main idea or thesis.

The *conclusion*—(usually the last paragraph) summarizes key points, provides a logical follow-up to the thesis and arguments, and is an insightful ending to the essay.

Examine "A New Perspective" and identify each of the above parts or components; then consider the conclusion closely. How does it link to the introduction (a device called "closing by return")?

Only Daughter

Memoir by Sandra Cisneros

Once, several years ago, when I was just starting out my writing career, I was asked to write my own contributor's note for an anthology I was part of. I wrote: "I am the only daughter in a family of six sons. *That* explains everything."

Well, I've thought about that ever since, and yes, it explains a lot to me, but for the reader's sake I should have written: "I am the only daughter in a *Mexican* family of six sons." Or even: "I am the only daughter of a Mexican father and a Mexican-American mother." Or: "I am the only daughter of a working-class family of nine." All of these had everything to do with who I am today.

I was/am the only daughter and *only* a daughter. Being an only daughter in a family of six sons forced me by circumstance to spend a lot of time by myself because my brothers felt it beneath them to play with a *girl* in public. But that aloneness, that loneliness, was good for a would-be writer—it allowed me time to think and think, to imagine, to read and prepare myself.

Being only a daughter for my father meant my destiny would lead me to become someone's wife. That's what he believed. But when I was in fifth grade and shared my plans for college with him, I was sure he understood. I remember my father saying, "*Que bueno, mi'ja*, that's good." That meant a lot to me, especially since my brothers thought the idea hilarious. What I didn't realize was that my father thought college was good for girls—for finding a husband. After four years in college and two more in graduate school, and still no husband, my father shakes his head even now and says I wasted all that education.

In retrospect, I'm lucky my father believed daughters were meant for husbands. It meant it didn't matter if I majored in something silly like English. After all, I'd find a nice professional eventually, right? This allowed me the liberty to putter about embroidering my little poems and stories without my father interrupting with so much as a "What's that you're writing?"

But the truth is, I wanted him to interrupt. I wanted my father to understand what it was I was scribbling, to introduce me as "My only daughter, the writer." Not as "This is my only daughter. She teaches." *El maestra*—teacher. Not even *profesora*.

In a sense, everything I have ever written has been for him, to win his approval even though I know my father can't read English words, even though my father's only reading includes the brown-ink *Esto* sports magazines from Mexico City and the bloody *¡Alarma!* magazines that feature yet another sighting of *La Virgen de Guadalupe* on a tortilla or a wife's revenge on her philandering husband by bashing his skull in with a *molcajete* (a kitchen mortar made of volcanic rock). Or the *fotonovelas*, the little picture paperbacks with tragedy and trauma erupting from the characters' mouths in bubbles.

My father represents, then, the public majority. A public who is disinterested in reading, and yet one whom I am writing about and for, and privately trying to woo.

When we were growing up in Chicago, we moved a lot because of my father. He suffered periodic bouts of nostalgia. Then we'd have to let go our flat, store the furniture with mother's relatives, load the station wagon with baggage and bologna sandwiches, and head south. To Mexico City.

We came back, of course. To yet another Chicago flat, another Chicago neighborhood, another Catholic school. Each time, my father would seek out the parish priest in order to get a tuition break, and complain or boast: "I have seven sons."

He meant *siete hijos*, seven children, but he translated it as "sons." "I have seven sons." To anyone who would listen. The Sears Roebuck employee who sold us the washing machine. The short-order cook where my father ate his ham-and-eggs breakfasts. "I have seven sons." As if he deserved a medal from the state.

My papa. He didn't mean anything by that mistranslation, I'm sure. But somehow I could feel myself being erased. I'd tug my father's sleeve and whisper: "Not seven sons. Six! and *one daughter*."

When my oldest brother graduated from medical school, he fulfilled my father's dream that we study hard and use this—our heads, instead of this—our hands. Even now my father's hands are thick and yellow, stubbed by a history of hammer and nails and twine and coils and springs. "Use this," my father said, tapping his head, "and not this," showing us those hands. He always looked tired when he said it.

Wasn't college an investment? And hadn't I spent all those years in college? And if I didn't marry, what was it all for? Why would anyone go to college and then choose to be poor? Especially someone who had always been poor.

Last year, after ten years of writing professionally, the financial rewards started to trickle in. My second National Endowment for the Arts Fellowship. A guest professorship at the University of California, Berkeley. My book, which sold to a major New York publishing house.

At Christmas, I flew home to Chicago. The house was throbbing, same as always; hot *tamales* and sweet *tamales* hissing in my mother's pressure cooker, and everybody—my mother, six brothers, wives, babies, aunts, cousins—talking too loud and at the same time, like in a Fellini film, because that's just how we are.

I went upstairs to my father's room. One of my stories had just been translated into Spanish and published in an anthology of Chicano writing, and I wanted to show it to him. Ever since he recovered from a stroke two years ago, my father likes to spend his leisure hours horizontally. And that's how I found him, watching a Pedro Infante movie on Galavision and eating rice pudding.

There was a glass filmed with milk on the bedside table. There were several vials of pills and balled Kleenex. And on the floor, one black sock and a plastic urinal that I didn't want to look at but looked at anyway. Pedro Infante was about to burst into song, and my father was laughing.

I'm not sure if it was because my story was translated into Spanish, or because it was published in Mexico, or perhaps because the story dealt with Tepeyac, the *colonia* my father was raised in, but at any rate, my father punched the mute button on his remote control and read my story.

I sat on the bed next to my father and waited. He read it very slowly. As if he were reading each line over and over. He laughed at all the right places and read lines he liked out loud. He pointed and asked questions: "Is this So-and-so?" "Yes," I said. He kept reading.

When he finally finished, after what seemed like hours, my father looked up and asked: "Where can we get more copies of this for the relatives?"

Of all the wonderful things that happened to me last year, that was the most wonderful.

Sandra Cisneros was born in Chicago, U.S. in 1954. She was instrumental in bringing the perspective of Chicana (Mexican-American) women into the field of literary feminism. Her first novel, *The House on Mango Street,* won the American Book Award from the Before Columbus Foundation in 1985.

I. *Response*
a. What do you think the author was trying to achieve with this memoir? What was she exploring in her own life?
b. In a few sentences, describe the picture you have in your mind of the father. Refer to the memoir for supporting details.
c. Selecting details is important when framing your writing. What details does Cisneros use to describe her childhood, and what is her purpose? What details does she select for her adulthood, and what is her purpose?
d. What are some variables that might contribute to people placing importance on one gender over the other?
e. Why do you think it is so important for children, no matter their age, to seek the approval of their parents? If you think about yourself as a parent someday, what qualities will you look for in your children?

2. *Vocabulary* With a partner, examine how Cisneros embeds Spanish words and terms throughout the memoir. What effect does this have? What format of type lets readers know that a word is in a different language? How has the author provided the translations smoothly, so that she does not distract the reader? For those words for which she does not provide a translation, how are we able to guess at their meaning?

3. *Language Conventions* *Sentence Fragments* When we are learning to write, we are warned not to use sentence fragments. Experienced writers, however, sometimes use sentence fragments for specific effects. Identify three sentence fragments in this memoir and read them aloud, along with the sentences that precede and follow them. With a partner, analyse the effect sentence fragments have on the way the sentences sound, the tone of the memoir, and the author's meaning.

Canadian novelist David Adams Richards
describes Newcastle, New Brunswick—
the town of his childhood.

My Old Newcastle

Descriptive Essay by David Adams Richards

In Newcastle, N.B., which I call home, we all played on the ice floes in the spring, spearing tommy-cod with stolen forks tied to sticks. More than one of us almost met our end slipping off the ice.

All night the trains rumbled or shunted their loads off to Halifax or Montreal, and men moved and worked. To this day I find the sound of trains more comforting than lonesome. It was somehow thrilling to know of people up and about in those hours, and wondrous events taking place. Always somehow with the faint, worn smell of gas and steel.

The Miramichi is a great working river.

There was always the presence of working men and women, from the mines or mills or woods; the more than constant sound of machinery; and the ore covered in tarps at the side of the wharf.

But as children, sitting in our snowsuits and hats and heavy boots on Saturday afternoons, we all saw movies that had almost nothing to do with us. That never mentioned us as a country or a place. That never seemed to know what our fathers and mothers did—that we went to wars or had a flag or even a great passion for life.

As far as the movies were concerned, we were in a lost, dark country, it seemed. And perhaps this is one reason I write. Leaving the theatre on a January afternoon, the smell of worn seats and heat and chip bags gave way to a muted cold and scent of snow no movie ever showed us. And night came against the tin roofs of the sheds behind our white houses, as the long spires of our churches rose over the town.

Our river was frozen so blue then that trucks could travel from one town to the other across the ice, and bonfires were lit by kids skating; sparks rose upon the shore under the stars as mothers called children home at 9 o'clock.

All winter long the sky was tinted blue on the horizon, the schools we sat in too warm; privileged boys and girls sat beside those who lived in hunger and constant worry. One went on to be a Rhodes scholar, another was a derelict at 17 and dead at 20. To this day I could not tell you which held more promise.

Spring came with the smell of mud and grass burning in the fields above us. Road hockey gave way to cricket and then baseball. The sun warmed, the ice shifted and the river was free. Salmon and sea trout moved up a dozen of our tributaries to spawn.

In the summer the ships came in, from all ports to ours, to carry ore and paper away. Sailors smoked black tobacco cigarettes, staring down at us from their decks; blackflies spoiled in the fields beyond town, and the sky was large all evening. Cars filled with children too excited to sleep passed along our great avenues lined with overhanging trees. All down to the store to get ice cream in the dark.

Adolescent blueberry crops and sunken barns dotted the fields near the bay, where the air had the taste of salt and tar, and small spruce trees seemed constantly filled with wind; where, by August, the water shimmered and even the small white lobster boats smelled of autumn, as did the ripples that moved them.

In the autumn the leaves were red, of course, and the earth, by Thanksgiving, became hard as a dull turnip. Ice formed in the ditches and shallow streams. The fields became yellow and stiff. The sounds of rifle shots from men hunting deer echoed faintly away, while women walked in kerchiefs and coats to 7 o'clock mass, and the air felt heavy and leaden. Winter coming on again.

Now the town is three times as large, and fast-food franchises and malls dot the roadside where there were once fields and lumberyards. There is a new process at the mill, and much of the wood is clear-cut so that huge acres lie empty and desolate, a redundancy of broken and muted earth. The river is opened all winter by an ice-breaker, so no trucks travel across the ice, and the trains, of course, are gone. For the most part the station is empty, the tracks fiercely alone in the winter sun.

The theatre is gone now, too. And those thousands of movies showing us, as children filled with happy laughter someplace in Canada, what we were not, are gone as well. They have given way to videos and satellite dishes and a community that is growing slowly farther and farther away from its centre. Neither bad nor good, I suppose—but away from what it was.

David Adams Richards, writer of poetry, short stories, essays, and novels, was born in 1950. His work, *Nights Below Station Street*—the first in a trilogy—won the Governor General's Award in 1985. Several other literary awards followed, including the Canadian Authors Association Literary Award for Fiction in 1991, and the Alden Nowlan Award for Excellence in English Literary Arts in 1993. In 2000, Richards shared the Giller Prize (with Michael Ondaatje) for his novel, *Mercy Among the Children.*

1. *Response*
a. What do you think the author's purpose was in writing this essay? How does he feel about his home as an adult? Provide evidence from the essay to support your view.
b. This is a sample of a descriptive essay: The author has used vivid sensory details and images to describe the town of his memory. List images that appeal to each of the senses. Why do you think this kind of imagery is so evocative and effective?
c. The third paragraph is one short sentence. Comment on its function and its place in the essay.
d. Consider the title and the author's play on words. How does the structure of the essay reflect the idea of old and new?

2. *Literature Studies* *Essay Structure* The author uses a chrono-logical structure to develop this descriptive essay. Trace this order in the essay. What is the period of time in which the essay ends? What do you think of this structure? How does it suit the author's subject?

3. *Film Study* Reread the paragraphs in which movies are mentioned. The author suggests that the movies they saw as children in Canada were not at all reflective of their lives. Describe a movie that you think is a fairly realistic depiction of your life, or of the lives of people your age. Alternatively, think of some movies that are aimed at your age group and explain how they are *not* realistic. Do you have a preference? Do you think movies reflect who we are or who we want to be? Discuss your ideas in a group.

Well-known journalist Rex Murphy pays tribute to
Canada's fifteenth prime minister on the day of his death:
September 28, 2000.

Pierre Trudeau

He Has Gone to His Grace

Tribute by Rex Murphy

The sad vigil the country went on a few weeks ago this afternoon reached its inevitable conclusion. The largest, liveliest, smartest, fiercest and most graceful public figure that Canada has had in modern times, and probably ever, has made an end.

He walked outside the boundaries of expectation in almost everything he did. He was intense, private and reserved and gave himself to the one profession, the one vocation, that most depends on exhibition, attention and continuous display.

He was radiantly intelligent, a full intellectual, powered with jesuitical resources of argument and reason, yet—on so many occasions—was the most visceral and passionate of our public figures.

He hailed from the province that, with reason, nursed doubts about its place in Confederation, was burdened by fears of its future and destiny. Yet he of all Quebecers was the one most powered by the certitude, by the absolute confidence, that Quebecers were larger by being Canadians, and that a lack of confidence was more a failure of nerve than a matter of politics.

He bore a symbolic relationship with his time. This angular, complex, multifaceted personality seemed to say things to this country outside the words of his speeches or his policies. There was some element within him, or of him, that acted like a summons to the Canadian imagination; to live a little larger, think a little more carefully, or bring more courage or daring to our dreams.

Pre-eminently, his life and his public career revolved around the idea of Canada. In any turn of crisis or act of state, from the storm of the FLQ to patriation of the Constitution, Pierre Trudeau acted from a conception of the whole country, and a determination to give body to this country's often vague and drifting sense of itself.

He paid the country the deepest tribute a real politician can: he believed in it with his brain and his heart, and gave the wit of the one and the heat of the other to enlarging and enlivening its possibilities and our citizenship.

He was no neuter. It is one of the grandest things we will say of his memory that, at times, he antagonized as much as he inspired; our affection for Pierre Trudeau was turbulent and always interesting. If citizens of this day lament that leadership is a game of polls and cozy focus groups there will always be the example of this man to remind us that convictions can be set in bedrock, and that adherence to principles is the most enduring charisma.

Canadians first admired Pierre Trudeau, halted before his presence in a kind of happy awe. Over time as we learned him, and if it is not presumptuous, he learned us, the admiration melted into, I think, a dignified affection.

He left politics larger than he found it. He added to the dignity of public life and did not subtract from it. His life and career spoke to everyone of the sheer power of excellence as an ideal. In this wide, mixed and imposing country, for the time he was with us Canadians knew they had one touch of grandeur outside the landscape.

Passion, intellect, honour and courage were his hallmarks. He was, in public life, the best that we had. It was an honour and a joy that he was around and a real grief that today so much, so very much of what is best about us, has made farewell.

He has gone to his grace, and that leaves so much less of ours.

Rex Murphy, born in Carbonear, Newfoundland and Labrador, began his CBC career in the early 1970s as a commentator/ interviewer for *CBC Here and Now.* He wrote and hosted the documentary *The Last and the Best,* which covered Newfoundland and Labrador's twenty-fifth anniversary in Confederation, and which won a Wilderness Award.

I. *Response*

a. Did this tribute help you to understand who Pierre Elliott Trudeau was? What additional information about him would you like to have? Where would you look for it?

b. From reading this article, what aspect of Trudeau's accomplishments or his character impressed you most?

c. What does the author mean by the second-last sentence: "He has gone to his grace ..."? How effective an ending do you think it is, and why?

d. What do you think are the most important qualities a nation's leader should possess? Which leaders in the world today do you think demonstrate these qualities? List leaders, their qualities, and how these qualities are demonstrated.

2. *Focus on Context* What knowledge do you have of Pierre Elliott Trudeau? Consider his life (public and private) and his contributions. As a class, brainstorm your knowledge of Canadian Prime Ministers. Record and list the top three according to how much knowledge you have about them. How does your knowledge of Trudeau compare with your knowledge of the others? What might be some reasons for this?

3. *Language Conventions* *Parallelism* Rex Murphy makes use of **parallel structure** in this selection. Identify the paragraph openers that follow this structure and then note the change from that structure to a different one. Why might the author have chosen not to use the same structure for every paragraph?

Parallel structure is the repeated use of the same phrase or sentence, or the repeated use of a similar sentence structure. Parallel structure can be used to create balance or place emphasis on certain lines.

This tribute was written for broadcast on national TV. Read the essay again, aloud, listening to the delivery. How is this structure suitable for an oral tribute like this one?

4. *Writing* *Tribute* Think of a person "who has gone to his [her] grace" and commemorate that person in a tribute of your own. You could try using a similar parallel structure in an essay form, or you could use forms such as a letter or poem.

Eulogies and written tributes to those who have died create moving stories and memories of a person's life. Photos, too, can pay tribute. When well-chosen, even just a few photos can reveal a life to us. Consider these photos, published in a newspaper following the death of Canadian writer Mordecai Richler.

Mordecai in Memoriam

Photo Tribute from
The Toronto Star
Wednesday, July 4, 2001

Artist as a Young Man:
Mordecai Richler during
a pensive moment.

Widespread Appeal:
Richler reads to kids from one of his
best-loved stories, "Jacob Two-Two
and the Hooded Fang."

Back to His Roots: Looking out over
old Montréal neighbourhood, 1979.

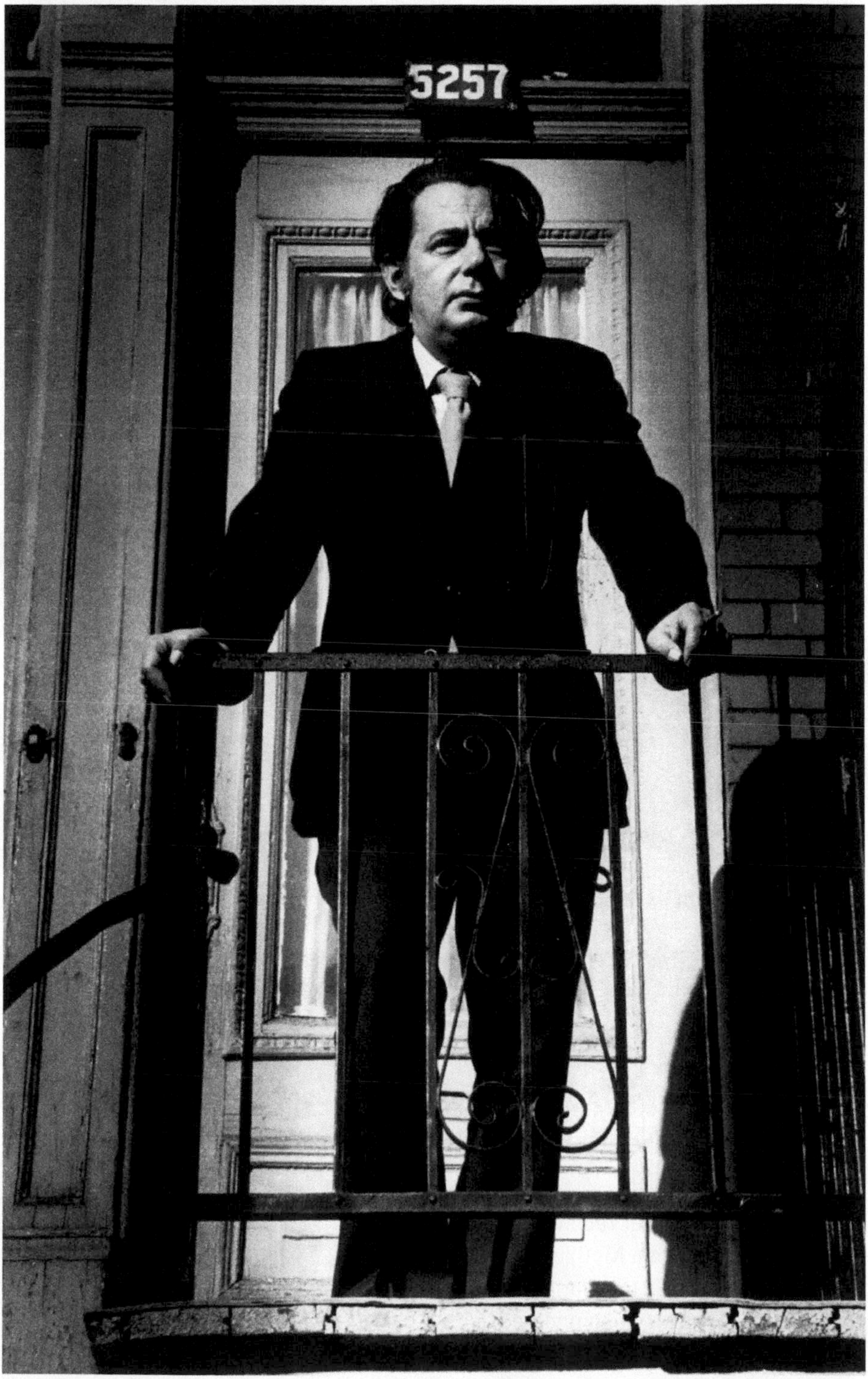
5257

Prix Parizeau: Mordecai Richler holds Aislin cartoon in Montréal spoofing Jacques Parizeau in 1996 with literary prize for Québec fiction in English. He called it the Prix Parizeau, given out by the Impure Wool Society, a thinly veiled reference to referendum-night remarks by the former Québec premier blaming the "ethnic vote" for the sovereigntists' defeat.

Family Toast: Richler with wife Florence and sons Noah (left) and Daniel.

Relaxed: Richler sits thoughtfully in a dressing room in Toronto, in undated photo.

Honoured: Richler receives honorary status from McGill University as university Chancellor Richard Pound looks on, in an undated photo.

Mordecai Richler was born in 1931 in Montréal, Canada. Before finishing his degree at Sir George Williams College in Montréal, Richler left for Europe, where he lived in London for twenty years. He achieved international acclaim with his novel, *The Apprenticeship of Duddy Kravitz*, set in Montréal and made into a film. His other works include novels *Cocksure* and *St. Urbain's Horseman*, which both won Governor General's Awards, and *Joshua Then and Now*, which was also made into a film. His essay collections include *Hunting Tigers Under Glass* and *Home Sweet Home: My Canadian Album*. Richler died in 2001. His fiction, essays, and columns revealed his outspoken and provocative nature.

I. *Response*

a. Which of the photos would you say gives you the most information about Richler? Why? What information are you given?

b. From these photos, what do you think Richler was like?

c. Which photo do you like the most, and why?

d. What, in particular, strikes you as interesting in these photos?

e. There were probably thousands of photos from which editors could have chosen to pay tribute to Richler upon his death. Why do you think these were among those chosen?

2. *Making Connections*

Mordecai Richler was a writer of varied genres: novels, screenplays, essays, and children's books. Read from some of Richler's works, as well as some of the biographical information on him. What do you learn about him that relates to what you perceived from the photos?

3. *Visual Communication* Photo Essay

Create your own photo essay about a Canadian you admire—living or dead, famous or not. Use photos that you take, or photos collected from print or digital resources. Choose shots that help convey the character of the person. Consider also the placement of your photos: Do you want them in chronological order? Juxtaposed? Experiment with choice and placement until you have the effects you want.

Alternatively, create a photo essay that pays tribute to your own life so far.

Frida Kahlo, a Mexican artist, died in 1954. In December 2001, the movie *Frida* was released to pay tribute to this popular artist. This article, published in April 2001, looks at some of the events surrounding the artist's popularity and the making of the movie.

Reviving Fridamania

Newspaper Article by Chris Kraul

Fridamania—the cult and the industry—may soon get a second wind.

Hollywood is finally making a movie on the tortured, colorful life of Mexican painter Frida Kahlo after a decade of abortive attempts. If the film is a hit, Mexico City could see a wave of Frida-inspired merchandising like the one that engulfed the capital a few years ago.

On an autumn day in 1997, you could on one day go to a Frida bar, see a Frida play, have a Frida dinner and load up on Frida T-shirts, calendars, cookbooks and key rings featuring her baleful, beetle-browed visage.

Overshadowed in her lifetime by her husband, the artist Diego Rivera, and ignored by the public for decades, Kahlo became an icon of popular culture. She was transformed into Mexico's Elvis, a "brand" that has sold several forests' worth of postcards, picture books and posters.

Fridamania began building in the late 1970s, spurred on by the interest of European feminists and Chicano muralists who saw her as a forerunner, said Raquel Tibol, author of *Frida Kahlo: An Open Life.* A 1983 biography by Hayden Herrera helped popularize the legend. Rivera willed all rights to his and Kahlo's images and intellectual property to the Mexican people after his death in 1957. And Mexico has made out handsomely, although not as well at it might have, because of weak copyright protection laws. To merchandise Kahlo legally, movie producers and souvenir manufacturers must pay royalties to the Mexican Central Bank.

Kahlo's house—la Casa Azul, or Blue House, where she lived, worked, was born and died—is Mexico City's Graceland, a museum now visited by an average of 300 pilgrims a day. They view the dozen Kahlo paintings on display, immerse themselves in the legend and pay homage to the artist's ashes—she died at age 47 in 1954—stored in an urn on the premises. But like all fads, Fridamania has subsided. Visits to the museum have declined 25 percent from the 1997 peak. Merchandisers report that demand for coasters, mirrors, calendars, key rings and desk

Frida Kahlo.

Use the imformation in the selection and in the above photo
to write a 25-word description of Frida Kahlo.

calendars has slipped significantly. The onslaught of books and theatrical productions—the latter now numbering at least 60—has slowed.

Frida is still there, just not everywhere.

One place she is these days: the city of Puebla, where Miramax Films began shooting this month on its production, starring Mexican actress Salma Hayek. Release is expected early next year.

The vagaries of pop culture and merchandising fads aside, Kahlo, who overcame polio, an almost fatal bus accident and other setbacks to become an accomplished artist, remains a powerful cultural force here. Ask a dozen museum-goers, art experts and Frida merchants why that is, and you get a dozen different answers. "It was her attitude before life that appeals to people, that of an indefatigable fighter who struggled against physical problems, the shadow of her famous husband, the social restrictions of womanhood," said Luis-Martin Lozano, director of the Museum of Modern Art in Mexico City.

I. Response
a. In your own words, write down five facts in your notebooks that you have learned about Frida Kahlo. Compare your facts with those of a classmate.
b. What is *Fridamania?* How did it start?
c. In your own words, define the term *powerful cultural force.*
d. How and why are Mexicans paying tribute to Kahlo?

2. Research and Inquiry Investigate the life and work of Frida Kahlo further, using Internet and library resources. Begin by recording any questions you had about Kahlo after reading this article. Choose an innovative format in which to present your research to others—for example, a short biography, visual essay, or eulogy.

3. Literature Studies *Bias and Tone* Reread the article and identify both its **bias** and **tone**. Does the author admire Frida Kahlo? What do words like *Fridamania* imply about the author's attitude toward the artist? Does the article remain objective and impersonal? Discuss the article with a partner, analysing the effect of the author's bias and tone on the reader.

Bias is the author's inclination or preference toward one stance that makes it difficult or impossible to judge something fairly. For example, a fan of Sylvester Stallone may be unable to write an objective or balanced review of his work. **Tone** is the implied attitude of the writer toward the subject or audience. The tone of a piece can be described as *angry, satiric, joyful, serious*, and so on.

Rewrite one paragraph of the article, using an opposing tone or bias. Discuss the effectiveness of this rewrite with your partner.

Canadian poet Al Purdy, known as "a poet of the people," died in June 2001.

The Awkward Sublime

Tribute by Margaret Atwood

I began to read Al Purdy's poetry about the same time it changed from being odd and ungainly to being remarkable—in the early '60s. I was just into my 20s, writing a lot of poetry but not liking much of it; like most young poets then, I wanted to be published by Contact Press—a highly respected, poet-run cooperative—and I read everything they issued; and thus I read Al Purdy's *Poems for All the Annettes* in 1962, when it first came out.

Al Purdy, 1996, by Frank O'Connor. Photo

I was somewhat frightened by it, and did not fully understand what he was doing. This was a new sort of voice for me, an overpowering one, and a little too much like being backed into the corner of a seedy bar by a large, insistent, untidy drunk, who is waxing by turns both sentimental and obscene. For a young male poet of those days, this kind of energy and this approach—casual, slangy, subversive of recent poetic convention—could be liberating and inspirational, and some found in him an ersatz father figure. But for a young female poet—well, this was not the sort of father figure it would be altogether steadying to have.

Then, in 1965, *The Cariboo Horses*—Purdy's breakthrough book—came out, and I found that the drunk in the bar was also a major storyteller and mythmaker, though still wearing his offhand and rather shabby disguise. This was poetry for the spoken voice *par excellence*—not an obviously rhetorical voice, but an anecdotal one, the voice of the Canadian vernacular. Yet not only that either, for no sooner had Purdy set up his own limits than he'd either transcend or subvert them. He was always questioning, always probing, and among those things that he questioned and probed were himself and his own poetic methods. In a Purdy poem, high diction can meet the scrawl on the washroom wall, and, as in a collision between matter and anti-matter, both explode.

"[Purdy] wrote about going to good hockey games
and fighting with the foreman at work ...
the kind of things that occupy ordinary people."

—Howard White, president of Harbour Publishing

It would be folly to attempt to sum up Purdy's poetic universe: like Walt Whitman's[1] it's too vast for a précis. What interested him could be anything, but above all the wonder that anything at all can be interesting. He was always turning banality inside out. For me, he was, above all, an explorer—pushing into nameless areas of landscape, articulating the inarticulate, poking around in dusty corners of memory and discovering treasure there, digging up the bones and shards of a forgotten ancestral past. When he wasn't capering about and joking and scratching his head over the idiocy and pain and delight of being alive, he was composing lyric elegies for what was no longer alive, but had been—and, through his words, still is. For underneath that flapping overcoat and that tie with a mermaid on it and that pretence of shambling awkwardness—yes, it was a pretence, but only partly, for among other things Purdy was doing a true impersonation of himself—

there was a skillful master-conjurer. Listen to the voice, and watch the hands at work: just hands, a bit grubby too, not doing anything remarkable, and you can't see how it's done, but suddenly, where a second ago there was only a broken vase, there's a fistful of brilliant flowers.

---

[1] **Walt Whitman:** American poet who wrote the radical and influential *Leaves of Grass,* 1855

Margaret Atwood's poetic reputation was established in 1966 when *The Circle Game* won the Governor General's Award. She has published numerous books of poetry, including the well-known collection *The Journals of Susanna Moodie: Poems.* She is also an award-winning novelist, winning the Governor General's Award in 1985 for *The Handmaid's Tale* and the Booker Prize in 2000 for *The Blind Assassin.*

I. *Response*
a. What does Atwood focus on in her tribute to Al Purdy? Why do you think she does not mention other aspects of his life?
b. How did Atwood's attitude toward, and appreciation of, Al Purdy's poetry change over the years?
c. What do you think of the tribute's title, which can be considered an **oxymoron**? In your own words, explain what you think the title means and what it refers to.

An **oxymoron** is a figure of speech that is a combination of contradictory words. One of the most common examples of an oxymoron is "jumbo shrimp."

2. *Focus on Context* Consider Margaret Atwood and her contribution to Canadian literature. Do some research, including reading a bibliography of her writing. Does her stature as a writer affect your response to the tribute? Explain.

Theme Connections

- *"Two Words,"* a story about the clever use of language, Vol. I, p. 51
- *"The Chariot,"* a poem about death, Vol. I, p. 207, and other poems in the cluster "Grief of Mind"
- *"Making Poetry Pay,"* an anecdote that profiles a poet, Vol. II, p. 40

Use Internet or print resources to find out who Susanna Moodie was and when she lived. As you read the following essay, consider contemporary Canada and its attitudes toward education.

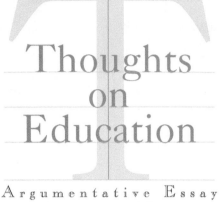

Thoughts on Education

Argumentative Essay
by Susanna Moodie

There is no calculating the immense benefit which the colony will derive from the present liberal provision made for the education of the rising generation.

A few years ago schools were so far apart, and the tuition of children so expensive, that none but the very better class could scrape money enough together to send their children to be instructed. Under the present system, every idle ragged child in the streets, by washing his face and hands, and presenting himself to the free school of his ward, can receive the same benefit as the rest.

What an inestimable blessing this is, and how greatly will this education of her population tend to increase the wealth and prosperity of the province! It is a certain means of calling out and making available all the talent in the colony; and as, thanks be to God, genius never was confined to any class, the poor will be more benefited by this wise and munificent arrangement than the rich.

These schools are supported by a district tax which falls upon the property of persons well able to pay it; but avarice and bigotry are already at work, to endeavour to deprive the young of this new-found blessing. Persons grumble at having to pay this additional tax. They say, "If poor people want their children taught, let them pay for it: their instruction has no right to be forced from our earnings."

What a narrow prejudice is this—what miserable, short-sighted policy! The education of these neglected children, by making them better citizens, will in the long run prove a great protection both to life and property.

Then the priests of different persuasions lift up their voices because no particular creed is allowed to be taught in the seminaries, and exclaim—"The children will be infidels. These schools are godless and immoral in the extreme." Yes; children will be taught to love each other without any such paltry distinctions as party and creed. The rich and the poor will meet together to learn the sweet courtesies of a common humanity, and prejudice and avarice and bigotry cannot bear that.

There is a spirit abroad in the world—and an evil spirit it is—which through all ages has instigated the rich to look down with contemptuous feelings of superiority on the humble occupations and inferior circumstances of the poor. Now, that this spirit is diametrically opposed to the benevolent precepts of Christianity, the fact of our blessed Lord performing his painful mission on earth in no higher capacity than that of a working mechanic ought sufficiently to show. What divine benevolence—what god-like humility was displayed in this heroic act! Of all the wonderful events in his wonderful history, is there one more astonishing than this—

> "That Heaven's high Majesty his court should keep
> In a clay cottage, by each blast controll'd—
> That Glory's self should serve our hopes and fears,
> And free Eternity submit to years?"

What a noble triumph was this, over the cruel and unjust prejudices of mankind! It might truly be termed the divine philosophy of virtue. This condescension on the part of the great Creator of the universe ought to have been sufficient to have rendered labour honourable in the minds of his followers; and we still indulge the hope that the moral and intellectual improvement of mankind will one day restore labour to her proper pedestal in the temple of virtue.

The chosen disciples of our Great Master—those to whom He entrusted the precious code of moral laws that was destined to overthrow the kingdom of Satan, and reform a degraded world—were poor uneducated men. The most brilliant gems are often enclosed in the rudest incrustations; and He who formed the bodies and souls of men well knew that the most powerful intellects are often concealed amidst the darkness and rubbish of uneducated minds. Such minds, enlightened and purified by his wonder-working Spirit, He sent forth to publish his message of glad tidings through the earth.

The want of education and moral training is the only *real* barrier that exists between the different classes of men. Nature, reason, and

Christianity recognise no other. Pride may say nay; but pride was always a liar, and a great hater of the truth. Wealth, in a hard, abstract point of view, can never make any. Take away the wealth from an ignorant man, and he remains just the same being he was before he possessed it, and is no way bettered from the mere circumstance of his having once been rich. But let that wealth procure for him the only true and imperishable riches—knowledge, and with it the power to do good to himself and others, which is the great end of moral and religious training—and a mighty structure is raised which death itself is unable to destroy. The man has indeed changed his nature, and is fast regaining the resemblance he once bore to his Creator.

The soul of man is of no rank, sex, or colour. It claims a distinction far above all these; and shall we behold its glorious energies imprisoned in the obscene den of ignorance and want, without making the least effort to enlighten its hideous darkness?

It is painful to reflect upon the vast barren wilderness of human intellect which on every side stretches around us—to know that thousands of powerful minds are condemned by the hopeless degradation of their circumstances to struggle on in obscurity, without one gleam of light. What a high and noble privilege has the Almighty conferred upon the wealthy and well-educated portion of mankind, in giving them the means of reclaiming and cultivating those barren minds, and of lifting them from the mire of ignorance in which they at present wallow, to share with them the moral dignity of thinking men!

A small portion of the wealth that is at present bestowed upon mere articles of luxury, or in scenes of riot and dissipation, would more than effect this great purpose. The education of the poorer classes must add greatly to the well-being and happiness of the world, and tend to diminish the awful amount of crimes and misery which up to the present moment has rendered it a vale of tears.

The ignorance of the masses must, while it remains, for ever separate them from their more fortunate brethren. Remove this stumbling block out of the way, and the hard line of demarcation which now divides them will soften, and gradually melt away. Their supposed inferiority lies in their situation alone. Turn to the history of those great men whom education has rescued from the very lowest walks of life, and you will find a mighty host who were in their age and day the companions, the advisers, the friends of princes—men who have written their names with the pen and the sword upon the pillars of time, and, if immortality can exist in a world of constant change, have been rendered immortal by their words or deeds.

Let poverty and bigotry do their utmost to keep such spirits, while living, in the shades of obscurity, death, the great equalizer, always restores to its possessors the rights of mind, and bids them triumph for ever over the low prejudices of their fellow-men, who, when reading the works of Burns or gazing on the paintings of Raphael, reproach them with the lowliness of their origin; yea, the proudest who have taste to appreciate their glorious creations rejoice that genius could thus triumph over temporary obstacles.

It has often been asserted by the rich and nobly-born, that if the poorer classes were as well educated as themselves, it would render them familiar and presumptuous, and they would no longer pay to their superiors in station that deference which must exist for the well-being of society. We view the subject with far other eyes, and conclude from analogy that that which has conferred such incalculable benefits on the rich, and helped mainly to place them in the position they now hold, could not be detrimental to the poor. The man who knows his duty is more likely to perform it well than the ignorant man, whose services are compulsory, and whose actions are uninfluenced by the moral responsibility which a right knowledge must give.

My earnest wish for universal education involves no dislike to royal rule, or for those distinctions of birth and wealth which I consider necessary for the well-being of society. It little matters by what name we call them; men of talent and education will exert a certain influence over the minds of their fellow-men which will always be felt and acknowledged in the world if mankind were equalized to-morrow. Perfect, unadulterated republicanism is a beautiful but fallacious chimera which never has existed upon the earth, and which, if the Bible be true (and we have no doubts on the subject), we are told never will exist in heaven. Still, we consider that it would be true wisdom and policy in those who possess a large share of the good things of this world, to make labour honourable, by exalting the poor operative into an intelligent moral agent. Surely it is no small privilege to be able to bind up his bruised and broken heart—to wipe the dust from his brow, and the tears from his eyes—and bid him once more stand erect in his Maker's image. This is, indeed, to become the benefactor both of his soul and body; for the mind, once convinced of its own real worth and native dignity, is less prone to fall into low and degrading vices, than when struggling with ignorance and the galling chain of despised poverty.

It is impossible for the most depraved votary of wealth and fashion *really* to despise a poor, honest, well-informed man. There is an aristocracy of virtue as well as of wealth; and the rich man who dares to cast undeserved contempt upon his poor but high-minded brother hears a voice within him which, in tones which cannot be misunderstood, reproves him for blaspheming his Maker's image. A glorious mission is conferred on you who are rich and nobly-born, which, if well and conscientiously performed, will make the glad arch of heaven ring with songs of joy. Nor deem that you will be worse served because your servant is a religious, well-educated man, or that you will be treated with less respect and attention by one who knows that your station entitles you to it, than by the rude, ignorant slave, who hates you in his heart, and performs his appointed services with an envious, discontented spirit.

When we consider that ignorance is the fruitful parent of crime, we should unite with heart and voice to banish it from the earth. We should devote what means we can spare, and the talents with which God has endowed us, in furthering every national and benevolent institution set on foot for this purpose; and though the progress of improvement may at first appear slow, this should not discourage any one from endeavouring to effect a great and noble purpose. Many months must intervene, after sowing the crop, before the husbandman can expect to reap the harvest. The winter snows must cover, the spring rains vivify and nourish, and the summer sun ripen, before the autumn arrives for the ingathering of his labour, and then the increase, after all his toil and watching, must be with God.

During the time of our blessed Lord's sojourn upon earth, He proclaimed the harvest to be plenteous and the labourers few; and He instructed his disciples to pray to the Lord of the harvest to send more labourers into the field. Does it not, therefore, behove those who live in a more enlightened age—when the truth of the Gospel, which He sealed with his blood, has been preached in almost every country—to pray the Father of Spirits to proportion the labourers to the wants of his people, so that Christian kindness, brotherly love, and moral improvement may go hand in hand, and keep pace with increasing literary and scientific knowledge?

A new country like Canada cannot value the education of her people too highly. The development of all the talent within the province will in the end prove her real worth, for from this source every blessing and improvement must flow. The greatness of a nation can more truly be estimated by the wisdom and intelligence of her people than by the mere amount of specie she may possess in her treasury. The money, under the bad management of ignorant rulers, would add but little to the well-being of the community, while the intelligence which could make a smaller sum available in contributing to the general good is in itself an inexhaustible mine of wealth.

If a few enlightened minds are able to add so much strength and importance to the country to which they belong, how much greater must that country become if all her people possessed this intelligence! How impossible it would be to conquer a country, if she could rely upon the united wisdom of an educated people to assist her in her hour of need! The force of arms could never subdue a nation thus held together by the strong hands of intellectual fellowship....

An ignorant man is incapable of judging correctly, however anxious he may be to do so. He gropes in the dark, like a blind man; and if he should happen to stumble on the right path, it is more by accident than from any correct idea which has been formed in his mind respecting it.

The mind which once begins to feel a relish for acquiring knowledge is not easily satisfied. The more it knows, the less it thinks of its own acquirements, and the more anxious it becomes to arrive at the truth; and finding that perfection is not a growth of earth, it carries its earnest longings beyond this world, and seeks it in communion with the Deity. If the young could once be fully persuaded that there was no disgrace in labour, in honest, honourable poverty, but a deep and lasting disgrace in ignorance and immorality, their education would be conducted on the most enlightened plan, and produce the most beneficial results.

The poor man who could have recourse to a book for amusement, instead of wasting a leisure hour in the bar-room of a tavern, would be more likely to promote the comfort and respectability of his family. Why should the labourer be debarred from sharing with the rich the great world of the past, and be unable to rank amongst his best friends the distinguished men of all creeds and countries, and to feel for these dead worthies (who, thanks to the immortal art of printing, still live in their works) the warmest gratitude and admiration? The very mention of some names awakens in the mind the most lively emotion. We recall their beautiful thoughts to memory, and repeat them with as much earnestness as though the dead spake again through our lips.

Of all the heaven-inspired inventions of man, there are none to which we are so greatly indebted as to the art of printing. To it we shall yet owe the emancipation of the larger portion of mankind from a state of mental and physical slavery. What floods of light have dawned upon the world since that silent orator, the press, set at liberty the imprisoned thoughts of men, and poured the wealth of mind among the famishing sons of earth! Formerly few could read, because manuscript books, the

A professional writer is an amateur who didn't quit.

Richard Bach

labours of the pen, were sold at such an enormous price that only men of rank or great wealth could afford to purchase them. The peasant, and the landholder who employed him, were alike ignorant; they could not obtain books, and therefore learning to read might well be considered in those dark ages a waste of time. This profound ignorance gave rise to all those superstitions which in the present enlightened age are regarded with such astonishment by thinking minds....

I have said more on this subject that I at first intended, but I feel deeply impressed with the importance of it; and, though I confess myself wholly inadequate to do it the justice it deserves, I hope the observations I have made will attract the attention of my Canadian readers, and lead them to study it more profoundly for themselves. Thanks be to God! Canada is a free country; a land of plenty; a land exempt from pauperism, burdensome taxation, and all the ills which crush and finally sink in ruin older communities. While the vigour of young life is yet hers, and she has before her the experience of all other nations, it becomes an act of duty and real *patriotism* to give to her children the best education that lies in her power.

Susanna Moodie, writer of poetry, short stories, articles, and novels, was born in Suffolk, England, in 1803. She became interested in humanitarian issues in the 1830s when her friend, the Scottish poet Thomas Pringle, introduced her to the injustices of slavery, and she wrote several anti-slavery tracts. In 1831, Pringle assisted Moodie in getting a collection of her poetry published. She moved to Canada with her husband in 1832, where they lived for six years on their bush farm. Her best-known book, *Roughing It in the Bush*, is a personal account of these difficult years spent in the Canadian wilderness. This was followed by *Flora Lyndsay; or Passages in an Eventful Life*, and *Life in the Clearings Versus the Bush*, which together create a trilogy about the immigration experience. Some of Moodie's novels include *Mark Hurdlestone; or The Gold Worshipper, Matrimonial Speculations*, and *Geoffrey Moncton; or The Faithless Guardian*. Moodie died in Toronto in 1885.

1. *Response*
a. Is Susanna Moodie in favour of publicly-funded education? Why or why not?
b. How convincing is Moodie's argument?
c. Do you agree with Moodie's position? Explain your own viewpoint on the issue of publicly-funded education.
d. Who was Moodie's original audience? What was her purpose in writing "Thoughts on Education"?

2. *Oral Language* *Group Discussion* Choose one passage within this essay and discuss Moodie's argument and viewpoint within a small group. Each group member should contribute one idea to this discussion. One member of your group can record the main points of your discussion. Another member can present these ideas to the class.

3. *Writing* *Letter* Write a letter to Susanna Moodie explaining the conditions of public education in your community in the present day. In your letter, incorporate a response to some of the points that Moodie raises.

4. *Language Focus* *Exclusive Language* Review the essay and consider the use of gender pronouns throughout. How does the language Moodie uses exclude particular people? What assumptions has the author made? Why or why not are these assumptions acceptable, given the context of this selection? In your own writing, what strategies do you use to maintain an inclusive tone or style?

Theme Connections

- *"Two Words," a story in which the main character is self-taught, Vol. I, p. 51*
- *"Young Soul," a poem that extols the importance of reading but also feeling, Vol. I, p. 189*
- *"Anything Worth Knowing" a poem about the value of education, Vol. I, p. 235*
- *"Did I Miss Anything?" a poem about the value of education, Vol. I, p. 236*
- *"Only Daughter," an essay that demonstrates the value of education, Vol. II, p. 48*

Screaming, shouting, and hitting—
abusive parents are spoiling their kids' sports.

Rink Rage

Magazine Article by James Deacon,

with Brenda Branswell in Montréal,
Susan McClelland in Toronto,
and Darryl Smart in Port Dover

When the Delhi Legion peewees travelled down the highway to play the Port Dover Pirates in February 2001, there was a fair bit on the line for both teams. The series winners would advance to the semifinals of the Ontario Minor Hockey Association's AE Peewee playoffs.... So about 200 parents and fans crowded into the arena in Port Dover and arranged themselves in the stands according to their community affiliation.

It was typical of peewee games at that level—12- and 13-year-olds a notch above house league—enthusiastic if not always polished. Early on, the Pirates won most of the battles along the boards, and took the lead as well. The action got progressively rougher. Several Delhi supporters began hollering at the two referees to crack down on what they saw as the Pirates' overly aggressive body checking, and in fact, Port Dover incurred most of the penalties.

That didn't satisfy some Delhi supporters. With five minutes left, when a Delhi player was penalized for hitting from behind, both of Delhi's coaches strenuously argued the call and were ejected. That provoked a couple of hotheaded fans, who hurled coins and a plastic water bottle onto the ice. Finally, with one minute and 38 seconds to go and Port Dover up 2-0, one particularly loud Delhi fan tossed a broom onto the ice. That was it for the officials. They halted play and, unable to identify exactly who the main offenders were, simply ejected all 200 spectators. The local provincial police detachment sent officers to protect the referees as they left the arena.

On the ice, the players were stunned by what they heard and saw coming out of the stands. "You don't pay attention to that stuff usually, but a couple of people in the stands were getting real mad at the refs," says Pirate defenceman Colton Organ, 13. When the broom hit the ice, Organ says, "we all just kind of looked at each other and shook our heads." The majority of fans did the same. It was, as one of the more composed Delhi parents said afterwards, "embarrassing."

No kidding. It was just a peewee hockey game, for crying out loud. It was supposed to be fun, yet it deteriorated into yet another example of out-of-control adults ruining their own kids' games. The bad behaviour is so common in hockey that it even has its own name—rink rage. In other incidents, some B.C. referees boycotted youth games to protest abuse from fans. A coach in Quebec was hospitalized after being attacked between periods by the father of one of his players. In Ontario, a coach was charged with threatening to kill a teenage referee. In Winnipeg, a police constable—already suspended from the force for a previous assault conviction—was arrested and charged with threatening another parent during his nine-year-old son's hockey game. And the worst news is that rink rage isn't confined to the rink. Similarly ill-tempered adults can be found spoiling kids' enjoyment of youth soccer, basketball, baseball and football games, among others.

The offenders are few—the vast majority of parents are supportive of their kids without being disrespectful of coaches, referees or other fans. And extreme behaviour is rare. There are tens of thousands of kids' games played every year in a variety of sports, and referees and sports associations contacted by *Maclean's* estimate that they are forced to eject spectators perhaps one per cent of the time. "Most of us just come out to support our kids," Delhi fan David Edmonds said about the incident in Port Dover. "It's too bad, really, because it's just a couple of people making the rest of us look bad."

While their shrill heckling may not always be profane or abusive enough to cause ejection, it poisons the atmosphere and drives volunteer coaches and low-paid referees out of the game. The Canadian Hockey Association says harassment is a major cause of attrition among referees, about 30 per cent of whom quit every season. In soccer, it's just about as bad: Manitoba soccer officials say that two-thirds of new referees recruited and trained in the province leave by the end of their first year.

Not that there weren't leather-lunged louts in the good old days. But experts say hostile behaviour at youth games is far more pervasive —and sometimes violent—than it was a generation ago. Consider what happened in the summer of 2000 at a children's recreational hockey practice in Reading, Mass., north of Boston. One player's father was so abusive to the man supervising a pick-up game that the arena staff asked the father to leave the building. But the man, 42-year-old Thomas Junta, came back to confront the volunteer supervisor, 40-year-old Michael Costin. The hulking Junta, six-foot-one and 275 lb., beat Costin, a single father of four, into unconsciousness while a crowd of young kids—including two of the victim's sons—watched in horror. Doctors pronounced Costin dead at the hospital, and Junta was charged with manslaughter. "It is a terrible tragedy," says Fred Engh, president of the Florida-based National Alliance for Youth Sports. "But given what's been happening out there, it didn't surprise me."

On a flight home after the National Hockey League All-Star Weekend in Denver, a 10-year-old boy was going through his bag of loot. He had, among other things, trading cards, a bunch of autographs and a cool replica all-star jersey. "Have fun?" someone asked. "It was awesome," the boy replied. His dad, sitting next to him, frowned and explained wistfully that, because of the trip, the boy had to miss his team's Saturday game back home. "Dad, it was against the last-place team," said the son. "It's not like we were going to lose or anything." "I know, I know," the father said, "but you missed a great chance to pad your stats."

Huh? For the kid, a pass into all-star weekend was better than a blank cheque at Toys "R" Us. But the father saw a lost opportunity to bolster his son's CV and to impress higher-level coaches. Parents' inflated ambitions, experts say, contribute to the intensified atmosphere surrounding youth games. "We're out there to put on recreation programs for kids, so they can have their fun," says Orest Zaozirney of the Edmonton Minor Hockey Association. "But you get parents who think they've got the next Gretzky."

This isn't the first generation of sports parents with stars in their eyes. But now they have dollar signs, too. Even modestly successful

> Only amateurs say that they write for their own amusement. Writing is not an amusing occupation. It is a combination of ditch-digging, mountain-climbing, treadmill and childbirth. Writing may be interesting, absorbing, exhilirating, racking, relieving. But amusing? Never!
>
> Edna Ferber

professional athletes can make millions these days, and expansion in all leagues has provided more jobs than ever before. The kids begin to look like meal tickets, when in fact lottery tickets is a better comparison. The odds of making it to the pro ranks are infinitesimally small— the Canadian Hockey Association estimates that less than one per cent of hockey-playing kids make it to the NHL.

"I think parents' expectations are greater than they ever have been," says Steve Larmer, a 39-year-old retired NHL all-star who, among other things, is now a volunteer coach of a novice (age 7 to 8) team in Peterborough, Ont. "They expect more not just from their kids, but from coaches and referees, too." Guy Blondeau, executive director of Hockey-Quebec, which represents about 350 minor hockey associations in the province, just shakes his head. "If parents stopped for a few minutes to think about the chances of their children having a career," says Blondeau, "I think they would reduce those expectations by a lot."

For a variety of reasons, modern parents are playing a bigger role than ever in their kids' recreation. "They are way more involved now than they were when I was a kid," says Larmer. "That's good in some ways, but sometimes they take it too far." As if to protect their "investment" in their future star, some adults hound their kids' coaches, demanding more playing time, all while pushing the child to excel. And that, says Jean Cote, a psychology professor at Queen's University in Kingston, Ont., is likely the most counterproductive approach parents can take. There are exceptions, of course—tennis's phenomenal Williams sisters and their all-controlling father come to mind. But Cote has studied the families of elite athletes and says the most successful competitors typically come from homes where parents are supportive without pushing their child too hard, or hollering at referees, or interfering with coaches. Parents who get too involved, Cote says, risk turning the kid off sport altogether. "It is quite consistent throughout our studies with elite athletes," Cote says, "that at a critical point, their parents let them choose what they wanted to do."

Beyond high expectations, experts say, the main reason for the sideline conflicts plaguing recreational sports is society as a whole. If otherwise sensible people can be enraged by traffic or by airline delays, why not by what they see at sporting events? "We are seeing an erosion of civility in society as a whole," says Engh, "and sports just mirrors what is happening all around us."

At a bantam (age 13 to 14) AA game in Thetford Mines, Que., in October 2000, a father confronted his son's coach during the intermission after the boy sat out the first period. The man allegedly hit the coach, Pierre Morin, in the face and slammed him to the ground. The attacker was ejected from the building and the injured coach took his place behind the bench for the rest of the game. Afterwards, Morin was taken to hospital where he was diagnosed with a dislocated shoulder. Clement Lajoie was charged with assault and uttering threats of death or bodily harm. His bail conditions forbid him from entering an arena or attending his son's hockey games. The case has not yet gone to court.

Youth sport couldn't exist without its referees and coaches, yet for years the culture surrounding the games has, if anything, driven them away. Dick Derrett, technical administrator for player and referee development at Manitoba Soccer, says that, for officials, dealing with rowdy adults is an ongoing battle. "Some of these parents get it in their head to win, win, win, and they don't care about the kids," Derrett says. "A lot of foul language is used right in front of the kids. For a referee, it is very frightening to be subjected to someone like that, not knowing what they are going to do."

It's not like refs are getting rich. It's a big deal if they receive $20 each to call a game in minor hockey, and they have to supply their own gear, including the striped jerseys. Veteran refs say it can be a lot of fun when the kids play well, the game goes smoothly and the fans enjoy themselves. But too often there is harassment and verbal abuse. In Nanaimo, B.C., local referees boycotted a weekend series of minor hockey games to protest the vicious taunting from so-called fans. Some attacks are not directed at the officials. "I've seen parents fighting in the stands, and heard people yelling racial slurs," says Cam Johnston, a longtime minor-hockey official in Mississauga, Ont. "One time, I saw two mothers pushing and shoving each other after a game, and there were their kids, just tykes, watching and crying. It was just terrible."

Before the start of the 2000-2001 season, the Edmonton Minor Hockey Association introduced something new to its player-registration process. Parents wanting to enrol their kids had to first sign a pledge to behave themselves at games. If they refused to sign, their children were not allowed to play. Simple as that.

Many sports organizations are reluctant to crack down on the hotheads for fear of alienating their members. Youth sports would simply collapse without the help of parents who volunteer as ticket-takers, drivers, fund-raisers, administrators and coaches. While practically every association admits there's a serious problem, they invariably claim their own group of parents is just fine.

Still, zero tolerance is spreading. The fair-play program adopted in Edmonton was pioneered by the Dartmouth Whalers Minor Hockey

Association in Dartmouth, N.S., in 1994. It promotes sportsmanship and equal ice time for players, and respect and restraint among spectators. It has resulted in a dramatic decline in verbal harassment of players and officials, leading nearby associations, which were initially skeptical, to adopt the same rules. In Laval, Que., after police were called to break up a fight in the stands between two parents, Hockey Laval introduced a code of ethics for parents, players, coaches, administrators and officials, and promised that parents will be required to sign the good behaviour pledge. "We want to sensitize people," says Dominique Roy, director of operations at Hockey Laval.

Experts say that approach will work over time. "One of the things we have to do," says Dale England, vice-president of officiating for the Winnipeg Minor Hockey Association, "is to teach parents to respect the game, the coaches, the players and the referees—all the things that go into making this activity happen." Engh, author of *Why Johnny Hates Sports*, says proactive education of parents is the only way to restore order on the sidelines. "Why do parents behave the way they do?" Engh asks. "There are many reasons, but the main one is that no one has ever told them they can't."

That education process has been slow, so youth sport officials hope that the embarrassing string of incidents this winter might prompt more sports to introduce their own fair-play initiatives. Or perhaps they should just listen to kids like Port Dover winger Craig Pineo, 13, who was out there trying to play a game while adults were screaming epithets and throwing debris and ultimately causing the game to be stopped. "I couldn't believe it was happening," Pineo said. "We knew it had nothing really to do with us, but it got a little scary. We were winning the game, but we just wanted to get out of there." And that is just wrong.

I. Response
a. Summarize the thesis of this essay in your own words. Compare your wording with that of other students and discuss the differences.

b. Identify the authors' use of examples to support the thesis. Remember that examples can include any of the following: narration of events drawn from the writer's experience; or statistics, facts, analogies, quotations, and anecdotes of events or incidents in others' lives. How have the authors organized the examples throughout the essay?

c. What seem to be the causes of rink rage? Do you think rink rage can be prevented?

d. If the offenders are few, why is the behaviour tolerated by so many? How do parents and children behave in your local sport competitions?

e. Why do you think some parents put this pressure on their children?

2. ***Visual Communication*** *Presentation* Prepare a visual presentation to encourage the prevention of parental violence connected with sports. You can focus on one sport or on sports in general. Choose your intended audience and purpose, and a suitable format; for example, a cartoon lampooning parents' "support" at a sports competition; a brochure for handing out to parents; a how-to video for parents; a videotaped skit about the problem; a PowerPoint (or similar) presentation; or a poster of rules for behaviour. Include a commentary about why your presentation would be effective in stopping sports rage.

3. ***Media*** *Studying Photos* Study the photos and captions that appear in the sports pages of a variety of newspapers and sports magazines for a given number of days. Using a chart or other graphic organizer, make observations based on the following: What is the subject of the photos? How many of them are of body contact or roughness? What types of shots are they—close up, wide angle, or middle distance? What message is conveyed by the caption? Is there a difference between the kind of shots taken of women's sport as opposed to men's? Study your findings and, in an oral report, share your overall observations.

   Then, assume that you are the photo editor of the sports page for your community's weekly newspaper. Using photos that you clip from newspapers and magazines, digital photos, and/or photos that you shoot, choose five photos that you would use on your sports page, and explain why you chose them.

Theme Connections

A simple cup of coffee turns out to be
not so simple after all.

Coffee

Process Analysis by Alan Durning

Beans

I brewed a cup of coffee. It took 100 beans—about one fortieth of the beans that grew on the coffee tree that year. The tree was on a small mountain farm in the region of Colombia called Antioquia. The region was cleared of its native forests in the first coffee boom three generations ago. These "cloud forests" are among the world's most endangered ecosystems.

The beans ripened in the shade of taller trees. Growing them did not require plowing the soil, but it did take several doses of insecticides, which were synthesized in factories in the Rhine River Valley of Europe. Some of the chemicals entered the respiratory systems of farm workers. Others washed downstream and were absorbed by plants and animals.

The beans were picked by hand. In a diesel-powered crusher they were removed from the fruit that encased them. They were dried under the sun and shipped to New Orleans in a 132-pound bag. The freighter was fueled by Venezuelan oil and made in Japan. The shipyard built the freighter out of Korean steel. The Korean steel mill used iron mined on tribal lands in Papua New Guinea.

At New Orleans the beans were roasted for 13 minutes at temperatures above 400 degrees F. The roaster burned natural gas pumped from the ground in Oklahoma. The beans were packaged in four-layer bags constructed of polyethylene, nylon, aluminum foil and polyester. They were trucked to a Seattle warehouse and later to a retail store.

Bag

I carried the beans out of the grocery in a brown paper bag made at an unbleached kraft paper mill in Oregon. I transported them home in an automobile that burned one sixth of a gallon of gasoline during the five-mile round-trip to the market.

Grinder

In the kitchen, I measured the beans in a disposable plastic scoop molded in New Jersey and spooned them into the grinder. The grinder was assembled in China from imported steel, aluminum, copper, and plastic parts. It was powered by electricity generated at the Ross Dam on the Skagit River.

I dumped the coffee into a gold-plated mesh filter made in Switzerland of Russian ore. I put the filter into a plastic-and-steel drip coffee maker.

I poured eight ounces of tap water into the appliance. The water came by pipe from the Cedar River on the west slope of the Cascade Mountains. An element heated the water to more than 200 degrees F. The hot water seeped through the ground coffee and dissolved some of its oils and solids. The brew trickled into a glass carafe.

Paper Cups

The coffee mugs were all dirty so I poured the coffee into a paper cup. The cup was made from bleached wood pulp in Arkansas. A fraction of the chlorine in the bleach was discharged from the pulp mill into the Arkansas River. In the river, the chlorine ended up as TCDD, which is often simply called dioxin. It is the most carcinogenic substance known.

Cream

I stirred in one ounce of cream. The cream came from a grain-fed dairy cow in the lowlands north of Seattle. The cow liked to graze on a stream bank and walk in the stream. This muddied the water and made life difficult for native trout.

The cow's manure was rich in nitrogen and phosphorus. The soils of the pasture where the cow grazed were unable to absorb these quickly enough, so they washed into the stream when it rained. The infusion of nutrients fertilized algae, which absorbed a larger share of the oxygen dissolved in the water. The shortage of oxygen made life more difficult for native trout.

Sugar

I measured out two tablespoons of sugar. It came from the canefields south of Lake Okeechobee in Florida. These plantations have deprived the Everglades of water, endangering waterfowl and reptile populations.

Alan Durning went to Washington D.C. after college, where he worked at the Worldwatch Institute as a research assistant. At the age of 21, his article on the dangers to the environment of animal farming, published in the *Los Angeles Times*, attracted national interest. Durning continued his work at Worldwatch, researching and publishing articles, and his book, *How Much Is Enough?: The Consumer Society and the Future of the Earth*, was published in 1992.

I. *Response*
   a. In this selection, the author details the processes that occur for him to have a cup of coffee. Briefly outline the steps in this process.
   b. What do you think Durning's purpose was in writing this? Explain the impression you are left with after reading it.
   c. Do you think that the ending provides a satisfactory conclusion? Explain.
   d. What environmental or ecological dangers does the author cite in this selection?

2. *Making Connections* With four or five classmates, discuss the following questions: What foods are manufactured in your area? What foods are imported to your area from other regions of Canada? From North America? From other continents? How much attention do you usually give to the source of what you eat and how it got to your table? Why might it be important to know where the food you eat comes from?

3. *Literature Studies* *Process Analysis* The type of organization or pattern for this selection is called **process analysis**. Look through some essay collections, magazines, or newspapers to find other examples of process

A **process analysis** shows how something is done. It gives information about a process, usually in the same order as the process itself.

analysis. Choose one to focus on and identify the steps in the process, perhaps by using a flow chart.

4. *Language Conventions* *Passive Voice* Alan Durning uses the passive voice in several paragraphs—something most writers usually try to avoid because it makes the writing less vivid and lively. Study the third, fourth, sixth, and ninth paragraphs, and identify the use of this voice. When the author uses "I" in the sentences, what voice does he use? What is the effect of this choice of voice and of sentence construction?

Blue Gold

"Canadians have something we need, and I don't mean hockey players."

Argumentative Essay
by Jim Hightower

Should we invade Canada with armed forces? Sure, they're nice people, and ever so peaceable. (It's going to be hard to work up much xenophobic hatred toward a country that thinks "jeepers" is an expletive, and that has "Be Polite" in its constitution.) But Canadians have something we need, and I don't mean hockey players. "Blue gold," it's been dubbed by a Canadian newspaper, but it's far more valuable than that implies, because the world can do without gold.

Water. That's what Canada has that parts of our country and much of the world might literally kill for.

Hell, you say, water's everywhere. Yes, but as Canada's Maude Barlow points out, less than half of 1 percent of all the water on the globe is drinkable. An author and agitator for common sense, Barlow heads the Council of Canadians and is founding chair of Action Canada Network, two grassroots groups working for progressive policies. "Worldwide, the consumption of water is doubling every 20 years," she writes in a stunning report called "Blue Gold: The Global Water Crisis." In a very short while, most of the world's people will face shortages or absolute scarcity. This is not a matter of seeing more stories of wretched African children dying in horrible droughts, but of imminent water crises in America (the Southwest, Florida, and California especially), Southern Europe, India, England, China, and other nations not usually thought of as facing massive water shortages.

Canada, on the other hand, has a blessing of *agua fresca*. Some 20 percent of the world's entire supply of fresh water is in its winding rivers and countless lakes. This reality has not dawned on Canadians alone; others are casting their eyes northward. But it's not countries making invasion plans—it's corporations.

To get their hands on the gold, the corporate grubbers first have to change how drinking water is managed. Instead of letting countries treat it as a commonly held resource allocated for the general good, they want it considered as a commodity traded by private investors for profit. Like oil or pork bellies ... only this is your drinking water they want to privatize. Will it surprise you to learn that those bratty globalization twins, NAFTA and the World Trade Organization, contain provisions that advance the commodity concept? Both baldly assert that "water, including ordinary natural water of all kinds," is merely one form of "goods," subject to the new rules of global trade.

We're talking about bulk sales here: not Evian, but whole lakes and aquifers bought and mined, rivers siphoned off, the Great Lakes themselves on the market. Barlow and others report that multinationals are ready to use supertankers, pipelines, canals, river rerouting, and other mammoth schemes to shift the product from the water-rich to those willing to pay top dollar:

- Nordic Water Company totes H_2O from Norway to thirsty Europe across the sea in giant, floating plastic bags.
- Global Water Corporation, a Canadian firm, has cut a deal with Sitka, Alaska, to haul 18 billion gallons of water per year from nearby Blue Lake to China—"Water has moved from being an endless commodity that may be taken for granted to a rationed necessity that may be taken by force," says GWC's chilling statement.
- The Great Recycling and Northern Development Canal involves building a dike across James Bay to capture water from 20 rivers that feed it, converting the bay into a giant reservoir, then building a network of canals, dams, and locks to move the water 400 miles south to Georgian Bay, where it would be "flushed through" the Great Lakes into pipelines that would take it to America's Sun Belt for lawn watering, golf course sprinkling, and other essentials.
- The McCurdy Group of Newfoundland hopes to "harvest" some 13 billion gallons of water a year from one of that province's lakes, pipe it to the coast, pump it into old oil tankers, and ship it to the Middle East for a hefty profit.
- One Monsanto executive, seeing a multibillion-dollar business opportunity, says bluntly: "Since water is as central to food production as seed is, and without water life is not possible, Monsanto is now trying to establish its control over water…. Monsanto [has launched] a new water business, starting with India and Mexico, since both these countries face water shortages."

What is written without effort is in general read without pleasure.

Samuel Johnson

"Canada," barked editor Terence Corcoran of the *Financial Post* in a 1999 editorial, "is a future OPEC of water"; he urged that the country begin trading this commodity. But thanks to citizen groups like Maude Barlow's, the Great Canadian Water Sale-a-Thon has yet to begin; their vigilance has produced a temporary moratorium on bulk sales. This might be a good place to add that Maude, and Canadians generally, are not saying, "It's our water and the rest of the world can go suck eggs." To the contrary, they are pushing for a public policy of sharing their bounty to meet the global water crisis, allocating water particularly to help those in need.

But the pressure is intense to simply let "the market" decide who needs it. And the big stick of "free trade" is being wielded to turn the water loose. Sun Belt Water Inc., based in Santa Barbara, California, has filed the first NAFTA water case. It had an agreement with a British Columbia company to ship water in tankers from B.C. to Southern California. But such an outcry ensued when the scheme became public that the provincial government enacted a moratorium on all water exports. The corporation sued Canada in 1998, claiming that its future profits were "expropriated" by British Columbia's export moratorium and that, under NAFTA's Chapter 11, the nice people of Canada owed it $468 million.

Money isn't enough, though. Sun Belt CEO Jack Lindsey is also outraged at what he perceives as Canadian stinginess: "California has 33 million people—more than the entire population of Canada. This is expected to double in the next 20 years, and they have been living in a permanent drought condition. In 20 years, the shortfall in California will be 4 million acre-feet of water [per year]—1 percent of what spills into the Pacific Ocean from British Columbia—and they're saying, 'Sorry, you can't have it?'" Such a humanitarian. Jack just wants a few drops for California's poor parched people.

What a crock. Bulk water deals have nothing to do with global need and everything to do with global greed. Privateers will deliver the water to whoever will pay the most—like Silicon Valley's water-gobbling high-tech companies and agribusiness corporations that suck up aquifers like insatiable sponges. Then there is Lindsey's snide comment about water that just "spills into the Pacific Ocean," a common refrain, as if water that isn't being used commercially is being "wasted." Never mind that water running to the sea is essential to the ecological cycle, delivering nutrients, sustaining fishing economies, replenishing wetlands, and doing much more useful chores than fattening the wallets of would-be water barons.

Jim Hightower is a radio commentator, bestselling author, and public speaker. This selection was taken from his book, *If the Gods Had Meant Us to Vote They Would Have Given Us Candidates.*

1. *Response*
   a. Discuss your response to this essay. How did you feel toward the author? Did this feeling change at any point? Explain.
   b. Is Canada being selfish with its policies concerning its "blue gold"?
   c. Why is the citizenry's vigilance important to the issue of water trade?

2. *Literature Studies* *Argumentative Essay* "Blue Gold" is an example of an argumentative essay. David G. Pitt writes, "Argumentative prose aims not so much to explain something as to convince or persuade others ..." These writing techniques can include making effective word choices; using irony; using the element of surprise or shock; using *hyperbole* (exaggeration); using the imperative voice; and using examples such as facts, statistics, events in real life, or quotations. With this list of techniques in mind, skim the essay to find out how Hightower has presented his argument and analyse its effectiveness.

3. *Oral Communication* *Discussion* Have a round-table discussion on the sale of water, with fellow students representing different countries. You should research the country's water resources and any policies on water consumption, and be prepared to present that country's needs and its possible stance on the issue.

4. *Media* *Ad* Create an ad based on your study of this essay and the water issue. You could, for example, promote Canada's sale of water; urge Canadians to resist the sale of their water; urge people to conserve water; promote the appreciation of our natural resources; or focus on the need for water in countries with few water resources.

5. *Making Connections* What do you think Alan Durning's ("Coffee") response might be to this essay? Support your response by thoroughly examining the opinions given in both "Blue Gold" and "Coffee." How does the way in which each writer presents his thesis differ?

*Mary Schäffer, photographer and pioneer at the turn
of the century, explored the Alberta rocky mountains
and captured an "unmapped country" on film.*

Hunter of Peace

Photo Essay by Mary Schäffer

Here's to a life of unnumbered
summers in the mountains,
with stars above by night,
sunshine and soft winds by day,
with the music of the waters
at our banquet.
Civilisation!
How little it means
when one has tasted
the free life of the trail!

Mary Schäffer Warren was born in Pennsylvania, U.S., in 1861. She was an explorer, watercolour painter, and photographer, returning time and again to Canada where she hiked the trails through the Canadian Rockies. She wrote the books *Untrodden Paths in the Canadian Rockies, Old Indian Trails,* and *A Hunter of Peace*, as well as many articles about the wildflowers and countryside of Saskatchewan and the Rockies. She died in 1939.

1. *Response*
a. Explain what you think the title "Hunter of Peace" means, given the introductory text and photos.
b. What would you say is the thesis of this photo essay? Express it by giving the essay a new title. You could also use a subtitle, if necessary.
c. What inferences or assumptions do you make from the photos? For example, what does the mood of the people seem to be? Who are they? What might their purpose be?
d. Imagine you are in one of the photos. Quickly, record the first words that come to your mind.

2. *Focus on Context*
What do you find out about Mary Schäffer from reading and viewing this essay? Use Internet and library sources to find out more about this photographer. Write a short biography for Schäffer, explaining how her photographic work was affected by her surroundings and the time in which she lived. What was her purpose in creating the photos? Who was her audience?

3. *Visual Communication* Photo Essays
Research to find another photo essay—other than the ones in this anthology —that appeals to you, on any subject, for example, showing another period in history or another location. Present this photo essay to a partner, explaining why it appeals to you.

Alternatively, create a photo essay to represent a period in history, a particular landscape, or a subject of your own. Take your own photos, if feasible, or select print and digital photos. Try a variety of sources. Make decisions about whether or not to include text, whether to use black and white or colour, or both, and about the placement of the photos. Do not forget to include a title. Ask a peer to assess your photo essay and its effectiveness.

4. *Film Study*
Choose one of these photos and consider the story it suggests to you. Jot down notes on the story and use them to develop a movie proposal or treatment (an outline for a movie that is used to sell the movie to a producer). Your proposal should include a title, list of characters, setting, storyline, and probable target audience.

You thought you knew

all about worms...

Worms
and the Soil

Expository Essay by Charles Darwin

Worms have played a more important part in the history of the world than most persons would at first suppose. In almost all humid countries they are extraordinarily numerous, and for their size possess great muscular power. In many parts of England a weight of more than ten tons of dry earth annually passes through their bodies and is brought to the surface on each acre of land; so that the whole superficial bed of vegetable mould passes through their bodies in the course of every few years. From the collapsing of the old burrows the mould is in constant though slow movement, and the particles composing it are thus rubbed together. By these means fresh surfaces are continually exposed to the action of the carbonic acid in the soil, and of the humus-acids[1] which appear to be still more efficient in the decomposition of rocks. The generation of the humus-acids is probably hastened during the digestion of the many half-decayed leaves which worms consume. Thus the particles of earth, forming the superficial mould, are subjected to conditions eminently favorable for their decomposition and disintegration. Moreover, the particles of the softer rocks suffer some amount of mechanical trituration[2] in the muscular gizzards of worms, in which small stones serve as mill-stones.

The finely levigated[3] castings,[4] when brought to the surface in a moist condition, flow during rainy weather down any moderate slope; and the smaller particles are washed far down even a gently inclined surface. Castings when dry often crumble into small pellets and these are apt to roll down any sloping surface. Where the land is quite level and is covered with herbage, and where the climate is humid so that much dust cannot be blown away, it appears at first sight impossible that there should be any appreciable amount of subaerial[5] denudation; but worm castings are blown, especially whilst moist and viscid, in one uniform direction by the prevalent winds which are accompanied by rain. By these several means the superficial mould is prevented from accumulating to a great thickness; and a thick bed of mould checks in many ways the disintegration of the underlying rocks and fragments of rock.

The removal of worm castings by the above means leads to results which are far from insignificant. It has been shown that a layer of earth, two tenths of an inch in thickness, is in many places annually brought to the surface per acre; and if a small part of this amount flows, or rolls, or is washed, even for a short distance down every inclined surface, or is repeatedly blown in one direction, a great effect will be produced in the course of ages. It was found by measurements and calculations that on a surface with a mean inclination of 9°26', two and four tenths cubic inches of earth which had been ejected by worms crossed, in the course of a year, a horizontal line one yard in length; so that 240 cubic inches would cross a line 100 yards in length. This latter amount in a damp state would weigh $11\frac{1}{2}$ pounds. Thus a considerable weight of earth is continually moving down each side of every valley, and will in time reach its bed. Finally this earth will be transported by the streams flowing in the valleys into the ocean, the great receptacle for all matter denuded from the land. It is known from the amount of sediment annually delivered into the sea by the Mississippi, that its enormous drainage-area must on an average be lowered .00263 of an inch each year; and this would suffice in four and a half million years to lower the whole drainage-area to the level of the seashore. So that, if a small fraction of the layer of fine earth, two tenths of an inch in thickness, which is annually brought to the surface by worms, is carried away, a great result cannot fail to be produced within a period which no geologist considers extremely long.

Archaeologists ought to be grateful to worms, as they protect and preserve for an indefinitely long period every object not liable to decay, which is dropped on the surface of the land, by burying it beneath their castings. Thus, also, many elegant and curious tessellated[6] pavements and other ancient remains have been preserved; though no doubt the worms have in these cases been largely aided by earth washed and blown from the adjoining land, especially when cultivated. The old tessellated pavements have, however, often suffered by having subsided unequally from being unequally undermined by the worms. Even old massive walls may be undermined and subside; and no building is in this respect safe, unless the foundations lie six or seven feet beneath the surface, at a depth at which worms cannot work. It is probable that many monoliths[7] and some old walls have fallen down from having been undermined by worms.

Worms prepare the ground in an excellent manner for the growth of fibrous-rooted plants and for seedlings of all kinds. They periodically expose the mould to the air, and sift it so that no stones larger than the particles which they can swallow are left in it. They mingle the whole intimately together, like a gardener who prepares fine soil for his choicest plants. In this state it is well fitted to retain moisture and to absorb all soluble substances, as well as for the process of nitrification.[8] The bones of dead animals, the harder parts of insects, the shells of land-molluscs, leaves, twigs, etc., are before long all buried beneath the accumulated castings of worms, and are thus brought in a more or less decayed state within reach of the roots of plants. Worms likewise drag an infinite number of dead leaves and other parts of plants into their burrows, partly for the sake of plugging them up and partly as food.

The leaves which are dragged into the burrows as food, after being torn into the finest shreds, partially digested, and saturated with the intestinal and urinary secretions, are commingled with much earth. This earth forms the dark colored, rich humus which almost every-where covers the surface of the land with a fairly well-defined layer or mantle. Von Hensen placed two worms in a vessel eighteen inches in diameter, which was filled with sand, on which fallen leaves were strewed; and these were soon dragged into their burrows to a depth of three inches. After about six weeks an almost uniform layer of sand four tenths of an inch in thickness was converted into humus by having passed through the alimentary canals of these two worms. It is believed by some people that worm burrows, which often penetrate the ground almost perpendicularly to a depth of five or six feet, materially aid in its drainage; notwithstanding that the viscid castings piled over the mouths of the burrows prevent or check the rainwater directly entering them. They allow the air to penetrate deeply into the ground. They also greatly facilitate the downward passage of roots of moderate size; and these will be nourished by the humus with which the burrows are lined. Many seeds owe their germination to having been covered by castings; and others buried to a considerable depth beneath accumulated castings lie dormant, until at some future time they are accidentally uncovered and germinate.

The challenge of nonfiction is to marry art and truth.

Phyllis Rose

Worms are poorly provided with sense-organs, for they cannot be said to see, although they can just distinguish between light and darkness; they are completely deaf, and have only a feeble power of smell; the sense of touch alone is well developed. They can therefore learn little about the outside world, and it is surprising that they should exhibit some skill in lining their burrows with their castings and with leaves, and in the case of some species in piling up their castings into tower-like constructions. But it is far more surprising that they should apparently exhibit some degree of intelligence instead of a mere blind instinctive impulse, in their manner of plugging up the mouths of their burrows. They act in nearly the same manner as would a man, who had to close a cylindrical tube with different kinds of leaves, petioles,[9] triangles of paper, etc., for they commonly seize such objects by their pointed ends. But with thin objects a certain number are drawn in by their broader ends. They do not act in the same unvarying manner in all cases, as do most of the lower animals; for instance, they do not drag in leaves by their foot-stalks, unless the basal part of the blade is as narrow as the apex, or narrower than it.

When we behold a wide, turf-covered expanse, we should remember that its smoothness, on which so much of its beauty depends, is mainly due to all the inequalities having been slowly leveled by worms. It is a marvelous reflection that the whole of the superficial mould over any such expanse has passed, and will again pass, every few years through the bodies of worms. The plough is one of the most ancient and most valuable of man's inventions; but long before he existed the land was in fact regularly ploughed, and still continues to be thus ploughed by earth-worms. It may be doubted whether there are many other animals which have played so important a part in the history of the world, as have these lowly organized creatures. Some other animals, however, still more lowly organized, namely corals, have done far more conspicuous work in having constructed innumerable reefs and islands in the great oceans; but these are almost confined to the tropical zones.

---

[1]**humus-acids:** acids in the humus, a brown or black substance resulting from the partial decay of leaves and other vegetable matter
[2]**trituration:** rubbing or grinding into very fine particles or powder
[3]**levigated:** ground to a fine, smooth powder
[4]**castings:** things thrown off or ejected
[5]**subaerial:** beneath the air, hence on the surface
[6]**tessellated:** laid out in a mosaic pattern of small, square blocks
[7]**monoliths:** in architecture, single large blocks of stone
[8]**nitrification:** impregnation of soil with nitrates, which serve as fertilizers
[9]**petioles:** the stalks to which leaves are attached

Charles Darwin was born in Shropshire, England, in 1809. After his education at Edinburgh and Oxford, he joined the English survey ship *HMS Beagle* on a voyage around the world. As a naturalist, he was expected to observe and report on the diverse geological formations, fossils, and living organisms found on the different islands and continents they visited. Darwin is best known for his controversial theories on evolution. In 1859 and 1871, he published his theories in *On the Origin of Species by Means of Natural Selection* and *The Descent of Man*. He died in 1882.

I. *Response*
    a. Why is Darwin so fascinated by worms?
    b. How do you feel about worms? Were your feelings toward worms changed by the information given in this essay? Explain.
    c. What is the thesis of this essay? Do you think Darwin proves this thesis? Explain.
    d. Summarize the main points of this essay.

2. *Focus on Context* Tell a partner everything you know about Charles Darwin. Listen as your partner does the same. Now, research to find out more about who Darwin was, and the time in which he lived. Discuss how this contextual knowledge influences your understanding or appreciation of "Worms and the Soil."

3. *Writing* *Character Sketch* Use the information in the essay and your imagination to develop a fictional character sketch for a worm protagonist or antagonist. Your story could be a horror, fantasy, drama, comedy, adventure, et cetera. Use your character sketch to develop a short story, movie treatment, novel outline, poem, or another format of your choice.

4. *Language Conventions* *Indicative Mood* Examine the use of indicative mood or mode (a verb form showing the manner of action—stating a fact or asking a question) within the essay. How is this mood appropriate to the purpose and content of the essay? What other mood is used in the essay (check a writer's handbook to find out the characteristics of imperative and subjunctive moods)? Where else would you expect to use indicative mood? How do you use indicative mood in your own writing?

A rocket launched into the aurora borealis
during a two-year peak in its activity
is helping scientists unravel the mysteries
of the northern lights.

Night
Spirits

Magazine Article by Candace Savage

One of the pleasures of a Canadian winter is the
night. Stars spangle the heavens, and between their radiant points,
the universe flows outward into endless black. We look up and feel
ourselves falling into cosmic emptiness—blank space without
matter or movement. But then, if luck is with us, the sky begins to
ripple with soft, shimmering curtains of light that fill this seemingly
empty cosmos with energy and life. Aurora borealis, or the northern
lights. So faint they are seldom seen in summer, these luminous
wraiths are a gift of winter's darkness.

The northern lights stand at the boundary between visible and
invisible worlds, giving us a glimpse into a little-known universe. In
times past, people thought that the lights must be spirits: fairies,
magic beasts or bright souls. Even today, while scientists have a
good idea of the physical forces involved, they still view the spec-
tacle of the aurora with old-fashioned awe.

Physicist Dave Knudsen, an assistant professor in the department of physics and astronomy at the University of Calgary, is a
case in point. Raised in Iowa (where the aurora rarely appears), he
was in his twenties before he first saw the northern lights in action.
Yet, despite the novelty of the experience, Knudsen was never in
any doubt about what he was looking at. "I've always been driven
by a desire to understand electricity and magnetism," he explains,
"and this was so obviously a display of electromagnetism. I knew
there must be basic laws governing it, but it was so inexplicably
complex. My mind was just racing with excitement!"

To Knudsen, the northern lights are more than a source of delight. To him they are a manifestation of turbulent forces that bluster and roil throughout the dark universe. "If you go even 100 kilometres above Earth, to the base of the auroral curtains," he says, "you already find yourself in a different world. The behaviour of the physical system is dramatically different there than what we find here on the ground. It's not hard to imagine that things get even more interesting and complex as you move farther out."

With this thought in mind, Knudsen recently initiated a multi-million-dollar international research project known as GEODESIC or, to give its full moniker: Geo-electrodynamics and Electro-Optical Detection of Electron and Suprathermal Ion Currents. The effort literally got off the ground in February 2000, when Knudsen and his team launched a sounding rocket (built by Winnipeg's Bristol Aerospace) from the Poker Flat rocket range, near Fairbanks, Alaska. The main purpose of the six-year study is to investigate the otherworldly behaviour of charged particles in and around the auroral curtains.

Space is occupied not by the solids, liquids and gases that we earthlings know so well. Instead, it is filled with a fourth state of matter known as plasma—a kind of improbably thin, electrically active vapour. Although natural plasmas are rare on Earth (found only in exotic phenomena such as ball lightning), they are exceedingly common in space. In fact, about 99 percent of the matter in the universe is thought to exist in the plasma state. Unlike air, which is electrically inert, plasmas consist of charged molecules and atoms that not only respond to familiar physical forces (such as pressure and gravity) but are also highly sensitive to electromagnetic fields. Pushed and pulled by all these conflicting forces, plasma is even more chaotic and dynamic than air, many times more changeable than weather.

Yet all the cosmic *Sturm und Drang*[1] of the plasma might pass us by unnoticed—if it weren't for the aurora. Like whitecaps on a storm-tossed sea, the northern lights are the visible crests of invisible plasma waves that batter Earth. (Much of this bombardment originates in the sun, which spews out streams of plasma as the so-called solar wind.) Drawn toward the polar regions of Earth along magnetic lines of force, plasma cascades ever downward until—about 1,000 kilometres overhead—it begins to run into atmospheric gases. As high-speed electrons in the plasma collide with oxygen and nitrogen in the air, the gases receive an energetic jolt, which they emit as faint bursts of colour

---

[1] ***Sturm und Drang:*** German, meaning, literally, storm and stress. Refers to a literary movement in Germany in the late eighteenth century.

(greenish white for oxygen, pink for nitrogen). When millions of energized molecules go off at the same time, the night sky begins to dance with all the tumultuous vigour of the plasma currents. Down on Earth, we look up and emit gasps of delight.

If we want to understand the cosmic forces that whirl through space, we cannot do better than to study auroral displays. "The northern lights provide us with a natural laboratory for studying plasma structures," says Knudsen. We can be pretty sure that whatever is simmering in the northern lights is boiling over somewhere else in the universe." For example, there are fine structures within the aurora—tubes less than 50 metres across—that appear to serve as a kind of charged-particle gun, or accelerator. Through some unknown mechanism, these tubes transfer energy from plasma to atmospheric ions and send them zooming off into outer space. If Knudsen and his GEODESIC colleagues can figure out how these accelerators work, they will have made a small contribution to understanding the northern lights and a larger one to solving an outstanding problem in plasma physics.

Northern Lights, Alberta, Canada by Daryl Benson. Photo

Examine this photo and record your thoughts and feelings on its content and composition. Use these notes to create a piece of writing (short story, folk tale, poem, essay, et cetera) that explores the impact that the northern lights have on humanity.

As the GEODESIC rocket blasted off from Poker Flat and through a display of northern lights, its payload of sensitive instruments took a rapid-fire series of measurements, at the rate of about 10 million bits per second. Translated into graphical images, these data trace the moment-by-moment behaviour of charged particles in a series of accelerators. The entire mission, from takeoff to crash landing in the frozen Beaufort Sea, took 17 minutes flat. But decoding and figuring out what the data mean will keep Knudsen and his colleagues busy until about 2003.

Meanwhile, Knudsen is preparing an instrument for another rocket that will be launched from Norway's Svalbard Archipelago in December 2001. Again, his plan is to make measurements inside accelerators. But his larger mission—the purpose that drives his research—is to understand the fundamental forces raging through the universe. They are out there every second, whether we can see them or not, dancing over our heads in the infinite darkness.

> ... writing is the action of thinking, just as drawing is the action of seeing and composing music is the action of hearing. And all that is inward must be expressed in action, for that is the true life of the spirit and the only way we can be continually discarding our dead and mistaken (sinful) selves and progressing and knowing more.
>
> Brenda Ueland

Candace Savage, a writer based in Saskatoon, Saskatchewan, was born in northern Alberta. She is the author of twenty books, including *Aurora: The Mysterious Northern Lights*, *The Nature of Wolves*, and *Bird Brains*. She writes about wildlife, the environment, natural sciences, and women's history, and received an Honour Book Award, Children's Literature Roundtable, in 1991 for her book, *Trash Attack!*

1. *Response*

a. What knowledge did you have of the northern lights before reading this article? Have you ever seen them? If you have not, how important is it to you to see them? If you have, describe how you felt when you saw them.

b. If you had lived in times long past, how do you think you would have explained the northern lights? What must it have been like to see them then?

c. Create a diagram to illustrate the author's description of the plasma and/or the aurora.

2. *Writing* Technical Report

Explaining scientific or technical information for a general audience can be difficult to do well. How has this author made the science of the northern lights easy to understand? Write a brief report explaining another natural phenomenon. Do some research, if necessary, and use some of the techniques that Savage uses.

3. *Language Conventions* Parentheses and Apposition

In expository writing, writers often need to convey as much information as possible in a succinct way. If they are introducing new vocabulary, they sometimes need to offer brief definitions within their sentences. Skim the report to see how Savage has used parentheses to offer additional or qualifying information, and how she uses **apposition** to offer definitions of terms. Examine a piece of your own expository writing to see how you can use apposition and parentheses more effectively.

Apposition is the relation of two parts of a sentence when the one is added as an explanation to the other. For example, in *Mr. Brown, our teacher, is on vacation*, *Mr. Brown* and *teacher* are in apposition.

4. *Making Connections*

Use library or Internet resources to find two more literature selections—for example, a poem, story, folk tale, myth, or non-fiction item—that are about the northern lights. Discuss these works with a small group, comparing any descriptions of the northern lights and the role they play in the various selections.

An encounter with a weasel
leads to Annie Dillard's reflection
on how she would like to live her life—
by yielding only to necessity.

Living Like Weasels

Analogy by Annie Dillard

A weasel is wild. Who knows what he thinks? He sleeps in his underground den, his tail draped over his nose. Sometimes he lives in his den for two days without leaving. Outside, he stalks rabbits, mice, muskrats, and birds, killing more bodies than he can eat warm, and often dragging the carcasses home. Obedient to instinct, he bites his prey at the neck, either splitting the jugular vein at the throat or crunching the brain at the base of the skull, and he does not let go. One naturalist refused to kill a weasel who was socketed into his hand deeply as a rattlesnake. The man could in no way pry the tiny weasel off, and he had to walk half a mile to water, the weasel dangling from his palm, and soak him off like a stubborn label.

I have been thinking about weasels because I saw one last week. I startled a weasel who startled me, and we exchanged a long glance.

Near my house in Virginia is a pond—Hollins Pond. It covers two acres of bottomland near Tinker Creek with six inches of water and six thousand lily pads. There is a fifty-five mph highway at one end of the pond, and a nesting pair of wood ducks at the other. Under every bush is a muskrat hole or a beer can. The far end is an alternating series of fields and woods, fields and woods, threaded everywhere with motorcycle tracks—in whose bare clay wild turtles lay eggs.

One evening last week at sunset, I walked to the pond and sat on a downed log near the shore. I was watching the lily pads at my feet tremble and part over the thrusting path of a carp. A yellow warbler appeared to my right and flew behind me. It caught my eye; I swiveled around—and the next instant, inexplicably, I was looking down at a weasel, who was looking up at me.

Weasel! I had never seen one wild before. He was ten inches long, thin as a curve, a muscled ribbon, brown as fruitwood, soft-furred, alert. His face was fierce, small and pointed as a lizard's; he would have made a good arrowhead. There was just a dot of chin, maybe two brown hairs' worth, and then the pure white fur began that spread down his underside. He had two black eyes I did not see, any more than you see a window.

The weasel was stunned into stillness as he was emerging from beneath an enormous shaggy wild-rose bush four feet away. I was stunned into stillness, twisted backward on the tree trunk. Our eyes locked, and someone threw away the key.

Our look was as if two lovers, or deadly enemies, met unexpectedly on an overgrown path when each had been thinking of something else: a clearing blow to the gut. It was also a bright blow to the brain, or a sudden beating of brains, with all the charge and intimate grate of rubbed balloons. It emptied our lungs. It felled the forest, moved the fields, and drained the pond; the world dismantled and tumbled into that black hole of eyes. If you and I looked at each other that way, our skulls would split and drop to our shoulders. But we don't. We keep our skulls.

He disappeared. This was only last week, and already I don't remember what shattered the enchantment. I think I blinked, I think I retrieved my brain from the weasel's brain, and tried to memorize what I was seeing, and the weasel felt the yank of separation, the careening splashdown into real life and the urgent current of instinct. He vanished under the wild rose. I waited motionless, my mind suddenly full of data and my spirit with pleadings, but he didn't return.

Please do not tell me about "approach-avoidance conflicts."[1] I tell you I've been in that weasel's brain for sixty seconds, and he was in mine. Brains are private places, muttering through unique and secret tapes—but the weasel and I both plugged into another tape simultaneously, for a sweet and shocking time. Can I help it if it was a blank?

What goes on in his brain the rest of the time? What does a weasel think about? He won't say. His journal is tracks in clay, a spray of feathers, mouse blood and bone: uncollected, unconnected, loose-leaf, and blown.

I would like to learn, or remember, how to live. I come to Hollins Pond not so much to learn how to live as, frankly, to forget about it. That is, I don't think I can learn from a wild animal how to live in

---

[1] *approach-avoidance conflicts:* theory in psychology—a person has opposing urges to do something and hold back at the same time

particular—shall I suck warm blood, hold my tail high, walk with my footprints precisely over the prints of my hands?—but I might learn something of mindlessness, something of the purity of living in the physical senses and the dignity of living without bias or motive. The weasel lives in necessity and we live in choice, hating necessity and dying at the last ignobly in its talons. I would like to live as I should, as the weasel lives as he should. And I suspect that for me the way is like the weasel's: open to time and death painlessly, noticing everything, remembering nothing, choosing the given with a fierce and pointed will.

I missed my chance. I should have gone for the throat. I should have lunged for that streak of white under the weasel's chin and held on, held on through mud and into the wild rose, held on for a dearer life. We could live under the wild rose wild as weasels, mute and uncomprehending. I could very calmly go wild. I could live two days in the den, curled, leaning on mouse fur, sniffing bird bones, blinking, licking, breathing musk, my hair tangled in the roots of grasses. Down is a good place to go, where the mind is single. Down is out, out of your ever-loving mind and back to your careless senses. I remember muteness as a prolonged and giddy fast, where every moment is a feast of utterance received. Time and events are merely poured, unremarked, and ingested directly, like blood pulsed into my gut through a jugular vein. Could two live that way? Could two live under the wild rose, and explore by the pond, so that the smooth mind of each is as everywhere present to the other, and as received and as unchallenged, as falling snow?

We could, you know. We can live any way we want. People take vows of poverty, chastity, and obedience—even of silence—by choice. The thing is to stalk your calling in a certain skilled and supple way, to locate the most tender and live spot and plug into that pulse. This is yielding, not fighting. A weasel doesn't "attack" anything; a weasel lives as he's meant to, yielding at every moment to the perfect freedom of single necessity.

I think it would be well, and proper, and obedient, and pure, to grasp your one necessity and not let it go, to dangle from it limp wherever it takes you. Then even death, where you're going no matter how you live, cannot you part. Seize it and let it seize you up aloft even, till your eyes burn out and drop; let your musky flesh fall off in shreds, and let your very bones unhinge and scatter, loosened over fields, over fields and woods, lightly, thoughtless, from any height at all, from as high as eagles.

Annie Dillard was born in 1945 in the U.S. She studied English, theology, and creative writing at college, and graduated with a Masters in English in 1968. After a near fatal attack of pneumonia in 1971, she decided to live life more fully, and spent the next year in Tinker Creek. Life among the forests, creeks, and mountains led her, at the age of 29, to write her world-renowned book, *Pilgrim at Tinker Creek*. In 1975, Dillard won the Pulitzer Prize for general non-fiction. Some of her other works include an autobiography of her early years called *American Childhood*, and a book of poetry, *Ticket for a Prayer Wheel*. She works as an adjunct professor of English at Wesleyan University in Connecticut.

1. *Response*
   a. Find an example of vivid description in this selection that allows you to see, almost like a picture or movie, what Dillard is describing. How has she made the picture real?
   b. Identify the four parts of this selection, and note the shifts in focus and tone from part to part. How has the author achieved these shifts? How has she linked the last part with her introductory paragraph—what image is repeated?
   c. In the third paragraph, the author uses the technique of contrast to make her point. Identify the series of contrasts and explain what she is contrasting, in a larger sense.

2. *Literature Studies* *Analogy* This selection uses an *analogy*; it uses a subject (a weasel) as a representation of something else, or to show us a likeness between two things. What does the weasel represent? List two other examples of analogies in your own reading, in movies, or TV shows, or in the way you explain things to others, either verbally or in writing. Use an analogy to write a short essay about a subject of your choice.

3. **Language Focus** *Poetic Language* Dillard uses a number of stylistic devices to give her writing a rhythm and fluidity that is almost poetic. She uses vivid language and images, alliteration, and *consonance, and assonance* (similar vowel sounds repeated in the same sentence(s)). Many of her sentences are balanced: Two or more sentences in succession, or two parts of a sentence will have the same number of syllables, or close to it. See the opening two sentences, for example. Skim the selection to look for examples of these devices and of others that make Dillard's writing so evocative. Keep a record of the techniques so that you can refer to them when you do your own writing.

4. **Making Connections** In the second part of the selection (the eleventh paragraph), Dillard makes a subtle reference to Henry David Thoreau's famous work, *Walden*, in which he writes, "I went to the woods because I wished to live deliberately, to front only the essential facts of life, and see if I could not learn what it had to teach, and not when I came to die, discover that I had not lived." How does this compare with Dillard's thesis?

5. **Visual Communication** *Collage* "Living Like Weasels," "Hunter of Peace," and "Stone Faces" all have points of similarity. Choose sentences from these selections that express similar thoughts or themes, and input the sentences on the computer or write them out. From these sentences, or using just words and phrases from the sentences, create a collage of this text. Experiment with fonts, type styles and sizes, and colour.

Theme Connections

- *"The Large Ant," a story about following instincts to survive, Vol. I, p. 150*
- *"The World Is Too Much With Us," a poem about rejecting civilization, Vol. I, p. 219*
- *"Stone Faces," an essay about art transcending necessity, Vol. II, p. 37*
- *"Hunter of Peace," a photo essay about leaving civilization behind, Vol. II, p. 90*

Media

Societies have always been shaped more by the nature of the media by which men communicate than by the content of the communication.

Marshall McLuhan

As you read the following selection, consider the original audience and the purpose of this article. Who benefits from having this article appear in a local paper?

Follows Family Stages a Reunion

Newspaper Article by Harry Currie

from the *Kitchener-Waterloo Record*, June 2001

"We are a beastly family, and I hate us!"

So says a member of the Bliss family in Noël Coward's play *Hay Fever*, which is being rehearsed for a run at the Gravenhurst Opera House and at Guelph's River Run Centre.

But this is a unique production, for the Bliss family is being played by the Follows family, who are together both as a family and a group of thespians for the first time in years.

Ted Follows, father of the crew, now lives in Kitchener with his second wife Susan, and the others are spread out across North America. Ted's first wife, actress Dawn Greenhalgh, has joined the family for this production, and their children Laurence, Edwina, Megan, and Samantha are all present, along with Megan's partner Stuart Hughes and Samantha's husband Sean O'Bryan.

Ted and Megan took a few moments in a break from rehearsals to speak about the experience.

"We're not there yet," said Follows, "but we're getting to be a beastly family. We're plowing our way through. It's an awful lot of work, with many interruptions going on. Rehearsals are being held up, and I know it can't be helped when it's for public relations, but it definitely slows us down. But all in all it's coming along fine."

Follows feels that the difficulty in the play is that the real story is hidden below the actual dialogue.

"Because it's Coward, people tend to think that it's all superficial," he said. "But that superficial dialogue is masking the hidden tensions which are there constantly. A character may look as though he's falling asleep, but the energy which drives the characters is very, very powerful and completely unstated.

"With the Bliss family, filled with selfishness, each one wants to outweigh any thoughts for the others' needs or desires, yet this is never really stated. It's what's not said that's important."

Megan is probably the best-known of the Follows children, with her now-legendary role as Anne in the film version of *Anne of Green Gables*. She arrived here after finishing a movie that brought her from the glitz and glamour to Smalltown, Ontario.

"You know what?" she said. "It's wonderful. It really is a refreshing change."

The family hasn't acted together like this since filming three episodes of TV's *The Littlest Hobo* back in the early '80s when they were just kids.

"By the end of the day we're exhausted," she said, "but it's so unique, and so great being together. I'm so grateful to have this time with my brother and sisters, and particularly with my parents.

"I see different siblings at different times, but it's been a long time since we've all been together. It's wonderful to spend time with my mother and father together, because they've been separated since I was 11. I feel really grateful for that."

Megan finds working with the whole family in a play very interesting.

"We know each other extremely well," she said, "and we're having a lot of fun with one another. I think we all really appreciate each other's sense of humour. That's important, because that seems to be a stronger bond than anything—at least we're not getting on each other's nerves yet."

The film Megan has just finished was shot in Montréal.

"The working title was *The Stork Derby*," she said. "It's a great Canadian story about a man named Charles Miller who was a millionaire in the '20s. He left a million dollars in his will to the woman who gave birth to the most children 10 years to the date of his death. The newspapers called it the Stork Derby. It should be shown during the next season."

Patriarch Ted said this whole experience was like real-time déjà vu.

"I feel as though I've gone full circle," he said. "I was doing this back in the forties —performing together, living together—and here we are once again. It's hard to believe it's happened." ◗

> A camera is an instrument that teaches people how to see without a camera.
>
> Dorothea Lange

A native of Moncton, New Brunswick, **Harry Currie** is a graduate
of four Canadian and British colleges and universities.
He has been a Director of Music in the Canadian army, worked
as an actor/singer/player/composer/arranger/conductor in Britain
for ten years, taught high school music and English, published
a thriller called *Debut for a Spy*. He is an entertainment writer
for *The Record* in Kitchener/Waterloo.

I. *Response*
a. Return to the introductory text at the top of this article
and respond.
b. What is a *thespian*? What connotations does this word
have? What synonym could be used in the place of *thespian*?
c. In your opinion, does this article provide a reader with
enough information about the play *Hay Fever* and its production? Explain.
d. Would you go and see a play you knew nothing about if
an actor you really liked was playing the lead role? Why or
why not?

2. *Media* *Publicity* The newspaper published this article because
many of its readers would be interested in local theatre. The
people producing the play would be eager to have this article
in the newspaper, since it might increase the public's interest
in seeing the play. This process of spreading news about a new
play, movie, book, or product is known as *publicity* or *public
relations*, and is the responsibility of a marketing department.
With a group, brainstorm ideas for spreading good publicity
about a new play in your community. Which of your ideas do
you think would be most effective? Why?

3. *Making Connections* Find a copy of Noël Coward's play,
Hay Fever. Read at least two scenes and, with a partner,
discuss why you would or would not like to see this play
performed. Which actors would you cast in the main roles?
Why? If you cannot find *Hay Fever*, research Noël Coward
and his writing.

Richard Curtis, the screenwriter of *Four Weddings and a Funeral*, reveals all about writing movie scripts. This article appeared in *The Observer* (a British newspaper) the week before the movie was released in the summer of 1993.

Four Rules and a Suggestion

How-To Article by Richard Curtis

Everyone who ever wrote a film hates Sylvester Stallone most of all. Apparently, he locked himself in a room for three days and wrote *Rocky*, the first one, which is a marvellous script and an excellent movie. But mostly things don't happen that way. Writing a film script is a stupidly long process, and for everyone except Sylvester, a pretty agonising one.

Three years ago I started writing a film called *Four Weddings and a Funeral*, which comes out this Friday. I'm sure my experiences with it can't be generalised about—but just in case there are any prospective screenwriters amongst you, here is my simplistic stab at Four Rules and a Suggestion for screenwriting.

My first rule is that you let things stew. I've twice written films straight after I thought up the idea, and they were both disastrous. In 1989 I thought of an idea for a film about dreams, complete, at a petrol station on the A40. I drove home and started writing frantically. Six weeks later it was finished. Six weeks and one day later it was in the dustbin. I reread it, and I realised it was well-constructed twaddle, it meant absolutely nothing to me. On the other occasion, I wrote a film for America, to please Americans, which I made up on the way to a "pitch-meeting." Two whole years of writing later, I attended another meeting at MGM—they told me they absolutely loved the film, provided I could change the character of the leading man, the second lead, the cameos, the dialogue and the jokes. I said that only left the title. They said they wanted to change the title too. So that's the first thing—it helps to let things stew in your head a while to find out if you really care. The process of filmmaking is SO DETAILED and SO LONG, nothing fraudulent is going to escape discovery.

My second rule is—try not to pitch. If you can avoid it, try not to get commissioned. Now this is a tough one, because most of us need the money—but the problem with pitching things, and with treatments, is that two people can read the same bit of paper and sit in the same room having the same discussion, but they never hear the same thing. One of them leaves intending to write biting social satire—the other happily describes how he's commissioned a sexy pants-and-knickers farce. Then, as the writer writes, the film comes to life, and changes. It's no longer a social satire, it's a dead serious state-of-the-nation film, moved from the original Westminster location to the brooding Shetland Islands. So you deliver your film, and the person who commissioned it is INEVITABLY disappointed. The next year is spent reconciling a film now called *Earthworm* with the original treatment, called *Sir Peter's Trousers*. So if you can write the thing first, at least the people who buy it, if they buy it, are under no misapprehension about what they're paying for.

On to rule three. If you possibly can, get your work edited by someone you love. My first film, called *The Tall Guy*, was a four-hour muddle before my best friend, Helen, got her hands on it. Five different times she read it and cut it down. The film that was accepted was the fifth draft by me and her. *Four Weddings* is a co-operation between me and my girl, Emma. She read every draft of every scene from the beginning of the process to the end. For a year I lived in terror of the fatal initials "C.D.B." scattered through everything she read. "C.D.B." stands for "Could Do Better." Once again, you're lucky if you can get this—but the thing about a friend, girlfriend, boyfriend, wife, or husband is that they understand what you're getting at. They have no hidden agenda—they want the film to be good, and to be your film—not just profitable and a perfect vehicle for Steve Guttenberg.

I stopped believing in Santa Claus when I was six. Mother took me to see him in a department store and he asked me for my autograph.

Shirley Temple

Rule four is—don't count the rewrites or it will drive you mad. These were the rewrites on *Four Weddings*—five for Emma before it was ever handed in. One after talking to Duncan, my producer, and Debra at Working Title, the production company. Then two big ones for Mike Newell, the director, and Duncan, as we tried to give every character proper stories, rather than just jokes. Then there was one after the first round of casting: actors reading the lines tend to show just how clunky the script is! The next rewrite came after Channel 4 expressed worries about it all being a bit "smart." Then the film was delayed for six months, so there was one long rewrite to fill the time and to try to crack the really knotty problems with the end. At one point, Emma and I escaped to Europe, and spent a month on one 2-minute scene. Then there was another rewrite during the second round of casting. Then one when our budget went from £3.5 million to £3.2. Then another one when it went from £3.2 to £2.7, which consisted of cutting down the cast: "a vicar," became "the vicar you saw earlier." After the read-through (when no one laughed at 15 percent of the "jokes" and DID laugh at 25 percent of the serious bits), there was another hefty hack. During rehearsals another. That's seventeen, and I've got a nasty feeling I've forgotten one or two. And the horrible thing about this rule is part two of it—don't resent the rewrites—the awful painful truth is that the script probably did get a bit better each time.

And so on to the suggestion: **I suggest that**—after you have let an idea stew, written the film you wanted without the compromises of commission, let it be brutally edited by someone you love and then rewritten it fifteen times—**you cast Hugh Grant as the lead**. It doesn't matter what the character is—if she's a middle-aged cop on the verge of retiring, Hugh will be perfect. If he's an Eskimo schoolboy—Hugh is exactly what you are looking for. This weekend *Four Weddings and a Funeral* may pass the thirty-million-dollar mark in America, and relatives in New York tell me that's really down to Hugh. If only we'd been canny, and cast him in the Andie Mac-Dowell, Simon Callow, and Rowan Atkinson roles as well, it could have been fifty million by now. And that's the hell of it. Whatever your script is like, no matter how much stewing and rewriting—if the punters don't want to sleep with the star, you may never be asked to write another one.

Publicity Shot from *Four Weddings and a Funeral*.

Richard Curtis is a well-known British scriptwriter. After graduation from university, he joined a team of writers to create *Not the Nine O'Clock News*. He also created the TV shows *Blackadder* and *The Vicar of Dibley*, and wrote the screenplays for the movies *Notting Hill* and *Bean*.

1. *Response*
a. How helpful did you find Curtis's advice about writing a screenplay? What piece of advice was most helpful? Least helpful?
b. In your opinion, does the humour within this selection make it more or less effective? Explain your answer to a partner.
c. What does the image accompanying the article reveal about the movie?

2. *Film Study* Use Internet and library resources to find out more about Richard Curtis and *Four Weddings and a Funeral*. If possible, view the movie and then write a movie review for it. Examine the features and structure of movie reviews in your local newspaper and use them as a model.

3. *Writing How-To* In a humorous way, Curtis provides some very helpful tips for writing a screenplay. Think of some activity at which you excel. Write at least four rules and one suggestion about this activity that would help someone doing it for the first time.

4. *Media Movie Industry* With a small group, discuss the process of making a movie, starting with the information provided in this article. (You may also wish to check out what Emma Thompson reveals about moviemaking in the following article.) What various jobs or roles are there in the movie industry? Which job appeals to you most? Why? What motivates the various people involved in the movie industry? For example, consider what might have motivated Thompson or Curtis to write their screenplays.

There are two cinemas: the films we have actually seen and the memories we have of them.
—*Molly Haskell*

This selection is from Emma Thompson's (star and screenwriter of the movie *Sense and Sensibility*) diary that she kept during the pre-filming and filming of the movie.

The Making of
Sense and Sensibility

Production Notes

by Emma Thompson

Production meeting in Oxford Street on a raw wintry morning on Monday 15 January 1995. Lindsay Doran (producer), James Schamus (co-producer), Ang Lee (director) and I had met previously this month to discuss the latest draft of the script, which is what we're all here to work through. Tony Clarkson (locations manager) and Laurie Borg (co-producer) already know one another but this is the first time the core personnel of the shoot have met to prepare.

Lindsay goes round the table and introduces everyone—making it clear that I am present in the capacity of writer rather than actress, therefore no one has to be too nice to me. It's 9 a.m. and everyone looks a bit done in. Except Ang, who brings self-contained calm wherever he goes. Just looking at him makes me feel frazzled in comparison, as though all my hair's standing on end.

Our first point of discussion is the hunt (during which, in this version, we witness the accident that kills Mr Dashwood). Where do we get a hunt? It seems to require at least twenty-five male stunt riders—or we hire a real hunt, like the Beaufort which was used on *The Remains of the Day*. Ang wants villagers and labourers watching and to see the fox being chased. My idea is to start the film with an image of the vixen locked out of her lair which has been plugged up. Her terror as she's pursued across the country. This is a big deal. It means training a fox from birth or dressing up a dog to look like a fox.

Or hiring David Attenborough, who probably knows a few foxes well enough to ask a favour. Laurie finally says it's impossible.

What Ang wants next is even more expensive: he's desperate for a kitchen scene in Norland Park (home to the Dashwoods—to be filmed at Saltram House in Devon) which would show the entire staff of Norland preparing a huge meal. I want a bleeding Mr Dashwood to be brought in through the kitchen door and laid on the table surrounded by all the raw joints of meat. As Ang and I enthuse about symbolism, Laurie gently reminds us of expense. These are costly scenes and the film hasn't even started.

I look around the table and realise—perhaps for the first time—that it's actually going to happen. After five years' work on the script (albeit intermittent), the sense of released energy is palpable. There are budgets, an office and several real people here. I glaze over for a second, in shock. Pulled out of reverie by James asking, yet again, what physical activities can be found for Elinor and Marianne. Painting, sewing, embroidering, writing letters, pressing leaves, it's all depressingly girlie. Chin-ups, I suggest, but promise to think further.

Photo from *Sense and Sensibility* by Clive Coote.

Examine this photo. How would you describe the relationship between the people in the photo?

We start to work through the entire script, adding, subtracting, bargaining, negotiating, trying to save money wherever we can. We get to the ballroom sequence and I suggest that we create several vignettes that occur in the background—a rich old rake forcing his attentions on a young girl whose greedy father affects not to notice, a fat matriarch surrounded by sycophantic cousins—a Cruikshankian taste of nineteenth-century greed and hypocrisy. More expensive than simply filling the room with extras but much more interesting. Laurie's eyes roll but he agrees that it's worth the effort and money.

I have a notion that it might be nice to see Colonel Brandon tickling trout—something to draw Marianne to him. Tickling trout is a mysterious old country method of catching trout; you tickle their tummies and when they're relaxed you whip them out of the water. I ask Laurie if it's possible to get trained fish. Lindsay says this is how we know I've never produced a movie. She tells us that two of her friends had read the script and thought I'd invented the pregnancy of Brandon's family ward for shock value. It's surprising to find such events in Austen, but after all, how many people know that there's a duel in *Sense and Sensibility*? When Lindsay asked me to adapt the novel I thought that *Emma* or *Persuasion* would have been better. In fact there's more action in *S & S* than I'd remembered and its elements translate to drama very effectively.

We get to the end of the script by 3.20 p.m. and Lindsay says, "Can we afford the movie we just described?" It's a long, complex script and the budget is pushing the limit. James is most worried about the number of shooting days. Doesn't seem enough. (In the event, our fifty-eight days stretched to sixty-five.)

Wander out into Oxford Street slightly dazed. "See you in April," I say to Laurie. Now everyone goes their separate ways to continue prep. Ang and James return to New York and work on budget and schedule from there. Lindsay returns to LA to produce and I go to West Hampstead and switch the computer on. Another draft ... I spend the rest of January in tears and a black dressing gown.

During February and March I revise the script constantly but the basic structure remains the same. Half a dozen new drafts hit the presses but by 2 April we settle on the final shooting draft. The hunt and kitchen scenes discussed at the January production meeting have both been cut due to budget and schedule constraints.

Never judge a book by its movie.

J.W. Eagan

In February, Ang, James and Lindsay return and the casting process begins. We start with Fanny. Everyone we see captures perfectly the balance of wifely concern and vicious self-interest. Ang says at the end of one day, "This is a nation of Fannys." It rings horribly true. Some characters are far more elusive, notably Lucy Steele and Willoughby, perhaps because of their hidden motives. Gemma Jones, Kate Winslet and Elizabeth Spriggs are so immediately Mrs Dashwood, Marianne and Mrs Jennings that we find it difficult to imagine anyone else in the roles. I'm excited about the fact that five of the actors I prevailed upon to perform a reading of an early draft last year are all hired by Ang: Hugh Grant (Edward), Robert Hardy (Sir John), Harriet Walter (Fanny), Imelda Staunton (Charlotte Palmer) and Hugh Laurie (Mr Palmer). Also that Hugh Grant, for whom I wrote Edward, has agreed to do it despite having become after *Four Weddings* the most famous man in the world. It's odd to be on the other side of the casting process. Even though Michelle Guish, the casting director, makes the circumstances as relaxed as possible, I am uncomfortably aware of how difficult it is for an actor to walk into a small room full of people staring at them. Lindsay is quite shy, James chats a bit, Ang seldom says anything at all and I make a lot of irrelevant noise whenever there's a long silence. Ang's principal criteria are unexpected. Physiognomy matters a great deal to him. Not whether a person is good-looking but the spaces between their lower lip and chin and between the bridge of the nose and forehead. Praxitelean proportions, virtually. After a first meeting with an actor there's a second during which we read scenes. I get the opportunity to play all the other roles and have a minor success with Sir John. Then a third when the scenes are put on video. Ang is not familiar with many British actors so we see people time and again until he's certain of what he wants.

"Can everyone in England act?" he says after a particularly engaging afternoon. Lindsay and I think about this one for quite some time before deciding that probably the answer is yes.

Ang presents a collection of intriguing contradictions. He does t'ai chi but his shoulders are constantly bowed, he meditates and smokes (not at the same time as far as I know), he hasn't an ounce of fat on him but eats everything going, especially buns. When I cooked roast beef for him he ate *all* the Yorkshire puddings—about eleven. He's forty years old and looks thirty.

As each role gets cast, the fact of the shoot becomes increasingly concrete. I rewrite scenes with the actors in my head. At the end of March I go away for two weeks, try to forget about the script and think about Elinor.

Emma Thompson was born in 1959 in London, England. She attended Newnham College at Cambridge University where she joined the Footlight Club, a group that performed comedies. Thompson, who is known first and foremost as an actress, won an Oscar for best screenplay for *Sense and Sensibility* in 1995.

I. *Response*
a. What is the most interesting or surprising detail about the production of movies that you discovered while reading this selection? Explain.

b. Discuss any references from this selection that you did not understand.

c. What impression of Ang Lee does Emma Thompson leave you with?

2. *Film Study*
With a small group, generate ideas for a movie that an audience of your peers would enjoy. Choose one idea and develop a proposal or pitch for it. Describe the genre (suspense, adventure, comedy, romance), theme, characters, and plot of your movie. Consider the tips provided in "Four Rules and a Suggestion" and "The Making of *Sense and Sensibility*."

3. *Making Connections*
Turn to the Drama unit in this book and find the scenes taken from *Sense and Sensibility*. Given these two examples, how would you describe Emma Thompson as a writer? Do you enjoy reading her work? Explain. How is her writing style different in both pieces? What are the reasons for these differences?

Theme Connections

- "*Four Rules and a Suggestion*," a how-to article about the movie script process, Vol. II, p. 115
- "*The Movie I'd Like to See*," a satirical commentary about what would make a good movie, Vol. II, p. 152
- "*The Dashwoods' Fate Is Decided*," an excerpt of the movie script written by Thompson, Vol. II, p. 199

Many news programs aren't just concerned with hard-hitting stories or current events. Many news programs, like the following, feature the actions and accomplishments of personalities in our communities.

Interview With Artist George Littlechild

TV Interview
written and produced by Kamala Todd

(Logo, title, and music for First Story *come up on screen. Cut to shot of narrator, standing in front of Vancouver harbour)*

Tatiana: Hi. I'm Tatiana Housty. And you're watching *First Story*. The show that takes you to the heart of the Urban Rez.

(Pan skyline, ending with shot of George Littlechild running along waterfront boardwalk. Host voice-over:)

Today on *First Story*, George Littlechild, a renowned Cree artist, tells us about his unique creative process.

(Cut to shot of sculpture/painting, being worked on. With George voice-over:)

George: The Trickster, the transformer, transforms the idea that art is lesson and makes it become reality. That's what the Trickster is for me, that's my understanding of Trickster …

Tatiana: Stay with us; *First Story* will be right back.

(Fade to text: "First Story *will return" Music up. Cut to commercial. Commercials end, and logo of hands back, music up, title up. Cut to host walking along beach)*

Tatiana: Vancouver has an abundance of art and we're treated to its various forms and mediums. On a beautiful day like today you can really see how you can get outside and enjoy the lifestyle. And for this reason, artists come here. George Littlechild is a well-known name in the art scene. He's known for his vivid colours and his accessible art. And when you speak to him, you realize that George is greatly influenced by the Trickster. In fact, the Trickster kicks him out of bed each morning to come down here for a jog. Storyteller, Kamala Todd, caught up with George for a chat about how the Trickster influences him.

(Cut to George sitting talking, panning down from tree branches waving in breeze)

George: That whole idea of transforming oneself from animal to human, and in that relationship to the animals and their hierarchy and their importance and they're all symbolic. Those symbols are very pertinent or important in my art.

(Pan up to tree, to George running. Kamala voice-over:)

Kamala: The artist has a gift: to express the world around them in new and provocative ways …

(Cut to George running along boardwalk)

… like George Littlechild, who is a renowned Vancouver artist of Cree heritage. He uses the power of the Trickster to influence how we look at the world.

(Cut to George sitting on beach, ocean in background)

George: The work is, in nature, it's intuitive. And I believe that as an artist, and as a vehicle for the information to come through.

(Cut to shot of can of brushes, bottle of paint with brush being dipped in. Pan up to sculpture being painted, golden head. Pan up to George as he speaks following lines. Medium shot of him, his paintings in background)

I'm very thankful for this talent. When I'm working on my art, it's a real place of serenity, calm. My studio, I think of it as a sacred place. A good place to go to and forget about what's going on out there.

(Cut to photo of George as a child)

I remember my artwork being shown in the display case in Grade 7, 8, or 9, I forget the year. And people would say, "*You* did that?"

All life's answers are on TV.

Homer Simpson

(Cut back to George, tighter head shot)

And to me that was the way that I won, in some regard. That people actually thought that, "Oh that person does have something good."

(Cut to George running along path, from behind. Music up. Cut to George from front, music down, George voice-over. During following speech cut to shot of feet running, move back to face)

George Littlechild at work in his studio.

This is a *still* (one frame captured from a movie or TV show) from the interview. Examine this image, and the directions included in this transcript. Discuss how the producers and directors tried to make this show appealing to its audience.

For me, running is sacred. To me it's like a real cleansing, and being in balance with the medicine world. And part of that is taking care of one's body, by exercising and you know nurturing it, and you love the end result. To me it's a real release. And here, *(speaking about ocean front park)* it's a place that just brings me back to the natural self of who I am, and how that environment ... how it affects me.

(Pan skyline, shoreline, trees, ocean. Cut to George sitting in park as before, tree branches waving around him)

These rocks, these trees, this ocean, the mountains, the sky. Even when it's torpid grey, it still is so ... beautiful. I think being brought up in the city you start to become so much of that environment that you don't really see nature around you. And one day I was looking at this ... grove of trees and I started to see the spirit of the tree, and I had never seen that before. And when I did, it just suddenly made me realize that each and every one of these trees has a spirit. And it was the most phenomenally important thing that could have occurred. And what I started to do was I painted this series called the Tree Spirits, with faces in the trees. And just realizing that, the respect for the earth, and respect for mother earth especially, and that each of these trees are sacred and they're providing life for us, and they're our friends.

(Cut to shot of trees, cut to painting of horses. Kamala voice-over:)

Kamala: George derives much of his inspiration from the natural world. The horse is his special guide.

(George voice-over:)

George: It's a very important Cree symbol, a Plains First Nations symbol.

(Cut to George in park)

And, uh, it's the animal that transcends the vision to the artist in the Cree culture. For years painting the horse and never knowing why I was painting it. And just realizing that horse was my friend. It's the most powerful experience.

(Cut to painting of boxers. Kamala voice-over:)

Kamala: George's art is a powerful experience. He tells stories and asks questions that some people don't want to touch.

(Cut to George in studio, working on gold head sculpture, paintings in background)

It is the Trickster at work, pushing us to gain new awareness.

(Cut to George on beach, sitting on driftwood speaking the following. Superimpose image of him at work in studio)

George: I think as human beings, we judge. We judge very harshly each other—and just being aware of that, and keep working through that, and where does that come from. And finding out where that comes from in order to address and deal with it.

(Cut to painting of two women, close-up on part of image, move out to see whole image, women in boat, city in background. Kamala voice-over:)

Kamala: What I find so uplifting about George's work is the way he deals with difficult and painful issues. Through his colourful imagery he has shown me a new and refreshing approach to healing.

(Cut to other paintings one by one. Cut to George painting)

George: I mean you watch the news and just see … how much catastrophe is going on, not only with mother earth but between nations, between people, and how we abuse each other, and I think the bottom line is to learn to respect and love each other, rather than continuously bringing each other down. I feel as an artist that … my gift is to be able to share some of my perspectives, but also some of the teachings that I've been taught.

(Close-up on brush painting. Back to George painting)

Trickster is a transformer, that transforms the idea of the art as the lesson, and makes it become reality. I think that's what the Trickster is for me. That's my understanding of Trickster. And through that lesson we receive teachings and in those teachings it's up to us to grow. Yeah, I think a lot of that part of my history, of dealing with foster care and, um, that whole issue in my life. I mean I did an art piece in a way that was a catharsis to let go of that. And I called that the Sixties Scoop; and it was a huge installation with personal testimonies from different people that had been raised in the sixties scoop. It was their stories plus my own.

(Cut to painting of children in foster care. Cut to George painting)

And for me, that was the end—it was letting go. It was time to move on. And so I see the work in many ways, as a conduit, a way of informing people, and also it changes their awareness.

(Cut to many of his works, scanning some. Music up. George voice-over:)

You know within my art I like to play with that idea. Humour versus the serious quality of the work but also it works together.

(Cut to George speaking, waving paintbrush, back at work on gold head)

And I think that's where the colour comes. I mean people can see the issue, they can visually, if they're informed by what's going on, but the colour in many ways seduces them. I mean you can't always take it so seriously, otherwise it's over … it's too much; you have to bring people to a good place and not always leave them in a sad or place of desperation. This work is more spiritual or fun, and I like to work with both. Both fun, humour, sadness, it's part of our history.

(Cut to singers, drummers, in studio. Music up, Kamala voice-over. Pan paintings, people in gallery.)

Kamala: Recently, George unveiled his latest work to family and friends. A colourful transformation series. It is only one of many ways that he shares his gift.

(Cut to George speaking at gallery)

George: Thank you all for coming out this evening. Enjoy the art, enjoy the food. All the friends that have supported me over the years, the family. I have a brother here this evening. It's just wonderful to be so supported and so loved, and this work is my gift back to you.

(Cut from painting to painting. Music up. Cut to people looking at art. Cut to classroom, George at front, long shot)

Kamala: George's vision goes far beyond his studio. He is an active leader and a role model in his community.

(Cut to George close-up in front of class, cut to student close-up, cut to teenagers in his studio, looking at paintings. Cut to George, at beach)

George: As an artist I'm constantly educating. I never ever thought I'd be an educator. But I am.

> I think that one's art is a growth inside one. I do not think one can explain growth. It is silent and subtle. One does not keep digging up a plant to see how it grew.
>
> Emily Carr

(Cut to George flipping through pages of a book that shows his artwork. George voice-over. Cut to George midway through following speech:)

I become more increasingly aware that what I'm to do here is to transform … the pain, or the history, the pain within the history. And it becomes more and more obvious in the work that I do in schools and lectures, is that … you know and in the workshops that I do, that it's to transform that energy, that negative energy and to make it positive. And that, I really believe, is why I'm here … what I was born to do, through this art, the gift that I was given.

And, um, one of the major themes that I like to go back to because I *enjoy* it—I really enjoy that transformation from human to animal spirit and in between and that essence, or that idea of what that would have been like years and years ago in traditional warfare transforming from self to animal spirit to attack your enemy, to go to places you couldn't go as a human. In relation to that, it's also those energies, and unblocking those energies that allow us to grow and … and to change and to achieve and to become better persons.

(Cut to paintings, close-up on various images. Music up. Kamala voice-over:)

Kamala: George Littlechild offers us new ways of looking at the world, ways to empower ourselves and move beyond our pain.

(Cut to George)

George: When you discuss your pain, when you discuss this history you bring it out in to the public, in to the world and we all become part of it. Because my story is your story.

(Cut to trees. Kamala voice-over:)

Kamala: I'm Kamala Todd for *First Story*.

(Music up. Logo up. Cut to commercial)

Kamala Todd is of Cree descent. She lives in Vancouver and works as a freelance video producer. She is the producer of *First Story* for British Columbia's VTV.

1. Response

a. With a partner, discuss this interview and what it reveals about George Littlechild.

b. What else would you like to learn about Littlechild? List at least three questions you would like to ask him. Do some research on the Internet to find answers to your questions.

c. Find examples of Littlechild's artwork and discuss the techniques he uses, as well as the content of the paintings.

d. Does the interviewer exhibit any bias in the questions she asks? Explain. Would you have handled the interview any differently?

2. Media *TV Interview* Skim this article and list the ways in which a TV interview is like or unlike interviews in other media formats. View several other TV interviews and list any common elements. What makes this selection a particularly effective interview? Discuss what makes a TV interview interesting and engaging.

With a partner or small group, develop a TV interview. You could interview someone of interest in your school, using a video camera to record the interview. You may wish to prepare questions beforehand.

3. Language Conventions *Interview Format* Examine the use of punctuation and other elements of design (such as the use of capitals, bold, or italic) within the transcript of this TV interview. List some rules for developing a TV script. Use those rules to script a short interview between yourself and a favourite actor or other personality.

4. Focus on Context This interview first appeared on the Aboriginal Peoples Television Network on a news program developed by that station, called *First Story*. Explain how the context in which this interview was developed may have affected its content. If CBC TV were to produce a documentary on Littlechild to be broadcast nationally, how do you think it might differ?

Theme Connections

- *"Art History,"* a speech about Aboriginal art in Canada, Vol. II, p. 29
- *"Stone Faces,"* an essay about the importance of art, Vol. II, p. 37
- *"Reviving Fridamania,"* an article about an artist, Vol. II, p. 62

Which newspapers do you read?
How often do you read a newspaper?
Which parts of the newspaper do you like most or least?

The*W*eekly

THE LAST COMMUNITY SIGNPOST

Newspaper Article by Catherine Dubé

Now that the mass media are busily scanning the four corners of the earth, the weekly newspaper is the only one still watching the neighbourhood. It is the one remaining link between the grass roots and the world.

A government minister serving food in a community kitchen is typical of the events covered by the local weekly newspaper. The news may seem trivial, except when the minister is Stéphane Dion and he receives a cream pie right in the face. Suddenly, the news takes on national scope.

Régent Gosselin, a photographer with *Les Nouvelles de l'Est*, owned by Transcontinental Group, was the only one to snap that memorable event on May 7, 1999, at Montréal's chic Resto-Pop restaurant. The next day, the photo from the Rosemont weekly made the front page of dailies across the country. Even media in Brussels, the world capital of pie-throwers, carried the item, along with the photo.

In close touch with events

Rarely does local news make its way abroad. The current generally flows the other way. "National and international issues filter down to the local news," says professor André A. Lafrance, head of the communications department at the Université de Montréal. "Local citizens know politics and the priorities of elected officials through the speeches of their members of parliament, ribbon-cutting ceremonies and community grants written up in their weekly paper."

Often a news item has to affect us personally before we pay attention, Lafrance says. Fifty years ago, conversations on the church steps filled that role. Events these days have international repercussions, however, and the weekly paper is the only medium able to reduce news to community proportions and thus link readers and current events. It is through its local athletes, for instance, that a community "participates" in the Olympic Games unfolding on the other side of the world.

Weeklies are not about to disappear. "Dailies have no interest in reporting small-town news," observes Florian Sauvageau, director of Université Laval's media research centre. "The local radio station could handle this role, but it has all but vanished, swallowed up by the big networks. The weekly is now the only medium that gives people news about their community."

The last village square

Small business openings and closings, the latest town council decisions, village festivals … Leafing through the weekly paper keeps people abreast of what is happening right around them. "It's the last remaining village square!" says Lafrance.

Anyone who thinks the news reported in weeklies attracts no interest should think again! According to a 1997 study by PMB, 81% of Québecers and 74% of Canadians had read a local newspaper within the past month.

Weeklies do not fill the same role everywhere. "Although everyone appreciates neighbourhood papers, people living in towns with no daily paper naturally expect much more from their weekly," points out Serge Bragdon, former president of the distribution division of Transcontinental Group, the second leading publisher of weeklies in Québec. This can be seen without having to venture very far from the big cities. Laval, for example, is Québec's second-largest city, adjacent to Montréal, yet it still has no daily newspaper of its own.

The people in Laval get their information from their local paper and the Montréal dailies. "Our paper fills the role of a daily," notes Jocelyn Bourassa, news director of *Courrier Laval*, published twice a week. That paper, distributed throughout the local area, is in addition to six neighbourhood weeklies covering the community scene. The six weeklies are also owned by Transcontinental Group.

The weekly is free

Unlike the advertising in daily papers and on radio and television, the many ads appearing in weeklies are not seen as a necessary evil, but rather as a source of information by many people. According to a three-year survey which Descarie & Complices completed this past summer for the association of Les Hebdos du Québec, 42% of respondents said that they regularly consulted the ads in weekly papers—twice as many as read the ads in dailies. An additional 42% read those ads from time to time.

"As a rule, ads in the print media are more informative than what you find on television," Professor Sauvageau notes. Bragdon points out that "the weekly is the paper of choice for local merchants." People read the weeklies to find out about the businesses in their vicinity. "The advertising you find in the weeklies reflects local life just as much as the news items do," says Lafrance.

Like it or not, advertising is the reason weekly papers are free. "Since it is part of community life, people expect the weekly paper to be free, just as the little favours neighbours do for one another are free," adds Lafrance.

So, even when it comes to advertising, the weekly stands out as the one remaining community signpost, the only medium left at the grass roots.

1. *Response*

    a. What conclusions about weekly newspapers does Catherine Dubé make? How does she support these conclusions? Do you agree or disagree? Explain.

    b. What do you think the future of daily and weekly newspapers will be like?

    c. Discuss the meaning and effectiveness of the title with a small group.

    d. Examine the structure of this article, and comment on its effectiveness.

    e. Skim the article and locate what Dubé compares weekly newspapers to. How effective are these comparisons?

2. *Vocabulary* Define the following terms using the context in which they appear: *grass roots, signpost, national scope, village square, community scene,* and *necessary evil.* Compare your definitions to those of a partner.

3. *Media* *Newspapers* Collect several examples of both weekly and daily newspapers. With a small group, discuss and analyse their features and content. What conclusions can you draw about the purpose, target audience, and effectiveness of these papers?

4. *Language Conventions* *Using Quotations* Examine how Dubé incorporates quotations from others within her article. How are these quotations introduced? How are they punctuated? How effectively do you use quotations within your own writing?

A media expert questions civic membership in the age of globalization.

The Accidental Citizen

Essay by Mark Kingwell

IT IS A COMMON EXPERIENCE in this, the age of casual multiculturalism. There I was, on a crowded 767, heading to London from Toronto, when I realized that nobody around me was speaking English—nobody at all, except the Québécoise flight attendant, who looked as if she might have preferred not to. The two Germans next to me were reading Ken Follett novels in translation. The man across the aisle was talking to his little boy in a mixture of Spanish and French, for reasons that escaped me. The two women farther up were, as far as I could make out, arguing in Italian.

Tourists on their way to the next destination? Maybe. International shoppers off to Harrods and Jermyn Street? Possibly—a man in the departure lounge had let it be known that he was just zipping over to Amsterdam for the weekend to pick up a few things he needed. Or were they just a group of all-sorts Canadians on their way to England? In the arrival area later there was a flurry of passports, a shuffle of multiple identities. The passengers conjured their variable selves without hesitation. Some of them, armed with logo-embossed briefcases and branded golf shirts, were clearly servants of a higher, corporate power: citizens of the world as it now lies, carved up into markets and territories, catchment areas and satellite PCS coverage zones. These new global citizens, whatever their mother tongue and regardless of their sometimes halting command of English, the lingua franca of the New Internationalism, all speak fluently the language of the customs declaration and the luggage carousel. They know the grammar of taxis and hotel shuttles and courtesy cars. *Which passport? Whichever gets me through the barrier faster.*

It is time for us to rethink the idea of citizenship, to reconceive the structures of political commitment and membership against the background of our shape-shifting world. These sky-people, harbingers of the world we are fast creating, are the first clues as to why. They tell us that old ideas of civic membership no longer compel our attention or answer our needs. Their presence is a reminder that the political structures to which those old ideas were wedded are not yet dead, but they are suffering—and are as nothing compared to the real powers of our world, the real centres of loyalty for most people (however undeserved that loyalty may often be). And if we are the sky-people ourselves, the ones who have found a reasonably comfortable place amid all these changes, who have the frequent-flyer programs and the higher degrees and the international connections, then the challenge is that much more proximate.

We begin with what is not news. Corporations and firms have not simply taken over the mechanisms of production and consumption. They have equally usurped our private selves and our public spaces. They have created bonds of belonging far stronger than any fractured, tentative nation could now hope to offer, providing structures of identity, ways of making sense of one's place in a complex world. They are also far more powerful, and richer, than many nations: the annual budget of France was only three-quarters of the combined value of America OnLine and Time Warner when those two media giants merged in January 2000, and Kmart's 1998 U.S. sales were equal to the estimated budget of the entire Russian military. But corporations are not democratic, and they do not possess the political legitimacy that is necessary to justify that kind of power. We have global markets, however unjust and skewed; and we have a global culture, however banal and enervating. What we don't have, but desperately need, is a global politics to balance and give meaning to these troubling universal realities.

Mark Kingwell was born in Toronto in 1963. He has taught at Yale, York University, and the University of Toronto in Scarborough, and has been a contributing editor for the magazines *Shift, Descant*, and *Saturday Night*. His essays, reviews, columns, and articles have appeared in publications such as *UTNE Reader, Adbusters*, and *Harper's*, and he is the author of *Better Living: In Pursuit of Happiness from Plato to Prozac* (which won the Drummer General's Award for Non-Fiction in 1998); *Dreams of Millennium: Report From a Culture on the Brink*, and *A Civil Tongue: Justice, Dialogue, and the Politics of Pluralism* (which won the Spitz Prize in Political Theory in 1996).

1. Response
   a. Mark Kingwell suggests that our loyalties are no longer connected to our nation or our citizenship. According to Kingwell, what are our "bonds of belonging" now connected to? Do you agree with this idea?
   b. Do you think you have the power to resist these "bonds" that Kingwell says are so strong? Do you want to? Explain.
   c. Kingwell uses the phrase "these troubling universal realities." Does what he has described in this piece trouble you? Explain.
   d. What does Kingwell mean by *sky-people*?

2. Literature Studies *Structure* When you read the first paragraph, what did you think the piece was going to be about? Why might the author have started in this way? How does the opening paragraph connect to the subsequent paragraphs? Keeping in mind the purpose of opening paragraphs, do you think this one is effective? Explain.

3. Vocabulary The author refers to some places and people with which readers may be unfamiliar. Look up any references that you do not know, along with any vocabulary that you were unable to figure out from its context. Afterward, consider how important it was to your appreciation of the piece to understand these references and words.

4. Critical Thinking In a small group, discuss the meaning of *globalization*. Where do you hear and see the word mentioned? How aware are you of the term and the issues that are involved? To extend the discussion, look through newspapers, news and world issues magazines, periodical indexes, and the Internet to find articles about globalization. What do the issues seem to be, as reflected by your findings? How do the issues affect you?

It has been said that arguing against globalization
is like arguing against the laws of gravity.
—Kofi Annan

What TV shows *do* chimps like to watch?
Read this interview to find out the media habits
of some primates.

Media Diet:
Jane Goodall

Magazine Interview by Karen Olson

Long before reality TV brought us soap operas set in remote jungles, Jane Goodall was giving viewers a glimpse inside the steamy, cliquish, and otherwise very similar world of chimpanzees. During the 1960s, Goodall's work as a brilliant observer of chimps in eastern Africa first captured the popular imagination. Today, the project she began some 40 years ago at the Gombe Stream Research Centre in Tanzania has become the longest uninterrupted field study of any animal group in the wild. Goodall's insight that chimps feel emotions and possess distinct personalities, much as humans do, has revolutionized how we view animals in general.

Now one of the most respected and beloved scientists in the world, Goodall travels almost constantly, speaking out on behalf of chimps and other threatened animals. As the roving ambassador of the Jane Goodall Institute, she encourages her audiences to recognize the power of individual action in protecting the environment. One of her passions, the Institute's Roots & Shoots program, encourages children to take an active role in helping animals as familiar as the birds and squirrels in their back yards. Another cause is the ChimpanZoo project, whose purpose is to study and improve the lives of the world's captive chimps.

Goodall is the author of numerous books, including *Africa in My Blood: An Autobiography in Letters* (Houghton Mifflin, 2000). She talked with assistant editor Karen Olson during a recent visit to Minneapolis.

K.O.: What are you reading these days?

J.G.: It's hard to find time to read while I'm traveling, but lately I've been jumping between two books. One is *The Courage of Children* by Peter Dalglish, founder of Street Kids International—who I hope to work with to help children in Dar es Salaam, Tanzania. The other is *Into the Wild*, Jon Krakauer's account of a young man who disappears in Alaska. I'm fascinated by attempts to get back to nature, both those that succeed and those that fail. It wasn't an overly long book, which I also appreciated. Big fat books are really intimidating when you're traveling all the time.

K.O.: Where do you get your daily news when you travel?

J.G.: In places like China, Taiwan, and remote parts of Africa, I usually rely on CNN, or, if I can get it, the BBC World Service, which I think is better. The World Service's radio version is super.

K.O.: The public television nature show has become an established genre. Do these glimpses into animal life help or hinder your cause?

J.G.: They're helpful, by and large, but on the other hand, very few accurately portray what's really happening. They come in two kinds: One is all doom and gloom, which people don't want to watch, and the other portrays animals living their own sweet little natural lives. The best approach would combine both views and stress what people can do to help.

K.O.: Speaking of television, you were in a lighthearted commercial a few years back co-starring chimps watching TV.

J.G.: Yes. I was reluctant at first, but the chimps only had to be interfered with long enough to catch them on film. What's more, the commercial didn't feature the cute and cuddly baby chimps you usually see on TV, a practice that bolsters the pet trade, which is horrendous. You got Frodo, our biggest male ever, and no one would want him in their living room.

K.O.: How do chimps really react to TV?

J.G.: We'd never show wild chimps television, but captive chimps love it, of course. They love the films about the Gombe chimps. If the chimps on the screen are excited, the chimps watching get excited too.

K.O.: How do chimpanzees communicate?
J.G.: They have a large repertoire of sounds, each with a different meaning. These sounds are not words, but they do communicate emotions: An appeal for help. An indication of danger. Hello. Here I am. Where are you? Listening. Anger. Fear. They also rely on a rich repertoire of touch and posture and gesture—embracing, patting on the back, kissing, holding hands, swaggering, tickling, punching—very much as we do. And among both chimps and humans, it seems, these gestures are triggered by the same kinds of contact and mean more or less the same thing.

K.O.: Do chimps make music?
J.G.: In the wild, they drum on tree trunks, which can't be very satisfactory because it doesn't really sound like much except from a distance. Chimps also display a rhythmic movement that's almost like dancing—a swaying from foot to foot that can be very majestic and beautiful. When they're lying down for the night, they may start calling on one side of the valley and the sounds will be taken up by chimps on the other side. But that's the closest they come to music.

K.O.: You've done some chat room conferences on the Web.
J.G.: Yes. I've done one or two of those, but they're not direct enough for me. These disembodied questions come in, and I don't like it. I prefer lectures.

K.O.: How has fame affected your life?
J.G.: I hated it at first. It's very British, you know, not to like that kind of thing. But I gradually began to realize that it was important for the media to be on my side if I wanted to get a message across. I don't think I've ever had a bad relation with the media. I've faced what I might call intelligently penetrating questions, but I've never been addressed in a hostile way. I recall a time when AIDS activists were protesting my position against the use

> The greatest danger before you is this: You live in an age when people would package and standardize your life for you—steal it from you and sell it back to you at a price. That price is very high.
>
> Granny D. (a.k.a. Doris Haddock)

of chimps for medical testing. They argued that those trying to protect the animals were condemning people to die instead. But even in that highly charged instance I found that the protesters and the press were willing to discuss the issue with me.

K.O.: What do you do in your down time?
J.G.: I talk to journalists.

K.O.: As a private person with a very public life, what sustains you?
J.G.: First, I don't think I've chosen this life, I feel I've been pushed into it. And what nourishes and sustains me, primarily, is the sense of my life as a mission. I feel I'm meant to be doing what I do. Second, there are the amazing people I meet, including the children I've encountered through Roots & Shoots. Today, for instance, I talked to 700 kids, and all of them sat in silence, listening intently for 50 minutes. Afterward, one of them came up and whispered in my ear, "I loved your talk and I love you, and you inspire me." And I'm inspired by them.

K.O.: If you had to make one law, what would it be?
J.G.: Laws alone are useless. We already have animal-protection laws that mean nothing because they're not enforced—and they never will mean anything until we get to people's hearts. That's why I put so much energy into working with children. But if I could wish one thing into being, never mind the law, it would be that we'd stop overpopulating the planet. It's a terrible situation, compounded in some places by the vast numbers of people who can't afford to move and thus totally destroy the land they're trapped on. Meanwhile, the affluent societies are overconsuming in the most horrifying way. In either case, there are just too many people.

K.O.: What is the essence of the message you're trying to deliver today?
J.G.: That every individual can make a difference, and that if we continue to leave decision making to the so-called decision makers, things will never change.

Karen Olson is Associate Editor for the *UTNE Reader.*

1. Response
a. Use the information provided in this article to describe Jane Goodall to a partner.
b. What other questions would you have liked Goodall to answer?
c. With a partner, discuss the effectiveness of this interview and the features of an interview that make this selection different from other non-fiction.

2. Oral Communication *Interview* With a partner, choose three appropriate questions from the selection, and ask each other these questions. You can adjust the questions slightly to make them more relevant. Generate three more questions to ask each other. Practise your interview, then deliver it to an audience of your peers.

3. Media *Animal Portrayals* With three or four classmates, discuss the use of animals in commercials, TV shows, and movies. What are the **codes** and **conventions** that seem to govern the behaviour of animals in these media? Generate five rules that you think producers and directors are following when they use animals. For example, rule one could be that all cats in sitcoms must ignore their owners.

Codes and **conventions** refer to the different ways in which each media product typically conveys meaning to audiences. For example, we expect certain kinds of movies to open with certain conventions, such as an action movie opening with lots of action, special effects, and maybe a chase scene.

Theme Connections

A Century of Cinema

Editorial by Susan Sontag

Cinema's hundred years seem to have the shape of a life cycle: an inevitable birth, the steady accumulation of glories, and the onset in the last decade of an ignominious, irreversible decline. This doesn't mean that there won't be any more new films that one can admire. But such films will not simply be exceptions; that's true of great achievement in any art. They will have to be heroic violations of the norms and practices that now govern moviemaking everywhere in the capitalist and would-be capitalist world—which is to say, everywhere. And ordinary films, films made purely for entertainment (that is, commercial) purposes, will continue to be astonishingly witless; already the vast majority fail resoundingly to appeal to their cynically targeted audiences. While the point of a great film is now, more than ever, to be a one-of-a-kind achievement, the commercial cinema has settled for a policy of bloated, derivative filmmaking, a brazen combinatory or recombinatory art, in the hope of reproducing past successes. Every film that hopes to reach the largest possible audience is designed as some kind of remake. Cinema, once heralded as *the* art of the twentieth century, seems now, as the century closes numerically, to be a decadent art.

Perhaps it is not cinema that has ended, but only cinephilia, the name of the very specific kind of love that cinema inspired. Each art breeds its fanatics. The love that cinema inspired, however, was special. It was born of the sense that cinema was an art unlike any other: quintessentially modern, distinctively accessible, poetic and mysterious and erotic and moral—all at the same time. Cinema had apostles (it was like religion). Cinema was a crusade. Cinema was a world-view. Lovers of poetry or opera or dance don't think there is *only* poetry or opera or dance. But lovers of cinema could think there was only cinema. That the movies encapsulated everything—and they did. It was both the book of art and the book of life.

As many people have noted, the start of moviemaking a hundred years ago was, conveniently, a double start. In that first year, 1895, two kinds of films were made, proposing two modes of what cinema could be: cinema as the transcription of real, unstaged life (the Lumière brothers) and cinema as invention, artifice, illusion, fantasy (Méliès). But this was never a true opposition. For those first audiences watching the Lumière brothers' *The Arrival of a Train at La Ciotat Station*, the camera's transmission of a banal sight was a fantastic experience. Cinema began in wonder, the wonder that reality can be transcribed with such magical immediacy. All of cinema is an attempt to perpetuate and to reinvent that sense of wonder.

Everything begins with that moment, one hundred years ago, when the train pulled into the station. People took movies into themselves, just as the public cried out with excitement, actually ducked, as the train seemed to move toward *them*. Until the advent of television emptied the movie theaters, it was from a weekly visit to the cinema that you learned (or tried to learn) how to walk, to smoke, to kiss, to fight, to suffer. Movies gave you tips about how to be attractive, such as: it looks good to wear a raincoat even when it isn't raining. But whatever you took home from the movies was only a part of the larger experience of losing yourself in faces, in lives that were *not* yours—which is the more inclusive form of desire embodied in the movie experience. The strongest experience was simply to surrender to, to be transported by, what was on the screen. You wanted to be kidnapped by the movie.

The first prerequisite of being kidnapped was to be overwhelmed by the physical presence of the image. And the conditions of "going to the movies" were essential to that. To see a great film only on TV isn't to have really seen that film. (This is equally true of those made for TV, like Fassbinder's *Berlin Alexanderplatz* and the two *Heimat* films of Edgar Reitz.) It's not only the difference of dimensions: the superiority of the larger-than-you image in the theater to the little image on the box at home. The conditions of paying attention in a domestic space are radically disrespectful of film. Since film no longer has a standard size, home screens *can* be as big as living room or bedroom walls. But you are still in a living room or a bedroom, alone or with familiars. To be kidnapped, you have to be in a movie theater, seated in the dark among anonymous strangers.

No amount of mourning will revive the vanished rituals—erotic, ruminative—of the darkened theater. The reduction of cinema to assaultive images and the unprincipled manipulation of images (faster and faster cutting) to be more attention-grabbing have produced a disincarnated, lightweight cinema that doesn't demand anyone's full attention. Images now appear in any size and on a variety of surfaces: on a screen in a theater, on home screens as small as the palm of your hand or as big as a wall, on disco walls and megascreens hanging above sports arenas and the outsides of tall public buildings. The sheer ubiquity of moving images has steadily undermined the standards people once had both for cinema as art at its most serious and for cinema as popular entertainment.

In the first years there was essentially no difference between cinema as art and cinema as entertainment. And all films of the silent era—from the masterpieces of Feuillade, D. W. Griffith, Djiga Vertov, Pabst, Murnau, King Vidor to the most formula-ridden melodramas and comedies—are on a very high artistic level compared with most of what was to follow. With the coming of sound, the image-making lost much of its brilliance and poetry, and commercial standards tightened. This way of making movies—the Hollywood system—dominated filmmaking for about twenty-five years (roughly from 1930 to 1955). The most original directors, like Erich von Stroheim and Orson Welles, were defeated by the system and eventually went into artistic exile in Europe—where more or less the same quality-defeating system was now in place, with lower budgets; only in France were a large number of superb films produced throughout this period. Then, in the mid-1950s, vanguard ideas took hold again, rooted in the idea of cinema as a craft pioneered by the Italian films of the immediate postwar period. A dazzling number of ambitious, passionate, artisanally crafted films of the highest seriousness got made with new actors and tiny crews, went to film festivals (of which there were more and more), and from there, garlanded with festival prizes, into movie theaters around the world. This golden age actually lasted as long as twenty years.

It was at this specific moment in the hundred-year history of cinema that going to movies, thinking about movies, talking about movies, became a passion among university students and other young people. You fell in love not just with actors but with cinema itself. Cinephilia had first become visible in the 1950s in France: its forum was the legendary film magazine *Cahiers du Cinéma* (followed by similarly fervent magazines in Germany, Italy, Great Britain, Sweden, the United States, Canada). Its temples, as it spread throughout Europe

and the Americas, were the many cinemathèques and film clubs spe-
cializing in films from the past and directors' retrospectives which
sprang up. The 1960s and early 1970s were the feverish age of
moviegoing, with the full-time cinephile always hoping to find a seat as
close as possible to the big screen, ideally the third row center. "One
can't live without Rossellini," declares a character in Bertolucci's *Before
the Revolution* (1964)—and means it.

Cinephilia—a source of exultation in the films of Godard and Truf-
faut and the early Bertolucci and Syberberg; a morose lament in some
recent films of Nanni Moretti—was mostly a Western European affair.
The great directors of "the other Europe" (Zanussi in Poland,
Angelopoulos in Greece, Tarkovsky and Sokurov in Russia, Jancso and
Tarr in Hungary) and the great Japanese directors (Ozu, Mizoguchi,
Kurosawa, Oshima, Imamura) have tended not to be cinephiles, perhaps because in Budapest or Moscow or Tokyo or Warsaw or Athens
there wasn't a chance to get a cinemathèque education. The distinctive
thing about cinephile taste was that it embraced both "art" films and
popular films. Thus, European cinephilia had a romantic relation to the
films of certain directors in Hollywood at the apogee of the studio system: Godard for Howard Hawks, Fassbinder for Douglas Sirk. Of
course, this moment—when cinephilia emerged—was also the moment
when the Hollywood studio system was breaking up. It seemed that
moviemaking had rewon the right to experiment; cinephiles could
afford to be passionate (or sentimental) about the old Hollywood genre
films. A host of new people came into cinema, including a generation
of young film critics from *Cahiers du Cinéma*; the towering figure of that
generation, indeed of several decades of filmmaking anywhere, was
Jean-Luc Godard. A few writers turned out to be wildly talented
filmmakers: Alexander Kluge in Germany, Pier Paolo Pasolini in Italy.
(The model for the writer who turns to filmmaking actually emerged
earlier, in France, with Pagnol in the 1930s and Cocteau in the 1940s;
but it was not until the 1960s that this seemed, at least in Europe,
normal.) Cinema seemed reborn.

For some fifteen years there were new masterpieces every month,
and one allowed oneself to imagine that this would go on forever. How
far away that era seems now. To be sure, there was always a conflict
between cinema as an industry and cinema as an art, cinema as routine
and cinema as experiment. But the conflict was not such as to make
impossible the making of wonderful films, sometimes within and sometimes outside of mainstream cinema. Now the balance has tipped
decisively in favor of cinema as an industry. The great cinema of the
1960s and 1970s has been thoroughly repudiated. Already in the 1970s

Hollywood was plagiarizing and banalizing the innovations in narrative method and editing of successful new European and ever-marginal independent American films. Then came the catastrophic rise in production costs in the 1980s, which secured the worldwide reimposition of industry standards of making and distributing films on a far more coercive, this time truly global scale. The result can be seen in the melancholy fate of some of the greatest directors of the last decades. What place is there today for a maverick like Hans Jürgen Syberberg, who has stopped making films altogether, or for the great Godard, who now makes films about the history of film, on video? Consider some other cases. The internationalizing of financing and therefore of casts was a disaster for Andrei Tarkovsky in the last two films of his stupendous, tragically abbreviated career. And these conditions for making films have proved to be as much an artistic disaster for two of the most valuable directors still working: Krzysztof Zanussi (*The Structure of Crystals, Illumination, Spiral, Contract*) and Theo Angelopoulos (*Reconstruction, Days of '36, The Traveling Players*). And what will happen now to Bela Tarr (*Damnation, Satantango*)? And how will Aleksandr Sokurov (*Save and Protect, Days of Eclipse, The Second Circle, Stone, Whispering Pages*) find the money to go on making films, his sublime films, under the rude conditions of Russian capitalism?

Predictably, the love of cinema has waned. People still like going to the movies, and some people still care about and expect something special, necessary from a film. And wonderful films are still being made: Mike Leigh's *Naked*, Gianni Amelio's *Lamerica*, Fred Keleman's *Fate*, Abbas Kiarostami's *Through the Olive Trees*. But one hardly finds anymore, at least among the young, the distinctive cinephilic love of movies, which is not simply love of but a certain *taste* in films (grounded in a vast appetite for seeing and reseeing as much as possible of cinema's glorious past). Cinephilia itself has come under attack, as something quaint, outmoded, snobbish. For cinephilia implies that films are unique, unrepeatable, magic experiences. Cinephilia tells us that the Hollywood remake of Godard's *Breathless* cannot be as good as the original. Cinephilia has no role in the era of hyperindustrial films. For cinephilia cannot help, by the very range and eclecticism of its passions, but sponsor the idea of the film as, first of all, a poetic object, and cannot help but incite those outside the movie industry, like painters and writers, to want to make films, too. It is precisely this conception of movies that must be defeated. That has been defeated.

If cinephilia is dead, then movies are dead too—no matter how many movies, even very good ones, go on being made. If cinema can be resurrected, it will only be through the birth of a new kind of cine-love.

News photo from premiere of *The House of Seven Gables.*

Crowds gather outside a theatre for the premiere of *The House of Seven Gables* on March 21, 1940. The film, based on Nathaniel Hawthorne's novel, is set in Salem.

Examine this image and discuss what going to the movies was like for people in this photo. What is going to the movies like for you?

Susan Sontag was born in New York City, U.S., in 1933. She was educated at universities in California, Chicago, and Paris, and at Harvard University. Her works include *Against Interpretation, Styles of Radical Will*, and *Under the Sign of Saturn* (essay collections); *Death Kit* and *The Volcano Lover* (novels); *On Photography* and *AIDS and Its Metaphors* (non-fiction books); and *I, etcetera* (a short story collection). Her novel *In America* won the National Book Award for fiction in 2000.

1. *Response*

a. With a partner, discuss Sontag's ideas and viewpoints in this editorial.

b. Which point from this editorial do you agree with most? Which point do you disagree with most? Explain why.

c. Define *cinephilia* to a partner. Discuss whether you consider yourselves cinephiles.

d. Discuss at least two reading strategies you used to read and understand this editorial.

2. *Film Study* With a small group, list ten movies that you have all seen in the past year. Use Sontag's two categories (1. bloated, derivative, and witless; or 2. great and one-of-a-kind achievements) to create a chart organizing these movies. Does everyone in the group agree with the categorization of each movie? Explain.

Review the glossary terms following this selection and use them whenever you discuss films.

3. *Making Connections* Find out more about one of the movies referred to in this article, using Internet and library resources. If possible, and if the movie is appropriate, view the movie. Write a short review of the movie, including your opinion of its quality.

4. *Critical Thinking* With a small group, discuss the following quotation from the selection. Present your opinion about this idea to the group, using examples to support it.

> To be sure, there was always a conflict between cinema as an industry and cinema as an art, cinema as routine and cinema as experiment. But the conflict was not such as to make impossible the making of wonderful films, sometimes within and sometimes outside of mainstream cinema.

Film Study Glossary

A **Classical Narrative Structure** is the most common way of telling stories in Hollywood films. It is called classical not because it is the oldest way of telling stories or even the best, but the most common.

A **climax** is the point in a film where the story's main conflict develops into a dramatic confrontation. It is the point where key struggles are waged and an eventual victor is determined.

Closure follows a movie's climax, and is the point where all of the major conflicts, issues, or ideas in a story are resolved.

Codes and **conventions** refer to the different ways in which each media product typically conveys meaning to audiences. For example, we expect certain kinds of movies to open with certain conventions—an action movie opening with lots of action, special effects, and maybe a chase scene; or a horror movie opening with shots of mist and a haunted house, with creepy music in the background.

Continuity editing is a strategy for linking together all the individual shots that make up a movie.

Genre refers to a style or type of film or TV show; for example, westerns, comedies, action-adventures, or horror pictures.

High contrast lighting uses harsh lines of light and shadows combined with dramatic streaks of blackness. The effect of this lighting style is often haunting and eerie, creating a sense of anxiety and confusion.

High key lighting means most shots in the film are brightly lit, with few shadows. This is the most common lighting style in Hollywood and is often assumed to be the "natural" look of movies.

The **hook** is the opening sequences in a film using the Classical Narrative Structure. These scenes are called the hook because they are meant to "hook" the audience's attention, and draw them into the story.

Low key lighting uses shadows and directed pools of light to create atmosphere and suspense. This lighting style generally suggests a sense of mystery.

Mise en scène (French for "to put in scene") refers to how space is used in individual shots to create symbolic meaning or dramatic effect throughout a movie.

Montage editing is a strategy for linking together individual shots in a movie. Montage editing is different from continuity editing in that it does not put shots together with a seamless flow, but presents them in a way that requires audiences to make their own connections between the images.

Myths are stories that help to organize how we understand ourselves and our communities, and prioritize certain values that a society holds dear.

A **negotiated interpretation** of a media text questions the dominant or intended meaning of the text, but does not attempt to rework the text's meaning in any significant way.

An **oppositional interpretation** questions the dominant meaning or explanation of the text, and uses the text for purposes other than those intended by the creator(s).

A **preferred interpretation** of a media text replicates the meaning intended by the text's producer(s).

Representation means that all media are symbols, or symbolic systems that refer to the outside world.

Verisimilitude means creating a sense of reality between two realms of experience.

With a partner, discuss a recent movie you have both seen.
What was the most true-to-life scene in the movie?
What action or scene from the movie would never occur
in real life?

The Movie
I'd Like to See

Commentary by Geoff Pevere

In the movie I'd like to see, credits would include what people were paid to make the movie.

In the movie I'd like to see, we'd see people working out with personal trainers all the time, which would explain why people in movies look like they work out with personal trainers all the time.

In the movie I'd like to see, waiters would chase after people who leave bars and restaurants without finishing their drinks or meals. They'd demand payment, and ask them if they think they're in a damned movie or something.

In the movie I'd like to see, sometimes people wouldn't be home when other people knock on their doors to confront them. Or, if they're home, they'd ask the confronter why they didn't just phone like people outside of movies do. Then slam the door.

In the movie I'd like to see, someone would explain why people in movies always carry paper grocery bags instead of plastic ones, and why their bags are always full of unwrapped produce like lettuce and oranges. Especially oranges.

In the movie I'd like to see, Bill Murray would play the president of the United States.

In the movie I'd like to see, someone would explain why all the women over the age of 35 have disappeared from the face of the earth.

In the movie I'd like to see, Julia Roberts would be dumped for Janeane Garofalo.

In the movie I'd like to see, watching cartoons wouldn't be a symbol of witless trashiness, but watching CNN would.

In the movie I'd like to see, unspeakably rich movie stars would not be permitted to play feisty working-class single mothers.

In the movie I'd like to see, people who get drunk don't sober up as soon as they enter the next scene. And they'd have hangovers that last the rest of the movie.

In the movie I'd like to see, high school students would still be played by people in their 20s, but their teachers and parents would be played by teenagers.

In the movie I'd like to see, a cranky old misanthrope would not be redeemed by his relationship with a precocious young child. He'd want to kill the brat.

In the movie I'd like to see, telemarketers would be calling to interrupt people all the time, just like in real life.

In the movie I'd like to see, there wouldn't be subliminal product placements, people would simply hold products up to the camera and say: "Buy this. They paid us huge to tell you to."

In the movie I'd like to see, someone would explain why movie tears always come from the centre of people's eyes, while non-movie tears tend to run from the corners of people's eyes.

In the movie I'd like to see, people would forget what they're saying sometimes, or they'd ask other people to repeat themselves because they weren't listening.

In the movie I'd like to see, major movie stars would be recognized by other people in the movie as major movie stars. "Hi Mel … I mean, um, Dave …"

In the movie I'd like to see, moments and ideas stolen from other movies would be credited on screen while they occur. Since they do this for cleverly sampled music, this seems only reasonable for creatively bankrupt movies.

In the movie I'd like to see, unattractive people would fall in love and live happily together.

In the movie I'd like to see, two people you'd just love to see get together keep missing each other and never do get together. Maybe they never even meet.

In the movie I'd like to see, serial killers would be portrayed as the boring pathetic creeps they usually are.

> What the mass media offer is not popular art,
> but entertainment which is intended to be consumed
> like food, forgotten and replaced by a new dish.
>
> W.H. Auden

In the movie I'd like to see, people would react to each other's cosmetic surgery. "Man you look so weird."

In the movie I'd like to see, all attractive, well-heeled professionals in their 20s would be sent to Third World coffee plantations and multinational athletic equipment sweatshops at the first sign of an "emotional crisis."

In the movie I'd like to see, Cher would play the Frankenstein monster. If she insisted on singing, that would be even better.

In the movie I'd like to see, all evocations of the '60s would come with a choice of Jiffypop-nostalgia musical cues, so we wouldn't have to endure The Doors, Buffalo Springfield, The Temptations or Jimi Hendrix any more. Better yet, there would be no evocations of the '60s.

In the movie I'd like to see, letters would no longer talk when opened. They'd sing.

In the movie I'd like to see, the bystander who gets knocked down on the sidewalk by other people chasing each other with guns would chase the other people with guns and pistolwhip them for being rude.

In the movie I'd like to see, aliens would invade the earth only to flee when they realize how stupid the movie they're in—and the planet they're on—is.

In the movie I'd like to see, people would spend more time going to crappy unrealistic movies and then complaining about how crappy and unrealistic movies have become.

Is this asking too much?

Geoff Pevere is a movie critic with *The Toronto Star*.

1. Response
a. Return to the discussion in the introductory text at the beginning of this article. How do you think Geoff Pevere would have responded to the movie you discussed?
b. What item on Geoff Pevere's list did you agree with most? Why?
c. Are there any items on the list that you thought were too extreme or radical? Explain.
d. What do you think motivated Pevere to create this list?
e. What is the overall tone of this selection? How is that tone achieved?

2. ***Film Study*** Review Pevere's list and discuss it in a small group. Together, brainstorm some ideas for additions to this list. List ten more items that you think should be added. Can you think of any movies that actually incorporate any of these items? If so, discuss the movie(s).

3. ***Media*** *Movie Trailer* Work with a small group to develop a proposal for a movie that incorporates at least five items from Pevere's list. Use that proposal to script and plan a movie trailer, remembering to feature Pevere's items. Discuss your production options, format, purpose, and audience. If possible, use a video camera to record your trailer, or present a live performance of the script. Ask your audience for some feedback on the production values of the trailer and the script.

4. ***Writing*** *Modelling the Selection* Use Pevere's commentary as a model to create a list of your own for another media form. For example, you could list what you would like to see in music videos, magazines, or sitcoms. Try to use a similar tone and structure to those used by Pevere. Discuss your list with others, assessing the effectiveness of your content, tone, and structure. Compare your list with a classmate who commented on another format. Are there similarities between your lists? If so, explain why this might be so.

5. ***Language Conventions*** *Parallel Structure* Examine the beginning of each paragraph and consider its effect on the reader. Why would Pevere choose to use a parallel structure for each paragraph? How effective is this use? Examine something you have written recently and consider how you could use parallel structure effectively.

Theme Connections

- *"My Old Newcastle," a memoir that refers to movie conventions, Vol. II, p. 52*
- *"Four Rules and a Suggestion," a how-to article about writing a script, Vol. II, p. 115*
- *"The Making of* Sense and Sensibility," *a diary about the making of a movie, Vol. II, p. 120*

*When it comes to portraying
individuals with disabilities,
Hollywood hasn't got a clue.*

Heroes
and Holy Innocents

Magazine Article
by Kathi Wolfe

Thanks to audio description and closed-captioning, blind and deaf moviegoers now are able to "see" and "hear" films. After a long struggle, people using wheelchairs are finding it easier to get into movie theaters. But once they're at the movies, people with disabilities rarely see true-to-life images of themselves.

Of course, Hollywood has presented unrealistic images of disabled people since its movie moguls first set up shop. Martin E. Norden, author of *The Cinema of Isolation: A History of Physical Disability in the Movies* (Rutgers University Press), writes, "the movie industry has perpetuated … stereotypes … so durable and pervasive that they have become mainstream society's perception of disabled people." Demeaning, patronizing stereotypes have marched across the silver screen for decades from that sweet innocent Tiny Tim in *A Christmas Carol* to Quasimodo, the villainous hunchback in *The Hunchback of Notre Dame* to the embittered blind veteran in *Scent of a Woman* (1992) and the idiot savant in *Rain Man* (1988). Disabled people aren't cheering as this parade of superheroes, venomous villains, and helpless victims goes by.

San Francisco State University history professor Paul Longmore says, "These stereotypes present disabled people as tragic, pathetic figures: Such films as *Whose Life Is It, Anyway?* (in which a man who has become quadriplegic begs to be allowed to kill himself) leave the audience thinking it's better to be dead than disabled." But disabled people today don't see themselves as symbols of evil, inspirational superheroes, or holy innocents (like that wise fool Forrest Gump). Though the disease-of-the-week flick still moves audiences to tears, most disabled filmgoers no longer view their lives as a two-hankie movie.

In the '90s movie *Living in Oblivion*, a comedy about the making of a small-budget picture, a dwarf named Mr. Tito complains about his role in a dream scene. He feels that he's only been cast because dwarfs symbolize weird emotions. Though Mr. Tito is a comic figure, his anger at being used as a symbol is shared by many with disabilities.

Leye J. Chrzanowski, editor-in-chief of the monthly newspaper *One Step Ahead—The Disability Resource*, asserts, "Hollywood has a hackneyed idea of disability. To add insult to injury, someone without a disability acting out this delusion is usually either an Oscar nominee or winner ... Every time we start breaking down stereotypes, we're slapped back into the 'helpless cripple' role by a *Love Affair* or a *Passion Fish*."

Are these views held only by the politically correct? Not at all, says George Covington, who was a special assistant to the quintessentially non-PC former vice president Dan Quayle. Covington, who is legally blind, says, "We're seen as 'inspirational,' and inspiration sells like hotcakes. My disability isn't a burden; having to be so damned inspirational is."

Mainstream Magazine editor William R. Stothers says, "If it was just entertainment, these images wouldn't worry me. But they help shape attitudes toward disability."

Do disabled people want to take the entertainment out of movies? To turn films with disabled characters into "eat your spinach" documentaries? No, says Mary Johnson, a former editor of *The Disability Rag Resource*, "but they want to see their reality reflected on screen."

Despite the stereotypes, some disabled people are hopeful about the movies. "As actors and writers, and from behind the cameras, we're pushing Hollywood hard to portray us in nonstereotypical ways," Stothers says.

Two recent independent films offer hope that this change can take place. *When Billy Broke His Head*, a dynamic documentary directed by Billy Golfus, has been shown on PBS and at film festivals. This film isn't (as Golfus himself says) an "inspirational cripple story." Instead the movie shows real-life disabled people: fighting for their civil rights, job hunting, and battling social service bureaucracies. *Twitch and Shout*, a touching but funny documentary directed by Laurel Chiten about people with Tourette Syndrome, has aired on the PBS program *P.O.V.* and at film festivals. The film shows not only what it's like to have this disorder but what it's like to encounter disability-based discrimination. The movie presents its subjects not as superheroes or objects of pity but as fully human human beings.

If the spirit of these films could somehow be transferred to Hollywood, the disabled wouldn't feel left out of the big picture on the silver screen.

Kathi Wolfe is a writer living in Falls Church, Virginia.

1. *Film Study* In your notebook, write a personal response to this article, and the points that Kathi Wolfe raises. Include your own experiences, ideas, and viewpoints about the portrayal of individuals with disabilities in movies you have watched.

With a small group, discuss movies you have seen, and how individuals with disabilities and other groups (teens, intellectuals, scientists, women) are portrayed, noting any stereotypes that you think exist. What stereotypes exist in the movies you like to watch most? What effect do these stereotypes have on you or other audience members? What do you think can or should be done about these stereotypes?

2. *Language Conventions* *Loaded Language* There are many groups and individuals who would object to the use of the word "disabled" as a collective noun, as Wolfe has chosen to use it. Many people would prefer terms such as *the physically or mentally challenged, individuals with disabilities,* or *people with special needs*. Discuss the issue of changing language trends, the language within this selection, and how **loaded language** can be used to stereotype or portray individuals negatively.

Loaded language is language that is intentionally chosen to evoke a strong response in a reader—usually an emotional response. It is also language that is highly connotative, conjuring in the listener much more than its literal meaning.

3. *Making Connections* With two classmates, role-play a conversation between Pevere, Sontag, and Wolfe. Use the information in each of these authors' selections and make connections between the selections, and between the ideas of each author.

Artists from around the world react to the terrorist attacks on New York and Washington.

Artists Respond to September 11, 2001

An eerie silence...

An Eerie Silence ...
by Sally-Ann Maslen, Australia.
Manipulated photo. Sept 13, 2001.

Untitled 2,
 by Bob Lake, United States.
Photo. Sept 30, 2001.

Eclipse 09.11.2001: Peace and Hate,
by Sergey Muravyev, Russia.
Painting. Oct 11, 2001.

Hope,
by Joy Yaffa, Canada.
Watercolour painting.
Sept 22, 2001.

Fire in New York,
by Blanka Lyszczarz,
Poland. Painting.
Sept 17, 2001.

No Words, 3,
by Gisela Vidalle, Argentina.
Pen-and-ink drawing.
Sept 23, 2001.

1. ***Visual Communication*** *Analysing Images* Discuss these images in small groups. What message does each image send to you? Does it send the same message to each member of the group? Why might the message be different for different people? How do these images make you feel? Which image is your favourite? Why? How do the captions for each image contribute to the meaning of the image?

2. ***Research and Inquiry*** Use Internet or library resources to find other works of art that were created in response to September 11, 2001. Choose one image and write an essay analysing its message, features, techniques, and content and how these elements work together. You should develop a clear thesis, an argument to support that thesis, and a conclusion.

**Read the title and teaser below and consider
whether you are being described here. Are you a
skeptical youth? An information-age cynic? Discuss.**

Peace a Hard Sell to Skeptical Youth

*Opponents of the U.S. Star Wars scheme find out heartstrings and
hippy-dippy nostalgia don't click with information-age cynics.*

Newspaper Article by David Beers

from *The Vancouver Sun*, February 2001

The greying peace movement is looking for fresh blood to
oppose America's latest "Star Wars" scheme. But how do you
lure recruits who may have been playing with Cabbage Patch
dolls and Transformer toys when the Cold War ended?

The answer stands 10 metres tall at the corner of Commercial and Broadway [in Vancouver], a day-glo image of a funky
young guy kick-boxing a warhead beneath the words "Bombs
Away." The billboard, similar transit ads and the Web site they
promote are the direct result of a close study of how to sell
nuclear fear, and activism, to 18 to 35-year-olds.

Irony works. Tugging at heartstrings doesn't. Make plenty of
neutral-toned information available to your inherently skeptical
audience. And avoid even a whiff of hippy-dippy. If there's one
thing youth distrust more than the military industrial complex,
it's their parents' nostalgia.

These are the findings of a Vancouver agency hired to
research and craft a just-launched media campaign for the
International Physicians for the Prevention of Nuclear War.
The aim of the campaign is to mobilize youth against Canadian
support for the U.S. national defence system, which sits at the
top of President George Bush's agenda.

Proponents of NDM say the system will shield North America by intercepting nuclear-tipped missiles fired by "rogue"
nations. Opponents claim the unproven technology is an expensive boondoggle in the making, may violate antiballistic missile
treaties, and will trigger a new global nuclear-weapons buildup.

"If the U.S. goes ahead on this, China and Russia have said they will respond by heightening the arms race," notes 24-year-old Sarah Kelly, who was one of several Bombs Away campaign spokespeople on hand last Tuesday at the billboard unveiling. "Keep heightening the arms race," reasons the fourth-year medical student at the University of British Columbia, "and eventually a nuclear weapon will be used."

Articulate, imbued with energy not only to study medicine but wrestle with geopolitics, Kelly is just what the doctor ordered for a flagging movement.

Indeed, as the Star Wars debate rekindles, peace activists in North America and Europe see a golden opportunity to replenish their membership, which plummeted around the time the Berlin Wall came down. Fresh troops are essential, they say, to tackle their larger aim: abolishing nuclear weapons altogether.

Seizing public attention for that cause proved daunting in an era when "presidents Bush and Clinton told people that we no longer lived under the threat of nuclear war and that the world was a much safer place," says Lynn Martin, Communications Director for the U.S. branch of IPPNW.

"While it is true that the numbers of nuclear weapons decreased under these administrations," Martin says, "there are still 30,000 nuclear weapons in the world today and the nuclear war-fighting plans and strategies remain unchanged. The U.S. and Russia each have about 2,500 strategic nuclear weapons on hair-trigger alert status and these are targeted at hundreds of cities. If just one modern nuclear weapon exploded over a large city—either by accident or intent—millions of people would die and millions more would be injured. The threat of nuclear war remains the greatest immediate public health threat in the world today."

If so, not just politicians, but popular culture fails to reflect such urgency. In 1964, Stanley Kubrick's black comedy *Dr. Strangelove* made a splash by ridiculing the notion that America's nuclear arsenal was failsafe. In 1983, the television movie *The Day After* used realism to shock viewers into imagining the consequences of nuclear war. In cineplexes now we find *Thirteen Days*, a retelling of the Cuban missile crisis that gets good reviews, but implies nuclear doom was confronted 40 years ago and, through cool Kennedy thinking, defused.

Sarah Kelly was born 15 years after that near conflagration. She was but nine years old in 1986, when the International Physicians for the Prevention of Nuclear War received the Nobel Peace Prize. Forgive her, then, if the antinuclear movement of old is little more than a grainy *Life* magazine photo in her mind. She and her friends "have seen pictures of our parents' generation marching for peace." But for Kelly, the persistent risk of Armageddon comes as a fresh discovery, and she says she is hungry to know and do more about it.

Optimistic but ironic

The 18 to 35 age group that includes Sarah Kelly is the subject of much scrutiny by marketing types. A Toronto-based research firm called D-Code has named them the Nexus generation, caught as they are between the Industrial and Information Ages, and sandwiched between the Baby Boom and Echo generations.

This demographic is the focus, too, of Amanda Gibbs, whose job at the Vancouver-based Institute for Media, Policy and Civil Society is to help put together media campaigns for non-profit organizations. According to Gibbs, the Nexus generation is "realistic, confident, optimistic, activist" and "incredibly media literate. Yet members of the Nexus gang are also born skeptics, steeped in the irony of the age."

When the International Physicians for the Prevention of Nuclear War decided it needed to appeal to the Nexus generation, it hired Gibbs and IMPACS to figure out how.

Gibbs developed some campaign approaches, then hired D-Code to run the ideas by a Nexus-aged focus group. Among the group's six carefully selected members: A social activist who'd worked at addiction recovery and sexual-assault centres. An arts publicist who'd sailed the Pacific on a youth cultural exchange program. A restaurateur and wine grower who specializes in organic ingredients. A hip-hop artist studying commerce and information technology. A screenwriter/graphic designer. And the founder of her own ecological gardening company.

Gibbs herself casually throws around terms like "marketing to the Web" and "fashion forward" and would seem to be naturally in tune with these Nexusers. But at age 30, she felt a bit dated as the cultural biases of the focus group revealed themselves.

For example, Gibbs is in love with atomic kitsch like those 1950s instructional films telling school kids to "duck and cover" at the first sign of a nuclear flash, or that famous *Dr. Strangelove* scene of Slim Pickens riding a falling H-bomb like a bronco. But such retroiconography doesn't register with the Nexus group. "They thought it was mouldy," Gibbs says.

Nor, despite the success of "Joe Canada" beer commercials, did the group respond to a nationalistic, us versus big, bad America approach. This was unanimously rejected as self-righteous and cutting against their ideal of the "global citizen."

A concept called "We said No Nukes" was intended to connect younger people with the peace protests of the past. But it fared no better. "Several of the D-Coders [saw] the activism in the 1960s as largely ineffective and its adherents as sell-outs to big business (or worse, their parents)," read the final report.

Many in the group liked a concept that blamed corporate greed for driving the nuclear-arms industry. But they doubted the broader appeal of that message across their generation. "'Sticking it to the man' is not going to push your 'social hot-button' if you work in a bank," said the report. Some might "feel as though the campaign message is attacking them, their lifestyle, etc."

More popular was a straightforward approach declaring that we face, even today, immediate risk of a nuclear catastrophe. But again, a caveat specific to those of Nexus age: "The message was traumatic in the '80s when Nexus was growing up. It made them feel vulnerable to powers beyond their control and it could still elicit a disempowering response if not supported by actionable steps," D-Code reported. As the gardening company owner said: "No more missile horror messages for me ... I still feel traumatized by the nuclear war movies of the '80s. ... It was such a negative way to be brought up in this world, thinking that it might blow up any second because of power-freak grown-ups."

The group went so far as to brainstorm its own slogans, and came up with "Bombs away." Gibbs pored over the report and, working with graphic designer Darren Carcary, and Raised Eyebrow Web Design, produced a campaign she believes speaks to the essence of her Nexus targets. The total budget of $50,000 left only enough to buy one billboard here [Vancouver] and one in Toronto, but those plus bus and subway ads in both cities are designed to drive eyeballs to the real engine of the campaign, the Bombs Away Web site.

"Before you can activate younger people, you have to educate them," theorizes Gibbs. The younger half of the Nexus generation, those aged 18 to 25, "don't watch, much less trust, TV," Gibbs maintains. Instead, surveys show they get more of their information from the Web than anywhere else. The Web fits their skeptical, hype-averse nature by allowing them to read as deeply and broadly on a topic as they desire, and it can give them timely updates and action advisories. When a notice gets picked up and spread exponentially in cyberspace, Gibbs says, that is a sign that the "viral marketing" approach to "web activism" is working, and very inexpensively.

Such buzz phrases were foreign to Dr. Mary-Wynn Ashford, co-president of IPPNW, when she came to Gibbs and IMPACS for help. Ashford, who is 60 and lives in Victoria, intended to hire the group to make a 20-minute video, a standard tool for her group in the past. Now she fully buys into the Web-driven strategy for youth, whom she's come to see are "information savvy and steeped in irony."

It did startle Ashford to see this age bracket reject "our traditional approach: forthright and emotional, based on love for the planet, wanting to protect children. Young people said all this stuff sounds like the '70s and our parents' generation."

Likewise, Debbie Grisdale, the Ottawa-based executive director of Physicians for Global Survival, says she took to heart the focus group's demand "for straight information, and no sense of patronizing, speaking down." But the group's taste for "sarcasm" surprised her.

Sarcasm may be in the ear of the beholder. UBC education professor Peter Seixas likes what he thinks he hears from the Nexus focus group. The former high-school teacher, a baby boomer, believes students need to approach media messages critically, as a corrective to the emotional pull of today's dominant media, television and film. "Perhaps well-educated young people have taken the lesson: 'Don't hit us over the head with a one-minute ad, don't give us preachy talk about love or death—we exist in a much more critical mind than that.' If so, that is something to celebrate."

Exporting the message

Ashford expects lessons learned from Bombs Away to be applied in campaigns in the nine other countries. Top of that list is the United States, where public opinion is the only weapon against well-financed lobbyists for military contractors.

"We have to affect voting in the U.S. Congress," Ashford declares. "If we do, other countries will fall in line." If veteran nuclear dissenters are having to start from scratch with a new pool of potential activists, the U.S. military establishment suffers no such loss of institutional memory. Case in point: the point man on National Missile Defence is the new U.S. secretary of defence, Donald Rumsfeld—who held his same post in the mid-1970s under President Gerald Ford.

The new U.S. president vows to up military spending by a third, adding another $100 billion a year, and he has made NMD a cornerstone of his campaign. If the program goes forward, firms like Boeing and Lockheed stand to gain from at least $60 billion US in new contracts, according to a conservative estimate by the Congressional Budget Office.

Some of that money will be spent in this country, Bush has suggested. That is the carrot. The stick, should Canada not cooperate, is the subject of much concerned speculation in Ottawa. There are hints the U.S. might punish Canada by ending our NORAD air surveillance alliance, most of which is bankrolled by the U.S.

Canadian industry leaders also fear a backlash in trade dealings. Opposition to NMD will lead to "inevitable repercussions ... on such diverse issues as softwood lumber, or how long it takes for cars to get across the Canada-U.S. border," Yves Poisson of Human Resources Development Canada has predicted.

So far Minister for Defence John Manley is taking a wait-and-see attitude, watching European, Chinese and Russian reactions to the project. His predecessor, Lloyd Axworthy, is clearly against it. "Do you want to spend upwards of 100 billion dollars [Cdn] on a system that is not yet proven, for limited protection? And trade that for division among allies and a potential arms race in the nuclear field? That is not exactly a sound proposition," says Axworthy, now director and CEO of the Liu Centre for Global Issues at UBC.

Axworthy scoffs at the notion that the U.S. might boot Canada out of NORAD. "It's a fallacy. We've just signed a five-year extension." Nor is he cowed by the prospect of trade sanctions. "Prime Minister Pearson opposed the Vietnam War, and Canada is still in good standing with the U.S."

"It is important at this moment that we have a strong public debate," says Axworthy, who will host a gathering of international

Performance artist and activist Troy Jackson, 30, was involved in creating a billboard campaign that puts a new face on the peace movement and social activism to appeal to the post-Cold-War generation.

experts on the NMD issue at the Liu Centre next week, culminating in a public forum Friday evening.

Getting youth into that conversation, and mobilizing them to act throughout North America and Europe is, in Axworthy's view, "essential."

"Young people show a pretty strong understanding of global issues," he says. "A lot better than our generation did."

David Beers is a well-known Vancouver journalist who writes regularly for *The Vancouver Sun*.

1. *Response*
a. Review what David Beers says about the Nexus Generation. Discuss the term *Nexus Generation*.
b. What methods would you suggest for effectively selling peace to your generation? Discuss your ideas.
c. What does *hard sell* mean? What connotations, if any, does the term have for you? Do you consider the use of this term appropriate or inappropriate? Explain.
d. Discuss how you would have responded to some of the advertising campaigns that are described in the article.

2. *Making Connections* Consider what "Peace a Hard Sell to Skeptical Youth" says about your generation. Would you agree with the way in which the article describes today's youth? Why or why not? Write a short essay, letter, or poem in response to this selection.

3. *Research and Inquiry* Find out the current state of the U.S. Star Wars plan using Internet and library resources. Report your findings to the class in an innovative way—for example, using a poster, PowerPoint presentation, music video, radio news broadcast, collage, et cetera. Include a reference to recent world events and what impact you think these events have on Beers' argument.

4. *Media* Selling to Youth With several classmates, examine at least five ads that you think target teenagers. Discuss the strategies these ads use and develop ideas for selling some of these products, services, or ideas more effectively. Redesign at least one of these ads, using your ideas.

Nairobi's hip hop scene asserts its African identity in the face of the bland imports of the global music industry.

TRANSLATE THIS!

NEWSPAPER ARTICLE BY ADRIAN COOPER

Kenya's demand for music and television can't be met by under-funded local industries, so a flow of pop culture from the West, a culture of brands and products, fills the gap. It isn't a lack of talent that stops broadcasters from going home-grown: it's simply cheaper for broadcasters to buy the entrails of television from the West than it is to commission indigenous pro-gramme-makers or encourage a self-sustained music industry. Radio is judged for the speed it serves the latest Eminem, Will Smith or Britney Spears, not for introducing new, local artists. Record shops, magazine stalls and nightclubs are no different, their fodder shaped by the idea that current means playing catchup with the West.

Wayua Muli, a young Nairobi journalist says: "We're not quite sure where we belong, so our greatest influence right now is from the States and from Britain. That's what teaches who we should be."

At the core of this cultural crossfire, Nairobi's blossoming hip hop scene is the most visible example of how young urbanites are latching on to the styles, symbols and language of imported music, television and film. Its genesis, during weekend jam sessions and talent contests in Nairobi's clubs, was simple mimicry: rappers were hailed for their skill as a parrot, not their ability to invent new rhymes and sounds. You had to look and act the part too: baggy jeans, sports shoes, baseball cap and an imitation American accent.

In response, a group of journalists, musicians and television producers in Nairobi is searching for ways to counter the biased flow of pop culture into Kenya.

"What we're trying to do is encourage the young people to maintain the culture and morality that Africa has," says Jimmi Gathu, a television producer who has turned the spotlight on local talent through a string of music shows. This self-conscious attempt to create local icons for young Kenyans to identify with is paralleled by the recent launch of East Africa's first youth culture magazine *PHAT!* The title is an acronym of *Pamoja Hip Afrika Tunawakilisha*, Swahili for "Together we represent hip Africa." "There's never been a

Kenyan musician on the cover of any magazine in the world," says Blaze, assistant editor of *PHAT!* "Talent in Kenya doesn't get a chance to be seen." It hasn't proved easy for the likes of Jimmi Gathu and Blaze to convince financiers, venues and broadcasters to focus on new groups and music made in Kenya. "You'd literally have to pay DJs to play your records," recalls Gathu from his own musician days.

Not until 1995, when artist Poxi Presha released a single *Total Bala* (Total Chaos) in Luo, one of Kenya's 44 ethnic dialects, did people realize the potential of rapping and singing in local languages. *Total Bala* "just hit the country like bushfire," says Bruce Odhiambo, the record's producer. "It crossed all language barriers and people realized they could do it in their mother tongue." A realization that struck a chord with rappers from Nairobi's Eastlands slum estates, who formed the Mau Mau collective—named after Kenya's freedom fighters from the 1950s.

Mau Mau group Kalamashaka's song *Tafsiri Hii*—which means "translate this!"—evoked

life in the Nairobi slums and became a major hit. Another Luo act, Gidi Gidi Maji Maji, released their debut album in 2001, *Ismarwa* (It's Ours).

Gidi Gidi Maji Maji researched the album by returning to their home province on the Kenyan shores of Lake Victoria, where they collected Luo myths and sayings, instruments and sounds that defined what Tedd Josiah, the producer of *Ismarwa*, says was a re-statement of identity: "If you're an African there are certain cultures, certain traditions that you've grown up with—our language, our musical styles—and we have to actually go back to those things."

The seeds that a new generation have scattered to define and encourage Kenyan culture are a direct response to the saturation of Western pop culture. *Umbia*, another track on a new compilation of Kenya's rising stars quotes the words of the late President Jomo Kenyatta: "Flare up as the flames of a fire. Consume the nation with your passion. Let the Kenyan culture sing loud and clear, echoing over the hills and ridges."

Adrian Cooper is a filmmaker and writer. In 1989, he worked on images for the documentary *The Forbidden Land*, which examined the growing divisions within the Catholic Church in Brazil. He is presently working on a music festival to help increase awareness of East African music and culture.

1. *Response*

a. Study the first and final paragraphs. How are they connected, or how is the theme of the article expressed in each? Then skim the paragraphs in between and trace how the author has led the reader from the introduction to the conclusion.

b. Why did some of the musicians in Kenya turn to their traditional cultural influences and move away from Western influences?

c. According to the article, in Kenya's music and TV industry, Western imports dominate the local scene—that is, viewers and listeners experience more Western (American or British) media than local media. Explain why this is so. In your opinion, do Western media also dominate other media—such as radio, newspapers, or magazines?

2. *Critical Thinking* In small groups, discuss or debate one of the following topics:

- Globalization threatens/enhances cultures.
- The media teaches us who we should be.
- Western influences are bad/good for other nations.

3. *Oral Communication* Group Discussion With a small group, discuss the article, using some of the following questions: What is meant by "the West," in global terms? What countries within these regions would you say hold positions of international power? Which countries' media texts dominate those of other countries? What effect do you think this has on other countries and cultures?

4. *Media* Marketing Music Imagine that, tomorrow, all music from the United States will be banned in Canada. In a group, plan an all-Canadian morning show for a radio station in your area that has a specific teen audience. Develop a sample *playlist*, (a list of the songs the station would play) arrange two interviews with guests, and write a brief mission statement (statement of intent) for your program.

Alternatively, plan an issue of a new Canadian magazine along the lines of *PHAT!* (the magazine described in the article). Choose a title, design the cover, and list the articles you would include in that issue. Also write a brief mission statement for your magazine.

Drama

Drama assumes an order. If only so that it might have—
by disrupting that order—a way of surprising.

Václav Havel

Duel

Stephen Fry and Hugh Laurie are British comedians. The following script is taken from their comedy show, *Fry and Laurie*.

TV Comedy Sketch
by Stephen Fry and
Hugh Laurie

Hugh and Stephen in period dress (that is, dressed in the garb of seventeenth-century gentlemen) on a misty heath, about to duel. There is a referee, and possibly some seconds. Hugh plays "Sir David" and Stephen plays "Mr Van Hoyle."

REFEREE:	Gentlemen, I believe you both know the purpose of this meeting.
STEPHEN:	Thank you Mr Tollerby, but we have no need of explanation. The circumstances are well known to us.
HUGH:	Quite right. Let us be about the business.
REFEREE:	Very well, gentlemen. Sir David, I understand the choice is yours—sword or pistol?
HUGH:	Sword.
REFEREE:	As you wish.

Hugh takes the sword and swishes it expertly.

HUGH:	Ha. The only weapon for a gentleman.
REFEREE:	Quite so. That means, Mr Van Hoyle, that you have the pistol.
STEPHEN:	Thank you, Tollerby.
REFEREE:	When I give the command, I shall expect …
HUGH:	Wait a minute.
REFEREE:	Is there something wrong, Sir David?
HUGH:	Well …
STEPHEN:	Quick man, the hour grows late …
HUGH:	Well it's just that when you said sword or pistol, I sort of assumed that we would both have the same one, if you know what I mean.
REFEREE:	Ah.

STEPHEN: I'm not with you.

HUGH: Well I said sword, assuming that meant we would both have a sword …

STEPHEN: Oh I see.

REFEREE: Mmm. Thing is, I've only brought one of each, unfortunately.

STEPHEN: Oh damn and blast.

HUGH: Sorry to make a fuss, but it seems a bit unfair otherwise.

REFEREE: No, I take your point, Sir David.

STEPHEN: Well is there somewhere we could get a sword?

HUGH: I doubt there'd be anywhere open at this time …
Excuse me!

Hugh dashes off and stops a pair of joggers in dayglo strip.

You wouldn't happen to have a sword on you, would you?

JOGGER: *(Not stopping)* Twenty past seven.

HUGH: Damn.

STEPHEN: Well … we're a bit stuck, really, aren't we?

REFEREE: Gentlemen, I realise that this is a bit of an improvisation, but needs must when the devil …

STEPHEN: Get on with it.

REFEREE: Right, how would it be if Mr Van Hoyle were to take the pistol but promise not to fire it?

HUGH: You mean, use the pistol as if it were a sword?

REFEREE: Exactly.

HUGH: Well, suits me.

STEPHEN: Wait a minute, wait a minute. That's hopeless. Wouldn't cut anything, look.

Stephen prods Referee with the pistol.

See?

HUGH: Perhaps you're right.

REFEREE: Well it was just an idea.

STEPHEN: You could try shooting with your … no, that won't work. Forget I spoke.

HUGH: Mm. How about fists?

REFEREE: You mean boxing?

STEPHEN: Oh Lord no. I'm no good at that at all. It hurts your knuckles.

HUGH: Well, I can't think of anything else … hang on I've got some matches here I think.

STEPHEN:	What, you mean set fire to each other?
HUGH:	Better than nothing. Oh no, actually, look, there's only one match left in fact.
STEPHEN:	We could nip across to that café and see if they have any forks …
REFEREE:	Gentlemen, if you'll bear with me—I have one last idea up my sleeve.
STEPHEN:	Well?

Referee reaches up his sleeve and pulls out a handkerchief.

HUGH:	A handkerchief?
REFEREE:	No, Sir David. *Two* handkerchiefs.
STEPHEN:	You're suggesting that we duel to the death with a pair of handkerchiefs?
REFEREE:	I realise it's not ideal, Mr Van Hoyle, but it would at least be fair …
STEPHEN:	It would take for ever. I've got to be in town by eight.
HUGH:	Well we haven't got anything else.

Stephen sighs.

STEPHEN:	Oh all right then. Better be clean, that's all.
REFEREE:	Perfectly clean, I assure you.

They each take a handkerchief.

Gentlemen, I believe you both know the purpose of this meeting?

Stephen and Hugh start hitting each other with handkerchiefs. ▶

… the theatre demanded of its members stamina, good digestion, the ability to adjust, and a strong sense of humor. There was no discomfort an actor didn't learn to endure. To survive, we had to be horses and we were.

Helen Hayes

Stephen Fry (left) and Hugh Laurie.

Hugh Laurie, born in Oxford, England in 1959, and
Stephen Fry, born in London, England in 1957, met while
attending Cambridge University. Emma Thompson (actor and
screenwriter of *Sense and Sensibility*) introduced the two men.
Since 1981, Laurie and Fry have been collaborating and
performing together. They were both in the movie
Peter's Friends and appear as Jeeves (Fry) and
Wooster (Laurie) in the BBC production, *Jeeves and Wooster.*

I. Response

a. What serious point does this comedy sketch make? Do you think the authors intended to make this point? Explain.
b. How would you describe the humour in this selection? What comic techniques do the authors use?
c. Did you guess the general outcome of this sketch? If so, at what point, and what were the clues that suggested the ending?
d. Do you think you would enjoy the *Fry and Laurie* comedy show? Why or why not?

2. *Drama* *Voice* Consider the emotion and emphasis you think the actors would have used in delivering this script. Choose four lines from one character in this selection and read them aloud as you think the actor would have done. Practise reading the lines, experimenting with different tones, expressions, and volumes. Deliver these four lines to an audience and ask for their opinion on the effectiveness of your delivery.

PERFORMANCE TIP Before any performance, do a few exercises to relax your mind and muscles, and prepare yourself for your audience. Remember also that how you perform a scene not only depends on your interpretation of the author's words and intentions, but also on who your audience is (younger students, parents, peers) and where they are (classroom, auditorium, community centre).

3. *Writing* *Comedy Sketch* In a small group, brainstorm ideas for a comedy sketch. Together, choose one idea and write a short script, using this selection as a model. What type of humour will you use? How will you make the script sound natural? Present your comedy sketch to the whole class.

4. *Language Conventions* *Interjections* Examine the use of **interjections** in this script and analyse their effect on the reader. Remember to include interjections in the comedy sketch you are creating in activity 3. Note the use of interjections and their effect in other scripts within the unit. Form some conclusions about their use.

Interjections are words—such as *oh, wow, ha, mmm*—that show emotion, often without any grammatical connection to other parts of the sentence.

Can reality programming go too far?

That's
Extraordinary!

One-Act Radio Play by Diana Raznovich

Translated by Rosalind Goldsmith

CHARACTERS

ALICIA	early forties
GASPAR	radio journalist, late twenties
MC	broadcaster, deep, rich voice

SCENE ONE

(SOUND: ALICIA walks, autumn leaves crackling under her feet. She pants as she climbs a hill. Wind in the tops of the trees. ALICIA stops.)

ALICIA: *(Inhales the fresh morning air)* It's nice here. Deserted. This is a good place to say goodbye to the world. Dawn. The rocks look black. The sky so dark and full of clouds. It seems somehow right for me to die under this stormy sky. *(Sings softly, sadly)* Goodbye beautiful clouds! We won't see each other again ... *(Pulls herself up)* Come on, let's not be gloomy at the last minute. *(Tries to be brave)* I'll die laughing! *(Laughs, tries to be cheerful, stops short. Admits to herself)* But ... I'm afraid. That's the truth. Those trees have turned their backs on me. They're hiding, and even the flowers shiver when they see my gun ...

(SOUND: She loads the gun.)

I'm trembling like you, my dear, beautiful red poppies!

(SOUND: She plays with the gun, loading it and unloading it.)

(Laughs anxiously) It's not easy to be the criminal and the victim at the same time! My own executioner ... Alicia's obedient assassin: Alicia. *(Breathes)* I must climb higher.

(SOUND: Stronger wind. ALICIA climbs. She stumbles into an enormous rock, sits on it)

(Out of breath) From up here my own life seems so far away, like some-one else's story. *(Sighs)* Pitiful story. At least it could do with a dignified ending.

> *(SOUND: All nature seems to unleash itself. The trees creak and stir in the wind. Dry leaves blown everywhere; continues underneath)*

How much time I've lost in lost causes! I don't blame anybody ... no. They won't even notice when I've gone, since they never noticed me when I was there. *(With irony)* Someone will say: Miss Alicia didn't come today. Today she didn't cross the blue bridge clutching all her papers. Today she didn't eat alone at Joseph's restaurant. Today she didn't talk to her mirror. Today she didn't stay stuck to the telephone waiting for him to call. Today she has missed all her appointments. *(Overcome)* Today ...

> *(SOUND: Wind howls furiously, swish of leaves)*

(Speaks to the wind, her voice battling against the gale) Blow wind! Come on, blow! Take away all my fear! Take away my love—the love I gave to Peter that he never gave to me! Blow white wind and fill me with your rage, your power! Give me all the strength I need to pull this trigger! *(Decided)* I'll count to three and then I'll do it. Then it will all be over for me. One ... two ... two ... two and ... two and ... One, two and— *(Furious with herself)* I can't! I can't!

> *(SOUND: Wind drops. Calms. A gentle breeze, becoming more and more distant. A few birds chirp.)*

And now the wind has stopped! And the sun! The sun's coming out! *(Daunted, frightened)* How am I going to have the courage to say good-bye to the rest of my days in front of that beautiful sun? Oh God! Why do you make things even more difficult for me? Give me back my storm!

SCENE TWO

> *(MUSIC: Theme music of the radio program "That's Extraordinary!"— a catchy upbeat tune breaking the mood of the previous scene)*

MC: *(Professional, enthusiastic, false voice)* Good morning, ladies and gen-tlemen! And welcome to another morning with your friendly radio! Stay with us for "That's Extraordinary!" The hottest radio program on the international airwaves! *(With the same demagogic tone)* As always, at your service to bring direct into your home: *life itself!* And so ... *(Emphatic, inquisitive)* Isn't death just one side, one facet, we might say, of life?

(MUSIC: Suspenseful)

Because we believe that death is an intimate part of life, we are bringing to you today, direct, live and on location, an actual suicide.

(MUSIC: Well-known march)

Yes, ladies and gentlemen! The extraordinary and more and more extraordinary! Today we present "Suicide on a Hilltop."

(MUSIC: March)

What you have just heard was the fantastic but real testimony of a woman about to kill herself, captured by our secret microphones, especially arranged so that you can enjoy listening to a real suicide in the comfort of your own home.

(MUSIC: Suspenseful)

(In a salesman tone, with professional pride) Our program has stopped at nothing. We've been following Miss "A" for the last eight days, since the time we knew she had decided to take her own life. And now we can present to you, live and direct into your own home: her final words.

(MUSIC: Chords of triumphal march music between each of the following words)

Unique! Unrepeatable! Shocking!

(MUSIC: Suspenseful; builds underneath)

(Speaks invitingly, as if to each listener) She, of course, has no idea about our extraordinary report today. She doesn't know that her final words are being transmitted to thousands and thousands of eager radio listeners. Neither does she know that we have sent our own intrepid reporter, Gaspar Wolf, to the scene to interview her live and on location. Hello Gaspar? Are you there?

SCENE THREE

GASPAR: *(Enthusiastic, close on)* Good morning, William. I'm here, hidden behind some shrubs, and from my vantage point I can see today's interviewee quite clearly—in fact, she's only about a stone's throw away.

MC: We have heard directly her conversations with the wind, the poppies, the sun and God, and I must say it has been stupendous to follow her final emotions at such close range. But our curiosity has no end. Tell us—what does she look like?

GASPAR: *(Syrupy)* She … what does she look like? She's … tall, fair, blue eyes. She's very pale, really … not of this world, white as a sheet … She's been lifting the gun to her head and then … pulling it back. She's wearing a charming suit of autumn shades, she's a woman of about forty … Oh, she has an air about her … she's a classic beauty … But hang on—she's moving her lips, she's … *(Stops himself. ALICIA has done something unexpected.)* Oh!! No!! No!! You can't imagine what I'm seeing, my God! Just a minute! She's lifted the gun to her head with more conviction this time. *(Enthused)* She seems totally decided!! Here we go! She's going to do it!!!

(MUSIC: Suspenseful. Drum roll)

MC: *(Low, intense, like a golf commentator)* You are listening to "That's Extraordinary!"—the program with an impact! And for those of you who may have just joined us, "That's Extraordinary!" presents to you today a person just like yourself or myself, a person who, within a few precious moments, will actually cross over that barrier that separates life from death.

(MUSIC: Triumphal march; continues underneath)

Stay tuned! Don't lose a second! Every second could be the last!

SCENE FOUR

ALICIA: Now … yes. Now I feel ready … I can do it. *(Like a presentiment)* It's like a strange force is pushing me over the edge to the other world—a death-like energy inside me but from somewhere else … *(Forcefully)* One, two and—

GASPAR: *(Interrupts violently, as if sprung from the earth)* Just a minute! Don't do it! Not yet!

ALICIA: *(Terrified)* Who are you? Where did you come from? *(Furious)* Go away! Now! Go on, leave me alone! Don't you realize that this moment belongs to me?

GASPAR: *(Trying to placate her)* Miss, please believe me. It's not my intention to stop you or to dissuade you from your decision. On the contrary …

ALICIA: Get out of here! *(Discovers a mini tape-recorder on GASPAR. Panicked)* Why are you carrying a tape-recorder?

GASPAR: You're carrying a weapon and I haven't asked *you* why.

ALICIA: *(Furious)* A tape-recorder can also be a weapon.

GASPAR: Possibly ... but not in my hands. *(Sincerely)* I am a good man. I earn an honest living.

ALICIA: *(Trying to calm herself down and to believe him at the same time)* If you're really a good man, please have consideration and respect for me.

GASPAR: Of course. Just tell me what you need.

ALICIA: *(With complete certainty)* I need to be alone.

SCENE FIVE

(MUSIC: Suspense music, with chords that finalize ALICIA'S last sentence)

MC: Well, dear listeners, we're at a crucial moment. *(Trying with each question to create emotional tension in the audience)* Will Gaspar succeed in his mission? Will he be able to offer us this direct and so-very-human testimony?

(MUSIC: "That's Extraordinary!" theme)

(In a hard-sell, advertising tone) You are listening to "That's Extraordinary!" The most successful radio program on the international airwaves.

(MUSIC: Catchy, upbeat "You have just won ..." tune)

And why are we successful? Because we stop at nothing to bring to your ears, raw and untreated, reality itself! At whatever the cost!

(MUSIC: Smooth, romantic melody)

(Suggestively) Alicia needs to be alone. *(Ironically)* She doesn't know that thousands of people are following her every move.

(MUSIC: Suspense music returns)

SCENE SIX

ALICIA: *(Fed up)* Didn't you say you would leave me alone?

GASPAR: *(In a penetrating, sympathetic tone)* You are going to be alone forever. Really alone. What's your hurry? Let me offer you my company ... as a friend.

ALICIA: There's no time left for that.

GASPAR: *(Wounded)* But I need you to help me.

ALICIA: *(Beside herself)* You want *me* to help *you*? Why don't you go and ask someone more …

GASPAR: *(Feelingly)* More … what?

ALICIA: More able to help you.

GASPAR: I need *your* help, Alicia.

ALICIA: *(Shocked)* How do you know my name? Who told you my name is Alicia?

GASPAR: *(Seductively)* When someone attracts me, really attracts me I mean, her name suddenly appears to me out of nowhere, as clear and bright as day. From the moment I saw you, I knew your name. I saw you … so distant, so beautiful, lost in the middle of this wood, at the very cliff edge of your own life, and I said to myself: Her name is Alicia.

ALICIA: *(Falling for the flattery for an instant)* Really? Nothing like this has ever happened to me before.

GASPAR: *(Leading her)* Nothing like … what?

ALICIA: *(Moved)* Nothing—magic. That someone could guess my name …

GASPAR: *(Taking advantage of the weak flank she has offered him)* It's not only your name that I can guess, Alicia …

ALICIA: *(Surprised)* What more can you guess?

GASPAR: *(In a carefully controlled, calculated voice)* Your deepest needs.

ALICIA: I don't need anything anymore.

GASPAR: I'm sorry to contradict you, but it seems so very clear to me that you do need something more, that you're asking for something, that you're even … crying out for something …

ALICIA: *(Shocked)* Me? Asking for something? For what?

GASPAR: *(Attempting to touch her in order to get the interview)* Love. Love, Alicia. Love. You are asking me for love.

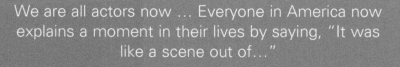

We are all actors now … Everyone in America now explains a moment in their lives by saying, "It was like a scene out of…"

Peggy Noonan

SCENE SEVEN

(MUSIC: Romantic, something worn out and in bad taste; continues underneath)

MC: *(Enthusiastic)* Yes! Oh yes! Now our own reporter Gaspar Wolf is really showing us how to reach the human soul. *(Demagogic)* I have tears in my eyes, and if my voice breaks … *(His voice breaks)* it's because *(With difficulty, as if about to cry)* I'm thinking of her, of Alicia. I can picture her enormous aquatic eyes mooring themselves in the penetrating gaze of Gaspar Wolf. His will be the last pair of eyes that she will see—the last pair of eyes that will look at her.

(MUSIC: Ends)

SCENE EIGHT

ALICIA: Why are you talking to me about love, now? I've looked for love all my life. Now I need to be alone, by myself.

GASPAR: *(Almost in secret)* Love cures all ills.

ALICIA: It's late … too late …

GASPAR: Give me a chance. *(Insistent)* Give yourself a chance.

ALICIA: A chance for what?

GASPAR: I want to do … an interview with you … before … before … you abandon us forever.

ALICIA: *(Bewildered)* An interview? With me? And who's going to be interested in this interview?

GASPAR: Lots of people, Alicia.

ALICIA: I don't understand …

GASPAR: You … could tell the world … what it feels like before you die. And since all of us are going to die sooner or later … who wouldn't be interested?

ALICIA: But what good is it to me to do an interview that won't come out until after I'm dead?

GASPAR: It will be for the good of humanity.

ALICIA: I have already said goodbye to humanity.

GASPAR: And above all it will be for the good of my family.

ALICIA: Your family?

GASPAR: *(Pathetic)* An interview like this could help us … financially.

ALICIA: I don't understand.

GASPAR: Excuse my … presumption, but you are in a position to do something really—an interview with someone who's about to take her own life—it's very original … They would pay me very well for it, and that would help my family to get out of the financial mess that we're in. It would mean my children could eat …

ALICIA: Your children are hungry?

GASPAR: *(Nervously)* Well, you see, I don't have any work right now. Well—actually—to be honest, it's been quite a while since I've had any work, since I've sold even a word.

SCENE NINE

(MUSIC: "That's Extraordinary!" theme)

MC: Extraordinary strategy of our reporter, Gaspar Wolf! He's demonstrating to us the techniques of the shrewd and clever journalist, the modern journalist without prejudice or fear … Will he pull off this final interview with Alicia by pretending to be a poor, unemployed father?

(MUSIC: Suspenseful; building)

Stay tuned to "That's Extraordinary!" The program that investigates humanity in the service of humanity!

(MUSIC: Theme music)

SCENE TEN

GASPAR: Well, now I've confessed to you *my* tragedy. *(Snivelling)* Only you can help me, Alicia. But it's true you have no reason to help me. You have already broken free from the chains of reality. Why should you bother about me? You have every right to throw me out, to insult me … *(Pitifully)* You could damn me to hell, Alicia, and I would understand perfectly.

ALICIA: Look, I—

GASPAR: *(False tears)* Yes?

ALICIA: I … never …

GASPAR: Do you want me to leave right now?

ALICIA: *(Confused, anxious)* Don't cry. Please don't cry, sir.

GASPAR: *(Cries)* It's nothing. It'll pass. Excuse my insolence. I'm going now.

ALICIA: I … look, don't go … I can do it … in a few minutes. I'll do the interview. At least my death will feed your children.

SCENE ELEVEN

(MUSIC: Happy, triumphant)

MC: *(As if GASPAR has scored a goal)* He scores! He scores! Our own Gaspar Wolf has broken through the defences of the unassailable Alicia, yes he has! Wonderful effectiveness in the approach, gentlemen, don't you think? This great offensive move on the part of our man means that we can now present to you a world première. Yes, for the first time anywhere in the world, ladies and gentlemen, an interview with a suicide a mere instant before her departure to the other world.

(MUSIC: Sports march)

Alicia leaves this world, valiant and resolute. And we will respect her unquestionable will. All we want is to be secret witnesses to her final confessions.

(MUSIC: Nostalgic, "We'll meet again"; continues underneath)

Alicia is not alone. Our white handkerchiefs are fluttering in the wind in gestures of: Farewell.

(SOUND/MUSIC: "Farewell" echoes and fades; harps, in bad taste)

We are like secret spies on her private journey of no return. Silent, hidden behind our radios large or small, you and I are the privileged witnesses to the unfolding of this final tragedy, while she, of course, is completely unaware of our presence.

(MUSIC: More intense, sentimental, nostalgic; continues underneath)

She is an unknown, an anonymous being from the anonymous city. But we have come to say goodbye. And although she doesn't know it, we have come to accompany her.

(MUSIC: Well-known children's tune; continues underneath)

Alicia too was once a little girl ... She too frolicked in the park with her little friends, surely unaware of what life had prepared for her.

(MUSIC: Children singing a well-known tune)

(Exploitingly) An innocent little girl who pranced about among the poppies, the same poppies that today bid her farewell.

(MUSIC: Sudden loud rock music; continues underneath)

And then Alicia became an adolescent. An adolescent who danced, happy and carefree, just like you ... or me, to the beat of rock and roll.

(MUSIC: Romantic Bolero music; continues underneath)

Until one day Alicia, also just like you or me, found love. The first love. The first kiss. *(Hums along with the music)* And perhaps it was then that she also came to know her first pain ...

(SOUND: Radio sound effect, intense rain; continues underneath)

Surely it was raining. And Alicia was walking in that rain, without her umbrella, thinking of him.

(MUSIC: "Singing in the Rain")

Then, one day, a day like any other day, it stopped raining. And Alicia, hardly realizing, began to laugh.

(SOUND: Radio sound effect, youthful, fun-loving laughter)

Whatever became of that youthful laughter? Who shattered it?

(SOUND: Radio sound effect, broken glass)

Who was it that suddenly slammed the door?

(SOUND: Radio sound effect, violent door slam)

Who was it that left her yet again in absolute and devastating solitude?

(SOUND: Radio sound effect, car starts, accelerates, screeches away)

Who? When? How was she brought to this final ending?

(MUSIC: "That's Extraordinary!" theme)

But enough of fantasies. Let's listen to the real Alicia.

(MUSIC: Soft music)

Let's hear what she herself has to say ...

SCENE TWELVE

(SOUND: Birds singing in the trees)

ALICIA: Well, what would you like to know, sir?

GASPAR: I was just listening to the birds singing and it seemed to me that their song was dedicated to you.

(SOUND: Singing and chattering of birds intensifies)

ALICIA: It's true. They're marvellous … with their feathers of all colours and their brilliant beaks … the way they fly. Look at that one perched on the top branch.

(SOUND: Happy cheeping of one bird)

If only I could perch on the highest branch and take to the air, flying towards the immense sky …

GASPAR: Have you ever tried?

ALICIA: Yes, I have tried.

(SOUND: Chattering of birds)

I have tried but I didn't get very far. And whenever I stopped to sing on the branches, usually I could only come out with a sort of "twip, twip," an insipid sound, not very joyful—or graceful for that matter. And most of the time the branch I was sitting on would break anyway, and I'd come crashing down to the ground.

(SOUND: Singing of birds intensifies)

They sing as if life were worth living … They sing innocently because they don't know anything about loneliness.

(SOUND: One bird sings alone, marvellously)

Can you hear that? That one sings better than the rest. He's a real virtuoso. *(Whistles to the bird, hoping for an answer)*

(SOUND: The bird answers, imitating Alicia exactly)

He heard me! He's answering me! *(Whistles again, this time a more complicated melody)*

(SOUND: The bird repeats the new tune)

GASPAR: He heard you! He is answering you!

ALICIA: Yes! I've made a friend! *(To the bird)* Let's see if you can do this tune. *(Whistles with more variations)*

> *(SOUND: The bird replies with exactly the same tune)*

Oh! This is really incredible! What have I done all my life that I never paid any attention to the birds? Why did I have to come to this extreme before I could even notice how beautiful, how generous nature is?

> *(SOUND: Now the bird suggests a tune)*

He's talking to me. Excuse me. I should reply. *(Whistles what the bird has just whistled)*

> *(SOUND: The bird speaks to her intently and at length)*

Oh! I think I understand what the bird is saying to me.

GASPAR: *(Impatient)* You and I were going to have a little conversation.

ALICIA: I'm sorry, it's just that at the last minute I'm discovering things I never dreamed of. I've been deaf, dumb and blind all my life. I'm just beginning to realize how lazy I've been, how I've—

GASPAR: Do we do this interview?

ALICIA: Wouldn't it be better to listen to the birds?

> *(SOUND: A real uproar from all the birds, a riot of happy singing)*

GASPAR: *(Fed up)* I didn't come here to listen to the birds sing, Miss.

ALICIA: I didn't either. But suddenly—

GASPAR: Let's just leave the little birdies aside …

ALICIA: Why?

GASPAR: What do you mean, why? You haven't come to this crucial point in your life just to amuse yourself with the singing of little birds. You came here to commit suicide. To commit suicide! Or have you forgotten?

ALICIA: I don't know …

GASPAR: What do you mean, you don't know?

ALICIA: Maybe I came here to discover the song of the birds.

GASPAR: That's not possible.

ALICIA: Everything's possible. *(Whistles to the birds)*

(SOUND: The birds answer her)

Do you hear them? They're talking to me. And do you know what they're saying?

GASPAR: They're saying that every person has an obligation to fulfil her destiny.

ALICIA: They're saying that life is worth the trouble …

(SOUND: Uproar of birds)

GASPAR: You're not seeing things clearly.

ALICIA: They're telling me to try again, not to be a coward, to wake up and live. Can you hear them? They're saying that life is always a risk … that to run away from this world is cowardice. That's what those birds are telling me.

(SOUND: Chattering of birds)

GASPAR: *(Losing control)* Enough of the stupid birds! Shut up! They're driving me crazy! I hate them!!

SCENE THIRTEEN

(MUSIC: "That's Extraordinary!" theme)

MC: *(Covering his anxiety)* It's all going according to plan, ladies and gentlemen. Our beloved Alicia has been deeply moved by the sweet singing of the birds, and this can only mean that in a little while she too will take to the air and fly, fly just like one of those little birds …

(MUSIC: Nostalgic)

One more bird among the thousands of birds that cross the night in glorious flight. She will fly … she will fly so high … and perhaps she will even reach the very source of light. Perhaps, from way up there, she will be able to see all of us, strolling through life … and perhaps she will even send us a sign so that we can recognize her.

(MUSIC: Vivaldi's "Gloria"; continues underneath)

She is ready to begin her flight. Her delicate wings have already begun to flutter. She is preparing herself for that eternal ascension …

ALICIA: You seem bothered, sir. What's the matter? It's not the birds, is it?

GASPAR: *(Trying to control his rage)* I was alone with you. Nobody was listening to us. It was like we were in our own glass bubble. And suddenly the place fills up with birds, talking birds, birds that talk to you. Look. You and I know that birds don't talk. You and I know that they chirp and that you are only hearing what you would like to hear.

ALICIA: Don't tell me you're jealous!

GASPAR: *(Romantic)* Very jealous.

ALICIA: *(Laughs)* Jealous of the birds?

GASPAR: Jealous of the birds.

ALICIA: They are asking me to live. And you?

GASPAR: I am not a bird.

ALICIA: Yes, I know that.

GASPAR: I am asking you to talk to me before you die.

ALICIA: To talk …

GASPAR: Yes, Alicia. I am asking you to talk to me in private before being silenced forever.

ALICIA: Of course. I understand. You want to appropriate my final words, isn't that right?

GASPAR: *(Implacable)* Good. I see you do understand. Speak to me, Alicia …

ALICIA: What do you want me to talk about? *(Lucid and ferocious)* You want me to entertain you with my romantic failures? Fine. The man I loved left me for my best friend. And now do you want to know about my personal frustrations? I wanted to be a dancer and I'm nothing. Do you know the taste, the smell of Nothing? Anything else? I have an alcoholic father who used to beat up my mother—who's paralysed. Is that the kind of news that sells?

GASPAR: Now we're on the right track, Alicia. It's the track of human beings, not birds, dear. So. Your father used to beat your mother?

ALICIA: And not only my mother, but my brothers and sisters too, and me. Are you taping? Is this what you want from me?

GASPAR: Yes, yes. I'm taping. Go on.

ALICIA: What else do you want to know?

GASPAR: Why did you come to this extreme, wanting to take your own life?

ALICIA: Because I didn't have birds around me ...

(SOUND: Cheering of birds)

GASPAR: That's nonsense!

ALICIA: And because I was alone and confused ... confused like I am now when I look at you.

GASPAR: I'm not confusing you.

ALICIA: You could tell me the same thing that the birds are telling me ... Now ... right now ... if ...

GASPAR: Alicia, we are human beings.

ALICIA: *(Desperate)* Say something ... Please. Don't leave me alone!

GASPAR: Fine. I say goodbye and good luck.

ALICIA: *(Very anxious)* That's all?

GASPAR: Now it's your turn to say goodbye.

ALICIA: Will a shot in the head sell? Is that what you're longing for?

GASPAR: *(Panicked)* Look, there's no need to point that gun at me.

ALICIA: *(Decided)* Now you answer me. The reason you don't want to help me to live is because you don't want to lose this interview. It's business, isn't it?

GASPAR: Put the gun down. We are civilized people. I didn't come here to die. I came here to—

ALICIA: To see me die! You want me to put the gun to my head, am I right? *(Sudden)* Who sent you? Who do you work for? Answer me or I'll kill you!

GASPAR: It's not my fault! It wasn't my idea! I work for the radio program "That's Extraordinary!" It's the truth, I swear.

ALICIA: "That's Extraordinary!"? You mean thousands of people are listening to this!? You mean that all that stuff about the humble, unemployed journalist was a lie?

(SOUND: A shot)

GASPAR: My God! Help! She wants to kill me!

(SOUND: Two shots)

ALICIA: Run away! Run away, coward!

(SOUND: One shot)

Coward! You can't even stand up to me. You want to sell my death for a good price! Well, I'm not going to give you the pleasure! I'm going to follow the birds' advice.

(SOUND: Happy cheering from the birds)

I'm going to take a gamble on life …

(SOUND: Cheering of birds)

Alicia is going to dare to start over again! Attention, audience of "That's Extraordinary!", wherever you are … *(To herself)* I suppose there are microphones hidden around here somewhere …

(SOUND: Rustling of leaves, bushes)

No one's going to make a circus out of my death! Do you hear? I'm throwing away this gun! I'm going to live! I'm sorry to have to disappoint the morbid, bloodthirsty audience …

(SOUND: Rustling of bushes, very close on)

I know my life is no good for business, for this sinister program directed by—

GASPAR: *(Secretly, whispering)* Hello, sound? Cut. Sound, cut. Cut the—

ALICIA: Aha! There it is! Give me that microphone! Give it to me! Attention, all of you in the audience of—

GASPAR: Sound—cut cut cut!! Hey—

(SOUND: Grunts, rustling, etc. A scuffle, very close on, over the microphone; continues underneath)

GASPAR: Don't you—give me that mike right now. Give me that!!

ALICIA: No I won't!!

(SOUND: Scuffling)

SCENE FIFTEEN

(SOUND: Radio interference, static)

MC: There seems to be … uh … some interference on the line, ladies and gentlemen. Regrettably we are forced to interrupt our transmission.

(MUSIC/SOUND: Static. "That's Extraordinary!" theme, sped up. Chattering of birds as on location. Sound is picked up again. Static, then:)

GASPAR: *(Struggling)* Would you give that to me? It's not yours, it's mine.

ALICIA: I want to talk to the audience. I want to tell them—

GASPAR: Shut up! Just shut up! Cut the sound! Cut cut cut cut cut—

(MUSIC/SOUND: Theme music, a few bars, static)

ALICIA: I'm alive! You can't gag me! I'm alive!

(SOUND: They scuffle, close on over mike)

Give me that earphone! I want to hear what they're saying!

(MUSIC: Theme established)

MC: And so, ladies and gentlemen, we have saved a life today! And is this not perhaps the mission of a humanitarian program such as our own?

(SOUND: Static)

ALICIA: Criminals! Liars!

(SOUND: Static)

GASPAR: Cut cut cut!

(SOUND: Static)

MC: We're not actually hearing Alicia very well just now, but we know that she's grateful. We have a few technical problems, uh … as I mentioned before there seems to be some kind of interference in our transmission. But doubtless if she could Alicia would want to say thank you to us all.

Drama of Trees by Robin Holtom. Oil.

Examine the painting above and consider its mood, style, techniques, and message. With a small group, discuss why it has been chosen to accompany this script.

> There is no better indication of what the people of any period are like than the plays they go to see.
>
> Edith Hamilton

(MUSIC: Triumphal march)

This has certainly been an unforeseen conclusion to our program today ... Marvellous! Alicia, grateful, deeply moved, is perhaps even now on her knees blessing "That's Extraordinary!" for saving her life ... And I must say it is wonderful to be able to do some good in this world, even from our own modest and humble program, "That's Extraordinary!"—the hottest radio program on the international airwaves! Until next week, friends!

(MUSIC: "That's Extraordinary!" theme)

Diana Raznovich was born in Buenos Aires, Argentina, in 1945. She published her first book of poetry by the age of 16. Because of the military regime, she left Argentina in 1976 and now lives in Spain. She is an internationally renowned playwright. This play aired on CBC Radio.

I. *Response*

a. Setting plays an important role in this selection. Discuss how the setting affects the action.

b. How is Gaspar's character different from that of Alicia? Which of these two characters earns the sympathy of the audience? Explain.

c. Do you think the ending is effective? Explain your answer.

d. Analyse the radio techniques and special effects the author has included, and assess their effect and effectiveness.

2. *Critical Thinking* This play deals with the sensitive subject of suicide in a humorous manner. Poll your classmates to see how many people think the subject matter and its treatment are or are not appropriate. Present these results in a bar graph. Along with the bar graph, write a paragraph in which you explain and analyse the results.

3. **Drama** *Satire* This play can be called a *satire*. What does it satirize? Is the satire effective? Share your findings with a partner. Discuss other examples of satires—plays, TV shows, novels, or poems. What do you like or dislike about satires in general? What might be difficult about performing a satire? With a small group, prepare a presentation of your favourite scene from this satire.

PERFORMANCE TIP Some comic scenes are funny to both the actors and the audience, while others could be described as *accidentally funny*—the audience might laugh at what happens to the characters, but the characters have to play the scene seriously. Consider how this advice applies to the scene you are presenting in this satire.

4. **Media** *Reality TV* This radio play is based on the idea of reality programming. Imagine that you work for a TV station that wants to come up with a new concept for a reality program. Write a memo to a studio executive in which you outline your idea. Include the advantages, as well as any possible drawbacks, to your idea. Assess the effectiveness and clarity of your proposal.

5. **Visual Communication** *Art Therapy* Reread this script, noting its use of symbols (birds, guns, trees, et cetera). Choose one of these symbols and create or find an image that depicts what the symbol represents in the script. Discuss your image with three or more classmates.

Theme Connections

The following script contains the opening scenes from the movie
Sense and Sensibility. Note that, in this selection, the structure is
different from stage plays and other selections you have already read.
As you read, refer to the abbreviations below
to help you understand the screenplay.

The Dashwoods' Fate Is Decided

an excerpt from the screenplay
for *Sense and Sensibility*
by Emma Thompson
(from the novel by Jane Austen)

ABBREVIATIONS

CAM	camera	EXT	exterior
cont.	continued	INT	interior
CU	close-up	POV	point of view
ECU	extreme close-up	V/O	voice over
EVE	evening		

0 EXT. OPEN ROADS. NIGHT. TITLE SEQUENCE.
A series of travelling shots. A well-dressed, pompous-looking individual (JOHN
DASHWOOD, 35) *is making an urgent journey on horseback. He looks anxious.*

1 EXT. NORLAND PARK. ENGLAND. MARCH 1800. NIGHT.
*Silence. Norland Park, a large country house built in the early part of the eight-
eenth century, lies in the moonlit parkland.*

2 INT. NORLAND PARK. MR DASHWOOD'S BEDROOM. NIGHT.
In the dim light shed by candles we see a bed in which a MAN (MR DASH-
WOOD, 52) *lies—his skin waxy, his breathing laboured. Around him two sil-
houettes move and murmur, their clothing susurrating in the deathly hush.*
DOCTORS. *A* WOMAN (MRS DASHWOOD, 50) *sits by his side, holding his
hand, her eyes never leaving his face.*

MR DASHWOOD: *(urgent)* Is John not yet arrived?

MRS DASHWOOD: We expect him at any moment, dearest.

(*MR DASHWOOD looks anguished.*)

MR DASHWOOD: The girls—I have left so little.

MRS DASHWOOD: Shh, hush, Henry.

MR DASHWOOD: Elinor will try to look after you all, but make sure she finds a good husband. The men are such noodles hereabouts, little wonder none has pleased her.

(They smile at each other. MRS DASHWOOD is just managing to conceal her fear and grief.)

MRS DASHWOOD: But Marianne is sure to find her storybook hero.

MR DASHWOOD: A romantic poet with flashing eyes and empty pockets?

MRS DASHWOOD: As long as she loves him, who*ever* he is.

MR DASHWOOD: Margaret will go to sea and become a pirate so we need not concern ourselves with her.

(MRS DASHWOOD tries to laugh but it emerges as a sob. An older MANSERVANT [THOMAS] now enters, anxiety written on every feature.)

THOMAS: Your son has arrived from London, sir.

(MR DASHWOOD squeezes his wife's hand.)

MR DASHWOOD: Let me speak to John alone.

(She nods quickly and he smiles at her with infinite tenderness.)

MR DASHWOOD: Ah, my dear. How happy you have made me.

(MRS DASHWOOD makes a superhuman effort and smiles back. She allows THOMAS to help her out. She passes JOHN DASHWOOD as he enters, presses his hand, but cannot speak. JOHN takes her place by the bed.)

JOHN: Father . . .

(MR DASHWOOD summons his last ounces of energy and starts to whisper with desperate intensity.)

MR DASHWOOD: John—you will find out soon enough from my will that the estate of Norland was left to me in such a way as prevents me from dividing it between my families.

(JOHN blinks. He cannot quite take it in.)

JOHN: Calm yourself, Father. This is not good for you—

(But MR DASHWOOD continues with even greater determination.)

MR DASHWOOD: Norland in its entirety is therefore yours by law and I am happy for you and Fanny.

(JOHN looks torn between genuine distress and unexpected delight.)

MR DASHWOOD: But your stepmother—my wife—and daughters are left with only five hundred pounds a year, barely enough to live on and nothing for the girls' dowries. You must help them.

(JOHN's face is a picture of conflicting emotions. Behind them is an ominous rustling of parchments.)

JOHN: Of course—

MR DASHWOOD: You must promise to do this.

(A brief moment of sincerity overcomes JOHN's natural hypocrisy.)

JOHN: I promise, Father, I promise.

(MR DASHWOOD seems relieved. Suddenly his breathing changes. JOHN looks alarmed. He rises and we hear him going to find the DOCTOR.)

Still from *Sense and Sensibility* with (from left to right) Kate Winslet, Gemma Jones, Emilie Francois, and Emma Thompson.

Examine the costumes and set in the above still. Use Internet sources to access other stills from *Sense and Sensibility*, or view the movie. In small groups, discuss the costumes and set, and the challenges in producing a movie set in an earlier time period.

JOHN: Come! Come quickly!

>   (*But it is we who share the dying man's last words.*)

MR DASHWOOD: Help them …

3 EXT. JOHN AND FANNY's TOWN HOUSE. LONDON. DAY.
Outside the house sits a very well-to-do carriage. Behind it waits another open carriage upon which servants are laying trunks and boxes.

FANNY: *(V/O)* 'Help them?'

4 INT. JOHN AND FANNY's TOWN HOUSE. DRESSING ROOM. DAY.
JOHN is standing in mourning clothes and a travelling cape. He is watching, and obviously waiting for, a pert WOMAN (FANNY DASHWOOD) who is standing by a mirror looking at him keenly.

FANNY: What do you mean, 'help them'?

JOHN: Dearest, I mean to give them three thousand pounds.

>   (*FANNY goes very still. JOHN gets nervous.*)

JOHN: The interest will provide them with a little extra income. Such a gift will certainly discharge my promise to my father.

>   (*FANNY slowly turns back to the mirror.*)

FANNY: Oh, without question! More than amply …

JOHN: One had rather, on such occasions, do too much than too little.
>   (*A pause as FANNY turns and looks at him again.*)

JOHN: Of course, he did not stipulate a particular sum …

5 INT. LAUNDRY. NORLAND PARK. DAY.
A red-eyed MAID (BETSY) plunges a beautiful muslin frock into a vat of black dye.

6 INT. NORLAND PARK. MRS DASHWOOD's BEDROOM. DAY.
MRS DASHWOOD is rushing about, mourning ribbons flapping, putting her knick-knacks into a small valise. The room is in chaos. A young WOMAN (ELINOR DASHWOOD) looks on helplessly.

MRS DASHWOOD: To be reduced to the condition of visitor in my own home! It is not to be borne, Elinor!

ELINOR: Consider, Mamma! We have nowhere to go.

MRS DASHWOOD: John and Fanny will descend from London at any moment, followed no doubt by cartloads of relatives ready to turn us out of our rooms one by one—do you expect me to be here to welcome them? Vultures!

(She suddenly collapses into a chair and bursts into tears.)

ELINOR: I shall start making inquires for a new house at once. Until then we must try to bear their coming.

7 INT. JOHN AND FANNY'S CARRIAGE. DAY.
JOHN and FANNY are on their way out of London.

JOHN: Fifteen hundred then. What say you to fifteen hundred?

FANNY: What brother on earth would do half so much for his real sisters—let alone half-blood?

JOHN: They can hardly expect more.

FANNY: There's no knowing what they expect. The question is, what can you afford?

8 INT. NORLAND PARK. DRAWING ROOM. DAY.
A beautiful young WOMAN (MARIANNE DASHWOOD) is sitting at the piano playing a particularly sad piece. ELINOR enters.

ELINOR: Marianne, cannot you play something else? Mamma has been weeping since breakfast.

(MARIANNE stops, turns the pages of her music book and starts playing something equally lugubrious.)

ELINOR: I meant something less mournful, dearest.

9 EXT. ROADSIDE INN. DAY.
JOHN and FANNY are waiting as the OSTLERS make the final adjustments to their carriage. The LANDLORD hovers, waiting for a tip.

JOHN: A hundred pounds a year to their mother while she lives. Would that be more advisable? It is better than parting with the fifteen hundred all at once.

(He displays some coins in his hand. FANNY removes one and nods.)

FANNY: But if she should live longer than fifteen years we would be completely taken in. People always live forever when there is an annuity to be paid them.

(JOHN gives the coins to the LANDLORD.)

10 EXT. NORLAND PARK. MARGARET'S TREE-HOUSE. DAY.

ELINOR comes to the foot of a large tree from which a small staircase issues.

ELINOR: Margaret, are you there? Please come down. John and Fanny will be here soon.

(A pause. ELINOR is about to leave when a disembodied and truculent young voice stops her.)

MARGARET: *(V/O)* Why are they coming to live at Norland? They already have a house in London.

ELINOR: Because houses go from father to son, dearest—not from father to daughter. It is the law.

(Silence. ELINOR tries another tack.)

ELINOR: If you come inside, we could play with your atlas.

MARGARET: *(V/O)* It's not my atlas any more. It's their atlas.

(CLOSE on ELINOR as she ponders the truth of this statement.)

11 INT. JOHN AND FANNY'S CARRIAGE. DAY.

JOHN and FANNY joggle on.

JOHN: Twenty pounds now and then will amply discharge my promise, you are quite right.

FANNY: Indeed. Although to say the truth, I am convinced within myself that your father had no idea of your giving them money.

JOHN: They will have five hundred a year amongst them as it is—

FANNY: —and what on earth can four women want for more than that? Their housekeeping will be nothing at all—they will have no carriage, no horses, hardly any servants and will keep no company. Only conceive how comfortable they will be!

12 INT. NORLAND PARK. SERVANTS' HALL. DAY.

The large contingent of SERVANTS who staff Norland Park are gathered in gloomy silence as ELINOR addresses them.

> There are people, who the more you do for them, the less they will do for themselves.
>
> Jane Austen

ELINOR: As you know, we are looking for a new home. When we leave we shall be able to retain only Thomas and Betsy.

(CAM holds on THOMAS *and* BETSY, *a capable woman.)*

ELINOR: *(cont.)* We are very sorry to have to leave you all. But we are certain you will find the new Mrs Dashwood a fair and generous mistress.

13 EXT. NORLAND PARK. DRIVE. DAY.
JOHN and FANNY's carriage approaches Norland.

FANNY: *(V/O)* They will be much more able to give *you* something.

14 INT. JOHN AND FANNY's CARRIAGE. DAY.
JOHN and FANNY are about to get out.

JOHN: So—we are agreed. No money—but the occasional gift of game and fish in season will be very welcome.

FANNY: Your father would be proud of you.

I. *Response*

a. Explain the relationships of each character to the others within the screenplay. Note the textual clues that reveal the types of relationships existing between the characters. Use a diagram or family tree to show how each character mentioned is related to the others. Discuss what the script reveals about each character.

b. In this opening segment of the screenplay, which characters do you think will be liked or disliked by the audience? In small groups, discuss your reactions to each character. Did each member of the group respond in the same way to the same characters?

c. What conflict is established in the opening scenes of this script? How do you think this conflict will be resolved?

d. The authors of this anthology chose the title "The Dashwoods' Fate Is Decided" for this excerpt. What do you think of this title? What else might this excerpt be called?

e. With a small group, discuss the tone of this selection and how that tone is established. Is the language the author uses appropriate for the setting? Explain.

f. List any words from the selection that you found unusual and develop definitions for them.

2. **Film Study** Watch the movie *Sense and Sensibility*. Does reading this screenplay add to your appreciation of the movie? Share your thoughts with your classmates.

3. **Drama** *Characterization and Conflict* Review your answers to 1.a, 1.b, and 1.c. With a small group, improvise a future scene between four of the main characters to perform for another group. Your scene should reflect the conflict and characters of the initial scenes in this movie. Make sure that your improvisation scene introduces or explains the conflict, and that the characters are then engaged in the conflict until some resolution is reached. Discuss the process of improvisation and the challenges of performing spontaneously.

> **PERFORMANCE TIP** Remember that conflict between characters is the basis for most action and the centre of the plot. Characters in conflict often want different things, so keep in mind what *you* want, as you perform. Actors in conflict act and react to one another, so consider how you will react to others as they voice what they want. Also remember that the personalities of the characters will be wrapped up in what they want, how they act, and how they react.

4. **Making Connections** Read the first three chapters of Jane Austen's *Sense and Sensibility*. In your opinion, did Emma Thompson successfully capture the tone of the novel and the essence of the characters? Explain.

5. **Language Conventions** *Abbreviations* Note the use of abbreviations throughout the screenplay. How do these help the reader? Is the use of abbreviations distracting at all? Explain. What reading strategies helped you read and understand this selection?

    Develop another scene for this screenplay using abbreviations, your understanding of the characters and their relationships, and your ideas from question 1.c.

Theme Connections

- *"Transients in Arcadia," a story in which characters worry about money, Vol. I, p. 37*
- *"A Pair of Silk Stockings," a story in which a character worries about money, Vol. I, p. 86*
- *"The Making of* Sense and Sensibility*," a diary that details part of the process of creating this script, Vol. II, p. 120*

Discuss what you know about Stephen Leacock,
his writing style, and the time period
in which he lived.

The Raft

An Interlude

Burlesque Act by
Stephen Leacock

(The kind of interlude that is sandwiched in for fifteen minutes between the dances in a musical review.)

(The curtain rises and the light comes on the stage slowly, gradually revealing a raft in the middle of the sea. The dawn is breaking. The raft has the stub of a mast sticking up on it and there is a chair on it and a litter of boxes and things. On the raft is A MAN. *He has on white flannel trousers, and a sky-blue flannel shirt, but no collar and tie. He stands up and looks all around the horizon, his hand shading his eyes. He speaks in a sepulchral voice.)*

"Lost! Lost! Alone on the Caribbean Sea." *(In a more commonplace voice)* "At least I think it's the Caribbean. It looks Caribbean to me. Lost! And not a woman in sight ... I thought that in this kind of thing there is always a woman. Ha! Wait! There's one!"

(He is much excited and gets a long spy-glass and shoots it in and out at different lengths, searching the sea.)

"No!—it's only seaweed ... Ba!"

(He goes and sits down on a chair and yawns.)

"I call this kind of thing dull! There's really nothing to do."

(He gets a box of shoe polish and starts to polish his shoes with a rag. Presently—)

"I think I'll look around for a woman again. It really is the only thing to do, on a raft—or anywhere else."

It is to be noticed that this piece is all ready to put on the stage. Actors anxious for dramatic rights may apply by telegraph or on foot.

(He takes his spy-glass and looks again.)

"By Jove! Yes! Yes! There's one floating in the sea right there. Quick! Quick!"

(In great excitement he runs over to the mast, where a little looking-glass hangs, and starts putting on a collar and tie, and brushing his hair in terrible haste ... He can't find his collar-stud, etc., etc., and keeps muttering—)

"I must keep calm—a woman's life depends on my getting this collar on."

(He looks over his shoulder.)

"She's floating nearer—"

(In the light of the rising sun THE GIRL is now seen floating nearer and nearer.)

"—and nearer—and she's a peach ... I *must* save her! I must plunge in after her."

(He stands in the attitude of a person about to dive into the sea, swinging his arms and counting.)

"One—two—*three*—" *(nearly dives but checks himself and goes on)* "four—five—SIX ... Ah, I forgot! I've no swimming costume ... Wait a bit, though!"

(He picks up off the raft a long, long pole with a hook on the end.)

"Ha!"

(THE GIRL is quite near now. He hooks her on the pole and hauls her on to the raft ... She sinks down flat on it, inanimate, her eyes closed, her face to the audience. Note: THE GIRL of course is not wet: that would only mess the act up.)

"What next? Ah, one moment."

(He runs over to a little bookshelf that is stuck up on the top of the mast, takes out a book, sits down in a chair, and reads aloud very deliberately.)

"'Rules for re—for, re-sus—for resuscitating the Damned—the Drowned: In resuscitating the drowned it must be remembered that not a moment must be lost.'"

(He settles himself more comfortably in his chair to get a better light to read by.)

"'Every minute is of vital—of vital'—humph, I must get my eye glass."

(He goes and hunts it up, polishes it and continues—)

"'Of vital importance. First, it is necessary to ascertain whether the heart is still beating.'—Ah!"

(He gets off his chair and on to the floor of the raft on his toes and hands, makes the motions of attempting to put his ear close down on THE GIRL'S heart, but keeps withdrawing it with sudden shyness.)

"Stop a bit."

(He goes and gets a cardboard box and takes out a stethoscope so long that, still standing up, he fixes it to his ears and it reaches THE GIRL'S body. He listens and counts, his head on one side and with an air of great absorption.)

"One."

(A long pause)

"One and a half."

(Another pause)

"One—eighty-five—right! She's alive!"

(He gets his book again and reads.)

"'The strength of the circulation being different in the male and the female sex, the first thing to do if the victim is a woman is to rub her—to rub her—'"

(He finds it difficult to read, and says conclusively—)

"The first thing to do is to rubber. Oh, yes I see: Now where shall I begin? I'll rub her hands."

(He takes one of her hands and strokes it very slowly in long loving strokes. After a moment he plucks at the lace cuff at her wrist.)

"Ah, a laundry mark! her name! I must read. Her life hangs on it. 'Edith Croydon!' What a beautiful name!"

(He goes on stroking her hand.)

"It doesn't seem to revive her. Oh, very well, there's nothing for it."

(He stands up with an air of great determination, and rolls back his cuffs.)

Good drama must be drastic.

Friedrich von Schlegel

"I must rub her legs."

(THE GIRL starts up.)

"Don't you dare! You're no gentleman!"

"Miss Croydon, you misunderstand my motives!"

(He walks away in a huff to the extreme end of the raft and stands with his back turned. THE GIRL meantime runs to the mirror and starts doing her hair, etc.)

"And for the matter of that, I *am* a gentleman. You'll find my card hanging there beside the mirror."

(THE GIRL picks down a large card that hangs beside the mirror and reads aloud.)

"'Harold Borus, Story Tale Adventurer, Rafts, Rescues and Other Specialities, Hairbreadth Escapes Shaved to Order.' Oh, Mr. Borus, I'm so sorry! Of course I know all about you—everybody does! I must apologize. Do come back to this part of the raft. Forgive me."

(BORUS, coming back, and taking her hand with emotion)

"Miss Croydon, there is nothing to forgive! If I have saved your life, forget it. Let us never speak of it. Think of me not as a hero, but only as a man!"

"I will!"

"And meantime, please make yourself comfortable. Do take this chair. The entire raft, I need hardly say, is at your disposition. You'll find the view from the east side most interesting."

"Thank you so much."

(They make themselves comfortable and intimate, she on the chair, he on the soap-box, with elaborate gestures of politeness.)

"And do tell me, Mr. Borus, how did you get here?"

"Very gladly. You won't mind if I begin at the beginning?"

"Must you?"

"It's usual ..."

"Oh, all right."

"Well then—" *(striking an attitude of recitation)* "Little did I think—"

"No, I suppose not."

"—when I left Havana in a packet—"

"Oh, Mr. Borus, who put you in a packet?"

"—in a packet-boat, that I should be wrecked on the dry Tortugas."

(THE GIRL, clasping her hands with agitation)

"The *Dry* Tortugas! Oh, Mr. Borus, have the Tortugas gone dry?"

"We had hardly left when a great storm arose … A monstrous wave carried away the bridge."

"Good heavens!"

"We struggled on. A second wave carried away the rudder, the propeller, the wireless apparatus and the stethoscope!"

"Great heavens!"

"We struggled on. A third wave carried away the bar. It was at once decided to abandon the ship and lower the boats."

(THE GIRL, perplexed)

"But why?"

"To look for the bar … In the confusion I was left behind. The storm subsided. I continued to make a raft out of a few loose iron beams fastened together by nuts."

"Fastened by nuts, Mr. Borus, but I thought you were the only one left in the ship?"

"—by nuts. This raft, Miss Croydon, cannot sink, it is all made of iron."

"How splendid! And now let me tell you my adventures."

"No, no, don't trouble, please. You're exhausted! Don't—you might faint!"

"Looking back" *(THE GIRL goes on very dramatically)* "it all seems a blank."

(BORUS, very hurriedly)

"All right, it's a blank. It's a blank. Let it go at that."

"Mr. Borus, I think you're terribly rude. You might let *me* tell *my* adventures!"

"Miss Croydon" *(very seriously)* "how many heroes are there in any story of adventure?"

"Only one."

"Well, I'm *it*. You must be something else."

(MISS CROYDON pettishly)

"I don't want to be. All I know is that I'm cold and I'm hungry, and I don't think that I'll stay!"

"Cold! Hungry!"

(He gets up and starts running round with animation, making preparations.)

"Cold! Ha! ha! I'll soon have a fire for you!"

"A fire, Mr. Borus, how can you possibly start a fire?"

(BORUS laughs.)

"A very simple matter, Miss Croydon, to a trained hero like myself."

(He has picked up an empty pan and set it on a box.)

"I do it simply with sticks rubbed together."

"By rubbing dry sticks together! How wonderful you are."

"I am."

(He picks up two or three very little dry twigs.)

"I take the dry sticks, *so*—"

"Yes! Yes!"

"And first rub them together, *so*—"

"Yes! Yes!"

"With a sort of twisting motion."

"Yes! Yes!"

"Then I put them in the pan with a bit of paper, *so*—" *(he takes out a matchbox as he speaks)* "and strike a match and light them."

(He lights the paper and the twigs and they blaze up in a little flame. EDITH CROYDON and BORUS warm their hands at it; she speaks.)

"How really wonderful!"

"Yes. It's the Peruvian method! And now for food and drink."

(The little fire presently flickers out, and has nothing more to do with the act.)

"Have you food and drink on the raft, Mr. Borus? I think you are simply superb."

"I am. Now let me see." *(He starts taking things out of a box.)* "What have we here? Tinned pâté de foie gras."

"Lovely!"

"Canned asparagus. Do you like canned asparagus?"

"Oh, I worship it."

"Tin of boneless pheasant."

"Oh, Mr. Borus, I'm just mad over boneless pheasant!"

> *(BORUS, taking out the cans and reading the labels,*
> *with exclamations from THE GIRL—)*

"Boneless pheasant—finless fish—spineless sardines—tongueless tongue—now what shall it be first?"

> *(BORUS with great empressement has just laid a little white cloth*
> *on a soap-box, and quickly spread out glasses and dishes and knives*
> *and forks till it has the appearance of an appetizing preparation.*
> *They both accompany it with exclamations of interest and delight.*
> *MISS CROYDON says)*

"Let me see. I think I'd like first, pâté de foie gras and finless fish, and just a teeny bit of shell-less lobster—and—and—"

> *(When suddenly BORUS has sprung to his feet with a sort of howl)*

"Oh, Mr. Borus, what is it?"

> *(BORUS, casting his hands to heaven—)*

"I haven't got—I haven't got—"

"Yes—yes—"

"I forgot—"

"Yes—yes—you forgot—"

"The can opener! Great heavens, we have no can opener!"

(THE GIRL exclaims—) "No can opener!" *(and falls forward on the table.)*

(BORUS):

"Stop! Wake up! I can open them!"

(He makes a wild attack on the tins, beating them, and stamping on them, and biting them, etc., etc. Presently he subsides in despair and collapses on the soap-box.)

"It's no good, Miss Croydon. We must eat the tins. You eat first. You are a woman."

"No, Mr. Borus, not yet. We can at least" *(she speaks with tragedy)* "we can at least drink. Let us drink before we die."

"You are right. We can drink before we die. It is more than a lot of people can do."

(He recovers something of his animation and begins taking out bottles and setting them on the table.)

"There! Bottled ale. Bass's bottled ale!"

"Oh, Mr. Borus, how divine! I just worship Bass's bottled ale."

"Now then, get your glass ready."

"Right."

(Then he leaps up again with a howl.)

"What is it, Mr. Borus—Oh, what is it?"

"The thing—the thing you open it with! I haven't got one!"

(They both collapse, BORUS slightly recovering, but gloomily):

"There's a way of opening these bottles with a fifty-cent piece ..." *(feeling in his pocket)* "but I haven't got a fifty-cent piece."

(MISS CROYDON, brightly)

"Oh, never mind, I think I have a dollar bill in my purse."

(Business here of trying to open the bottle by holding a dollar bill over it. At last BORUS says):

"It's no good, Miss Croydon. We must resign ourselves to our fate. If we must die" *(he takes a noble attitude)* "you are a woman. Die first!"

(There is a sadness and then MISS CROYDON says):

"Mr. Borus, it's getting dark."

(BORUS looks up at the sky.)

"Yes, the sun will soon set."

"Already, Mr. Borus?"

"Yes, Miss Croydon. Night comes quickly in the tropics. Look, the sun is setting."

(The sun, seen as a round, red disk at the back of the stage,
begins to set in jumps, about a yard at a time. When it has got near
the bottom it takes a long whirl up again and then goes under.
The stage is half dark.)

BORUS: "It is night!"

"Night! Here on the raft? Oh, I mustn't stay."

"Miss Croydon, I intend to treat you with the chivalry of a hero. One moment."

(BORUS takes an oar and sticks it up, and takes a big gray blanket
and fastens it across the raft like a partition, so as to divide the raft in two.)

"Miss Croydon" *(says BORUS, looking over the top of the blanket)* "that end of the raft is absolutely *yours*."

"How chivalrous you are!"

"Not at all. I shall not intrude upon you in any way. Good-night."

"Good-night, Mr. Borus."

(They each begin making preparations for sleep, one each side of the curtain.
BORUS stands up and puts his head over again.)

"You'll find a candle and matches near your bed."

"Oh, thank you, Mr. Borus, how noble you are."

"Not at all."

(After another little interlude BORUS puts his head over the top again.)

"I am now putting my head over this blanket for the last time. If there is anything you want, say so now. And remember if you want anything in the night do not hesitate to call me. I shall be here—at any moment. I promise it. Good-night."

"Good-night, Mr. Borus."

(They settle down in the growing darkness for a few minutes as if falling asleep. Then all of a sudden a bright light, a searchlight, comes shining over the sea, full on the raft. They both start up.)

"Oh, Mr. Borus, look, look, a light—a ship!!"

BORUS: "A light—a ship! They may have a corkscrew! We're saved. Look—it's a large yacht—a pleasure yacht."

(There are voices heard.)

"Raft, Ahoy!" *(and shouts)*

MISS CROYDON: "A pleasure yacht! Oh, then I recognize it!"

"You recognize it?"

"It's the yacht I fell out of this morning."

"Fell out of—"

"Yes. You wouldn't let me tell you …"

(There is a call across the water.)

"Raft ahoy! Stand by! We're lowering a boat."

BORUS: "Saved! Saved! But there is just one thing I want to say before we go aboard … Miss Croydon—Edith—since I've been on this raft I've learned to love you as I never could have anywhere else. Edith, will you be my wife?"

(MISS CROYDON, falling into his arms):

"Will I? Oh, Harold, that's what I fell out of the yacht for!"

(Curtain)

Dr. Stephen Butler Leacock was born in England in 1869 and immigrated to Canada with his parents in 1876. Although Leacock was a distinguished professor in the economics and political science department of McGill University, he is best known for his more than 60 books, particularly his humorous works. This great Canadian, who was considered the world's best-selling humorist during his lifetime, died in 1944.

I. *Response*

    a. Which of the two characters appeals to you more? Explain.

    b. What makes this play a **burlesque**? Is it successful as a burlesque? Share your responses in a class discussion.

> A **burlesque** is a literary or dramatic composition in which a serious subject is treated ridiculously or with mock seriousness.

    c. Did you find the ending of this play predictable? If so, explain what clues allowed you to predict the ending accurately.

2. *Drama* *Performing Burlesque* With a small group, discuss how this burlesque might be presented and any challenges there might be in presenting it. How could these challenges be overcome? Work together to prepare a presentation of this script.

> **PERFORMANCE TIP** Prepare for your performance by considering the gestures and movements you will make. Note that, in burlesque, the actions and emotions of the characters may be exaggerated. How will you use gestures, facial expressions, and movement to portray the emotions of the characters effectively? Practise displaying various emotions in front of a mirror.

3. *Focus on Context* *The Raft* was originally written in 1923. If this play were written today, how would it be different? What would account for these differences? Discuss these questions in small groups.

4. *Language Conventions* *Standard Structure* This play can be difficult to follow because Leacock has not used a conventional script structure. What has he done instead? Why might he have done so? Imagine you are planning to direct this show and you want to make the script easier for your actors to read. Do this by taking half a page of dialogue and writing it like a typical script. Use other scripts from this unit as models.

5. *Making Connections* With a partner, role-play a conversation between Borus from this selection and Aunt Bev from *Venus Sucked In*. Consider how the setting of each play and the time period in which it was written affect the characters' attitudes, actions, and beliefs. Which character do you find it easier to identify with? Why?

Just prior to the following excerpt, Cyrano arrived at a play and threatened a performer who offended him—Montfleury. Montfleury was halted just as he began to recite the opening lines of a play called *La Clorise* by Baro. This excerpt opens with the audience's reaction to Cyrano's actions and arrogance.

Introducing Cyrano

AN EXCERPT FROM THE STAGE PLAY
CYRANO DE BERGERAC
FROM ACT 1, SCENE IV

by Edmond Rostand

CHARACTERS

YOUNG MAN
CYRANO
OLD BURGHER (business man)
LADY INTELLECTUALS
BELLEROSE (actor)
CROWD
JODELET (actor)
LE BRET (friend of Cyrano)
MEDDLER

YOUNG MAN: *(To Cyrano)* Tell me, sir, what reason do you have to hate Montfleury?

CYRANO: *(Graciously, still seated)* I have two reasons, my callow young friend, either of which would be sufficient. The first is that he's a deplorable actor who brays like an ass and wrestles ponderously with lines that ought to soar lightly from his lips. The second—is my secret.

OLD BURGHER: *(Behind him)* But you're high-handedly depriving us of *La Clorise*! I insist …

CYRANO: *(Respectfully, turning his chair toward the BURGHER)* Sir, your pigheadedness can't change the fact that old Baro's verse is worthless. I feel no remorse at having deprived you of trash.

LADY INTELLECTUALS: *(In the boxes)* Oh!—Our Baro!—My dear, it's … How dare he!—Such insolence!

CYRANO: *(Gallantly, turning his chair toward the boxes)* Fair ladies, blossom and be radiant, fill our dreams with longing, soften death with a smile, inspire poetry—but don't judge it!

BELLEROSE: What about the money that will have to be refunded?

CYRANO: *(Turning his chair toward the stage)* Now there's the first sensible thing that's yet been said! Far be it from me to impose hardship on practitioners of the Thespian art. *(Stands up and throws a bag onto the stage.)* Here, take this purse and be quiet.

CROWD: *(Astonished)* Ah!—Oh!

JODELET: *(Quickly picking up the purse and weighing it in his hand)* At this price, sir, I'll be glad to have you come and stop our performance every day!

CROWD: Boo! Boo!

JODELET: Even if we must all be booed together!

BELLEROSE: Please clear the hall!

JODELET: Everyone out, please! *(The spectators begin leaving while CYRANO watches with satisfaction, but they soon stop when they hear the following scene. The ladies in the boxes, who have already stood up and put on their cloaks, stop to listen, and finally sit down again.)*

LE BRET: *(To CYRANO)* This is madness!

MEDDLER: *(Who has approached CYRANO)* What a scandal! Montfleury, the great actor! Don't you know he's protected by the Duke de Candale? Do you have a patron?

CYRANO: No!

MEDDLER: You don't have a …

CYRANO: No!

MEDDLER: What? You have no great lord whose name protects …

CYRANO: *(Annoyed)* For the third time, no! Must I say it a fourth? I don't rely on some remote patron for protection. *(Puts his hand to his sword.)* My protector is always near at hand.

MEDDLER: Are you going to leave the city?

CYRANO: That depends.

MEDDLER: But the Duke de Candale has a long arm!

CYRANO: Not as long as mine ... *(Pointing to his sword)* ... when I give it this extension!

MEDDLER: But surely you wouldn't dare ...

CYRANO: I would.

MEDDLER: But ...

CYRANO: Go now.

MEDDLER: But ...

CYRANO: Go! Or tell me why you're looking at my nose.

MEDDLER: *(Petrified)* I ...

CYRANO: *(Moving toward him)* Do you find it surprising?

MEDDLER: *(Stepping back)* You're mistaken, my lord ...

CYRANO: Is it limp and dangling, like an elephant's trunk?

MEDDLER: *(Stepping back again)* I didn't ...

CYRANO: Or hooked like an owl's beak?

MEDDLER: I ...

CYRANO: Do you see a wart at the end of it?

MEDDLER: I ...

CYRANO: Or a fly walking on it? What's unusual about it?

MEDDLER: Nothing, I ...

CYRANO: Is it a startling sight?

MEDDLER: Sir, I've been careful not to look at it!

CYRANO: Would you please tell me why?

MEDDLER: I was ...

CYRANO: Does it disgust you?

MEDDLER: Sir ...

CYRANO: Does its color seem unhealthy to you?

MEDDLER: Sir!

A mold is used to make a mask of Cyrano de Bergerac's nose for a performance of the Royal Ballet.

CYRANO: Is its shape obscene?

MEDDLER: Not at all!

CYRANO: Then why that disdainful expression? Do you find it, perhaps, a little too large?

MEDDLER: *(Stammering)* Oh, no, it's quite small ... very small ... diminutive ...

CYRANO: What! How dare you accuse me of anything so ridiculous? A small nose? *My* nose? You've gone too far!

MEDDLER: Please, sir, I ...

CYRANO: My nose is *enormous*, you snub-nosed, flat-faced wretch! I carry it with pride, because a big nose is a sign of affability, kindness, courtesy, wit, generosity, and courage. I have all those qualities, but you can never hope to have any of them, since the ignoble face that my hand is about to meet above your collar ... *(Slaps him. The MEDDLER cries out in pain.)* ... has no more glory, nobility, poetry, quaintness, vivacity, or grandeur—no more *nose*, in short—than the face that my boot ... *(Turns him around by the shoulders)* ... is about to meet below your waist! *(Kicks him)*

French dramatist **Edmond Rostand** was born in 1868 in Marseilles, France, and died during a widespread influenza epidemic in 1918. He is best known for his play *Cyrano de Bergerac*, written in 1897. Other plays include *The Romancers* and *Chantecler.*

1. *Response*
a. In this segment of the play, Cyrano does not reveal his second reason for hating Montfleury. With a partner, speculate on Cyrano's second reason.
b. How would you describe Cyrano's actions? How would you describe the reactions of those around him?
c. Reread the description Cyrano gives of himself at the end of this selection. Would you agree with the qualities that Cyrano ascribes to himself? Explain.
d. What do you think the author intended with this scene? Why would he have chosen to introduce Cyrano to his audience in this way?

2. **Drama** *Dialogue* This selection is an excellent example of dialogue. It might best be delivered in a *rapid-fire style* (delivered at high speed, with no pauses; very forceful on the part of Cyrano and timid on the part of the Meddler, with constant interruptions). With a partner, practise the exchange between the Meddler and Cyrano. Take turns assuming either role. In your opinion, which role is more challenging? Why? Reflect on other performances you have done during this unit. What did you learn about performing with others? Do you find it difficult? What strategies might help you work together to develop a unified performance?

> PERFORMANCE TIP When performing a scene, it is important to consider its context: When and where does it take place? What does the place look or feel like? What are the characters doing in this place? Where do the characters come from? What were the characters just doing? What will the characters do next? How much do the characters know? How much does the audience know? Reflect on these questions as you perform the scene between the Meddler and Cyrano.

3. **Focus on Context** With a small group, discuss the play and what you know of the whole story of *Cyrano de Bergerac*. Do you think this was a suitable excerpt to take from the play? Was the introductory text sufficient to help you understand the excerpt? Does the excerpt effectively introduce the character of Cyrano? Explain. To answer these questions, research this play on the Internet or by using print resources, if necessary.

4. **Language Conventions** *Imperative Voice* Examine how most of Cyrano's lines are phrased—short, emphatic commands in an imperative voice or mood. How does Rostand juxtapose the speech of others against Cyrano's lines? What effect does this have? How does the imperative voice help develop the reader's perceptions of Cyrano's character?

5. **Film Study** Several movies have been made based on this script. Investigate these movies using Internet or print resources. In a small group, discuss how you could use the story of Cyrano and give it a new slant for a twenty-first century audience. Develop a proposal for your movie, including notes about setting, costumes, actors, genre, and target audience.

Four women—all related—one small apartment

Venus
Sucked In
A Post-Feminist Comedy

One-Act Radio Play by Anne Chislett

CHARACTERS

KATHY	sixteen
LIZ	Kathy's mother, forty-five
BETTY	Kathy's grandmother, sixty-seven
BEV	Kathy's aunt, thirty-seven

The play takes place in real time. We follow Kathy throughout. Everyone else is "on" or "off" in keeping with their spatial relationship to her. Fortunately, the apartment is small, with the entrance directly into the living room and the kitchen close by. The apartment is in a large, ordinary highrise in mid-town Toronto.

SCENE ONE
(Fantasy/speech)
(MUSIC: JOAN Baez, "Diamonds and Rust.")

(SOUND: Mike is raised. KATHY clears her throat. She adopts a public-speaking mode: quite natural and informal but with a touch of projection, opening up to an imaginary audience. She improvises the speech, sometimes with revisions and asides to herself.)

KATHY: *(Internal. Public address)* "Modern Women." Some modern women have deliberately decided to live in the world's crummiest apartment. Take my mother, for instance. If she had set out to find the place I would most absolutely hate to move in to, she couldn't have done better than this building. Her excuse is that it's in our old neighbourhood, and I'm still going to the same school. That's so I won't have *two* traumas to cope with. Well, if walking out of a perfectly good marriage and a perfectly great house were really going to make my mom into the greatest female artist since … *(Shrug)* I don't know who, uh … whom … ruining all our lives might be worthwhile. But as it is, the whole situation is just totally embarrassing. Like this afternoon, on the way back from the movie, Janet—she's my best friend—asked to come in so we could work on our speeches. I had to tell her that Sunday is now my mother's designated day for painting, and this apartment is so small her easel takes up our whole living room. I can't even have anybody in my room, because the walls are too thin. You see, on Sunday …

LIZ: *(Way off)* Kath?

KATHY: *(Internal. Public address)* … nothing, but nothing, is allowed to disturb Mom's concentration.

LIZ: *(Off)* Kath?

KATHY: *(To herself)* Wait a minute … how come the easel's covered up?

SCENE TWO
(Living room)

LIZ: *(Coming on)* Kathy, I asked you to get me a coat hanger.

KATHY: Sorry. I didn't hear you. *(SOUND: Closet door opens, coat hangers, plastic and wire; continues underneath)*

LIZ: What were you doing? Talking to yourself?

KATHY: Of course not.

LIZ: Your lips were moving.

KATHY: I was practising my public speaking. *(Passing hanger)* Here.

LIZ: Oh, not plastic. A wire one. I want to straighten it out. *(SOUND: Rummaging through more coat hangers)*

KATHY: Are coat hangers a new painting technique or something?

LIZ: Don't be sarcastic.

KATHY: I wasn't.

LIZ: Then don't be silly. *(Going off)* Come in the kitchen for a minute, will you?

SCENE THREE
(Small kitchen)

KATHY: Mom, I kinda need to work on my speech.

LIZ: *(Coming on as KATHY nears her)* Well, I kinda need you to hold the flashlight. *(Her voice becomes muffled as she sticks her head inside a dishwasher.)* Shine it in there where the hose connects.

KATHY: What are you looking for?
(SOUND: A coat hanger being poked into dishwasher's orifices. LIZ'S voice shows the strain of arm and neck stretching.)

LIZ: Whatever's clogging this thing.

KATHY: Yech.

LIZ: Yech is right. The dishes are dirtier than when I put them in.

KATHY: Is this going to take long? *(SOUND: Clinks and clanks; continues intermittently)*

LIZ: I hope not. *(Sounds of effort as she digs at clog)* So … are you going to win the contest again this year?

KATHY: Not with the topic I got stuck with.

LIZ: What is it?

KATHY: "Modern Women." I can't think of a single angle that hasn't been used a million times.

LIZ: You could talk about the sexism girls your age run into.

KATHY: I don't run into any.

LIZ: Sure you do. You must. *(SOUND: Clinks stop. Dishwasher door closes)*

KATHY: Not as far as I know.

LIZ: Give the dial a spin. *(SOUND: Dial turns. Mechanical sputter)*
Darn.
(SOUND: Dishwasher door opens. Clinks and clanks; continues underneath)
What about career choices? What if you want to be an engineer?

KATHY: I don't.

LIZ: But if you did … I can tell you I'd worry. *(Idea)* Hey, how about gun control? There's a feminist issue for you.

KATHY: The topic is "women," not "feminism." I want it to be upbeat.

LIZ: Well … we're sure to have more women prime ministers in future.

KATHY: I'd have a better chance with something that lets me smile a lot.

LIZ: Why? *(Outrage on the rise)* Are the boys expected to smile?

KATHY: *(Declining the challenge)* Look, thanks for trying to help, okay?

LIZ: No! It's not okay. Do boys look for topics that let them smile?

KATHY: How should I know! Mom, I have to be ready for the assembly tomorrow.

LIZ: Oh, Kathy. Why do you always leave assignments till the night before?

KATHY: I've been practising since Friday.

LIZ: Where? At the movies or at the skating rink?

KATHY: You were the one who suggested I call Janet.
(SOUND: Dishwasher door closes underneath)

LIZ: Because your father disappointed you. I'd have saved my sympathy if I'd known you had a speech to write.

KATHY: I don't "write" it, Mom. I prepare it, like … in my mind.

LIZ: In your mind?

KATHY: Yeah. It has to sound spontaneous, so I practise by making up stuff about whatever occurs to me.
(SOUND: Dial turns. Mechanical sputter)
So it doesn't really matter if I'm at a movie or at my desk.
(SOUND: Dishwasher door opens)

LIZ: Good. Then it won't matter if you're at the sink, washing dishes by hand.
(SOUND: Dishes taken from dishwasher to sink; continues underneath)

KATHY: What do we need dishes for? Aren't we sending out for pizza?

LIZ: There's been a change of plans.

KATHY: How come?

LIZ: Your Aunt Bev phoned while you were out. She invited herself to dinner.

KATHY: Oh, great!

LIZ: For you, maybe. I'd just mixed my paints.

KATHY: You could have said no.

LIZ: Well, she said she has some news …

KATHY: Why didn't she tell you on the phone?

LIZ: She wanted to see me in person. *(Beat)* All right, so I'm a sucker. I couldn't bring myself to say no.

KATHY: You still don't have to cook. Aunt Bev likes pizza.

LIZ: But it is Sunday. And I thought it wouldn't be much trouble to thaw a few chicken breasts.
(SOUND: Water taps turned on, water running; continues underneath)
That was before I discovered there wasn't a clean pot or pan in the kitchen.

KATHY: *(Hesitant)* Mom? …

LIZ: What?

KATHY: Maybe … if you called Dad, he'd come over and fix the dishwasher?

LIZ: *(Dismissive)* Come on, Kath, pick up a tea towel.

KATHY: He's probably finished at his office by now …

LIZ: Oh, don't be silly.

KATHY: I bet he could have that thing working in five minutes flat. (SOUND: *Taps turned off*)

LIZ: Kathy, you want to know about modern women? I'll tell you about modern women. They've ended up alone at forty-five in rotten cheap apartments, with rotten lazy superintendents. They've been brought up to believe they are utterly hopeless when confronted with a mechanical problem. But modern women are going to learn to make it on their own! They will wash every dish in the city of Toronto before they will ever again trade their personal integrity for some jerk who knows how to repair appliances.

KATHY: Cute, Mom.
(SOUND: *Aggressive dishwashing; continues underneath*)
Except I think the principal would dock me for false generalization.

LIZ: The principal is a man, naturally.

KATHY: No, she's a woman. It's just no big deal with her.

LIZ: What's no big deal?

KATHY: She doesn't think men are all jerks. And she's not paranoid about them trying to keep her in chains, either.

LIZ: I'm paranoid? Is that what you're saying?

KATHY: Well … I mean … maybe some men did try to keep your generation down.

LIZ: Maybe?

KATHY: Yeah, but the principal's younger, so her attitude is more "now."

LIZ: What do you mean "now"?

KATHY: You know, more like Aunt Bev's than like yours.

LIZ: (*Flaring*) Really! Then you should ask your Aunt Bev for help, shouldn't you?
(SOUND: *Dishwashing fades out*)

SCENE FOUR
(*Fantasy/speech*)

KATHY: (*Internal*) Sisters. (*Public address*) "Modern Women and their Sisters." Have you ever seen that Bell Canada commercial? The one where this girl calls her sister because she needs a soft shoulder? Well, those two girls are definitely not my Mom and Aunt Bev. I figure it's because Mom is jealous. You see, Aunt Bev has her "personal integrity," which in my mother's mind means her chosen career, whereas Mom wasted fifteen years doing graphic art just to make money. She says that was Dad's fault because he insisted on a middle-class lifestyle. Except now, without him, she has to waste even *more* time on commercial stuff to pay the rent. The thing is—Aunt Bev makes twice as much money at her journalism, *and* she's got a great guy too. Sam not only does his share of the housework, he makes all their meals, on top of bringing her a long-stem rose every day. In other words, he's exactly the kind of guy Mom wanted my dad to be. But the weird thing is—Mom is always down on Aunt Bev for putting her own desires before anyone else's ... which is exactly why Mom walked out on Dad—so she could do the same herself. Not that she does. In fact, my mom can find more reasons not to do what she says she wants than anybody I ever heard of. *(To herself. Idea)* Hey ... maybe ... I could make a really fun speech about her totally screwed-up behaviour. Yeah ... like ... my mother says her art is going to be a priority in her life ... that is unless ... let's see ...

SCENE FIVE
(Kitchen)
(SOUND: Dishwashing fades back up; continues underneath)

KATHY: So, Mom, how much painting did you get done today?

LIZ: I told you. I hadn't touched the canvas when the phone rang ...

KATHY: *(Internal. Public address. Following her train of thought)* Unless the phone rings. *(SOUND: Apartment intercom buzzer; off)*

LIZ: What are you mouthing?

KATHY: That's the buzzer.

LIZ: Not already. Get it, will you? *(SOUND: Dishwashing noises recede)*

SCENE SIX
(Entrance way/living room)
(SOUND: Apartment intercom buzzer)

KATHY: *(Presses "Talk")* Who is it?

BETTY: *(Through intercom)* The Queen of England.

KATHY: Mom, what's Granny doing here? *(SOUND: Apartment intercom buzzer)*

LIZ: *(Coming on)* For heaven's sake, press the door button.

KATHY: *(To intercom)* You have to wait for the middle elevator. *(To LIZ)* Did she phone and invite herself too?

LIZ: I phoned her.

KATHY: I see.

LIZ: I thought if I was cooking for you and Bev ... I might as well cook for Mother.

KATHY: Mom, do you realize we've been here two months and you haven't finished one single picture?

LIZ: I would have today ... if the dishwasher hadn't screwed up.

KATHY: I guess dishwashers want to keep women in chains too.

LIZ: That's a very snide remark.

KATHY: Well, you always blame Dad for not letting you paint. It seems to me *(Quoting)* "the problem is simply your own lack of commitment."

LIZ: Is that what your father told you?

KATHY: I mean, look at this afternoon ...

LIZ: Yes, look at it! Who is supposed to take you out of my hair on Sunday?

KATHY: It's not Dad's fault he had to work.

LIZ: Kathy, I will not tolerate any quotations from that jerk about my lack of commitment, understand!

KATHY: What makes you think Dad said it?

LIZ: You didn't come up with an idea like that by yourself. If it wasn't your father, who was it?

KATHY: If you must know, it was Aunt Bev.
(SOUND: Knock on apartment door; off)

LIZ: *(Taken aback)* Bev told you I lacked commitment?

KATHY: I heard her tell Gran ...

LIZ: Now come on. You're making that up.
(SOUND: Knock on apartment door)

KATHY: Here's Gran. Since you don't believe me—

LIZ: *(Overlapping)* Kathy!

KATHY: ... you can ask her yourself.

LIZ: *(Overlapping)* Kathy!
(SOUND: Door opens)

KATHY: Hi, Gran. Mom wants to—

LIZ: *(Overlapping)* Don't you dare!

BETTY: *(Off)* Elizabeth, what's wrong?

LIZ: Nothing, Mother. Come in.
(SOUND: Door closes underneath)

BETTY: *(Moving on)* I could hear you two shouting since I left the elevator.

LIZ: We were having a discussion. The door is paper thin.

BETTY: Yes, I suppose. *(To KATHY)* Kathy, I'm surprised to see you home on a weekend.

KATHY: Dad had a computer crash.

BETTY: *(Judgemental)* I see.

KATHY: *(Defensive)* Well, he couldn't help it.

LIZ: Come and sit down, Mother. I'll move my easel ...
(SOUND: Easel moved underneath)

BETTY: Oh, are you trying to paint again?

LIZ: What do you mean "trying"?

BETTY: *(Beat)* Trying to find time, of course. May I see it?

LIZ: *(Defensive)* No! *(Recovering)* Not yet. Not until it's finished. Open the closet door, Kath.

BETTY: Beverly and Sam aren't here yet?
(SOUND: Closet door opens. Rattle of coat hangers as easel is put in; continues underneath)

LIZ: Actually … Sam had to go see his father. He's back in hospital.

BETTY: I was wondering why Beverly was honouring us with her presence.

LIZ: *(Laughing)* You couldn't expect her to cook her own dinner. Speaking of which … I'd better get to it.

BETTY: May I give you a hand?

LIZ: No, no … you and Kathy have a chat.

KATHY: Mom, I need to work on my speech.

LIZ: Perhaps your grandmother can help you.

KATHY: It's about modern women, remember?

LIZ: Kathy!

BETTY: Never mind. *(Moving off)*

I'm going to inspect your balcony for a bit.

LIZ: Mother, you haven't been here three seconds.

BETTY: *(Off)* Yes, but I couldn't smoke in the cab either.
(SOUND: Standard apartment balcony door opens. Hum of city noise, very low. Door closes)

LIZ: For Pete's sake, Kath, your speech has waited this long. Go out and try to be nice *(Moving off)* for a change.

KATHY: In a minute, okay?

SCENE SEVEN
(Fantasy/speech)

KATHY: *(Internal)* Anyway, where was I? Oh, yeah. *(Public address)* "Women's Confusing Behaviour." Teachers always tell us to talk about what we know, and the woman I know best is my mother. Well, I find the way she acts very confusing. She says her art is important, but not as important as answering the phone, fixing the dishwasher, or making dinner. Like today with Aunt Bev … Mom could have told her she was busy. I mean, I understood since I was a kid, if Dad has to work, he has to work, and there's no sense whining about it. I have to admit I didn't mind Mom being there. But it's like Dad says … if you want something you have to go get it. I guess the point is … well … if women want to—no.

If modern women want to get ahead in the world, I mean if they want to make it as artists or something, then they better not act like my mom. They should act like my dad instead. *(To herself)* Not bad … but it's kinda … it's a downer.

SCENE EIGHT
(Living room)

LIZ: *(Off)* Kathy!

KATHY: I'm on my way. *(SOUND: Balcony door opens. Hum of city noise; continues underneath)*

SCENE NINE
(Balcony. Flick of cigarette lighter)

KATHY: Gran, are you on your *second* cigarette already?

BETTY: *(Puffs)* If it bothers you, feel free to go inside.

KATHY: *(Ironic)* Great view, eh? If you like parking lots.

BETTY: Perhaps your mother will find a nicer neighbourhood. *(Puffs)* When your house is finally sold.

KATHY: Dad says if Mom forces him to sell in today's market, we won't even cover the mortgage.

BETTY: Kathy *(Beat)* shouldn't you be working on your speech?

KATHY: Well … *(Becoming intimate)* I'm sort of making one up about Mom, but … *(SOUND: Balcony door closes. City noise continues underneath)*

Gran, do you believe Mom has a chance of becoming famous?

BETTY: Well, she was "quite well known" once. She even had a one-woman show.

KATHY: Oh, that. *(Meaning ancient history)* That was before I was born.

BETTY: Really? What a coincidence.

KATHY: *(Takes point)* Okay, Gran. But women with commitment manage to have kids *and* a career. That is, if they have talent too.

BETTY: I think your mother has talent.

KATHY: *(Very intimate)* Go take a peek at that canvas in the closet … just take a peek.

BETTY: I wouldn't dream of doing such a thing without permission!

KATHY: Gran, it's gross, really gross. The whole canvas is this nude woman … being swallowed by an oyster!

BETTY: *Rising* from the oyster, surely. Like *Venus Rising?*

KATHY: No … she's being swallowed … the body is all stretched out and her mouth is open like she's screaming. Believe me, nobody, but nobody in their right mind is ever going to buy it.

BETTY: I'm not an expert in

modern art, and I doubt if you are either.

KATHY: Gran, please … listen, for Mom's own good, don't you think you should have a talk with her … you know … about the divorce?

BETTY: Kathy, I'm hardly in a position to give anyone advice.

KATHY: But you're her mother!

BETTY: I know I am. That's why she has to invite me over on Sunday afternoons. Now, if you've nothing more to say, I'm going back inside.
(SOUND: Balcony door opens. City noise continues for a moment, then fades)

SCENE TEN
(Fantasy/speech)

KATHY: *(Internal. Public address)* "Modern Grandmothers." Modern grandmothers aren't what they're supposed to be. They aren't grey-haired, they aren't

loving, and they're no help to their granddaughters at all. *(To herself)* Boy, is that ever a dead end.
(SOUND: Apartment buzzer; off. Hum of city noise comes up underneath)
Maybe Aunt Bev … if I can get her alone … *(Calling to LIZ)* It's okay, Mom. I'll answer it.
(SOUND: City noise fades)

SCENE ELEVEN
(Entrance way/living room)

KATHY: *(To intercom)* What's the password?

BEV: *(Intercom)* Chocolate Orange Ice Cream.
(SOUND: Door buzzer)

KATHY: *(To intercom)* All right! *(To LIZ)* Mom, I know you were joking when you suggested it, but would you be mad if I do a speech about Aunt Bev?

BETTY: I suppose you can't get more modern than your aunt.

LIZ: *(Comes to kitchen doorway)* The "me" generation belonged to the seventies, Mother.

KATHY: She's "now" enough to buy gourmet ice cream, and she does have a perfect relationship.

LIZ: *(Moves back into kitchen)* Oh sure ... without any "commitment" on either side.

KATHY: *(Calling)* I knew you'd be mad.

LIZ: *(Off)* I'm not mad. I'm putting the potatoes on.
(SOUND: Angry rattle of pots; off)

BETTY: Kathy, you aren't thinking of telling your class about Beverly and Sam, are you?

KATHY: Why not? Oh, Gran ... lots of people don't bother with marriage anymore. At least if she and Sam break up they don't have to go through a divorce.

BETTY: No, and your aunt will get even less out of the ordeal than your poor mother.

KATHY: Relationships are about love, Gran. Not money.

BETTY: Life is never so simple as when you're sweet sixteen.

KATHY: You don't have to patronize me.

BETTY: Then *you* stop patronizing *me*.

LIZ: *(Coming on)* What's going on? Kathy, are you being rude?

KATHY: She always talks to me as if I were a child.

BETTY: And she talks to me as if she knows the answers to everything. Well, you don't, little girl. You don't even know the right questions.

LIZ: Oh, come on, you two!

KATHY: Mom, what does she mean?
(SOUND: A knock)

LIZ: Nothing, Kathy. Nothing that concerns *you*!
(SOUND: Door opens)
(Tense) Hi, Bev. Come in.

BEV: *(Panting)* Liz, what's wrong?
(SOUND: Door closes)
(Panting) I could hear you three shouting from halfway down the hall.

LIZ: We were having a discussion.

BETTY: It seems the door is especially thin.

BEV: *(Starts to breathe more normally)* The door may be, but the tension in here is ten feet thick.

BETTY: Beverly, dear, you sound like you ran up the stairs.

BEV: Yes, I missed my workout this morning.
(SOUND: Closet opens, rattle of hangers; continues underneath)

LIZ: *(Slightly off)* Bev, I've put your stuff in the closet, okay?
(SOUND: Closet door closes)

BEV: Oh wait, there's a bottle in my bag ...
(SOUND: *Closet door opens*)
(*Slightly off*) Hey ... is that your painting stashed in there?
(SOUND: *Closet door slams*)

LIZ: Yes, it's stashed! Whose fault do you think that is?!

BEV: What?

LIZ: I had no "lack of commitment" till you phoned!

KATHY: Mom!

BETTY: Girls, are you arguing already?

LIZ: Mother, stay out of this!
(SOUND: *Clinking pot lid and hiss of water boiling over in kitchen; off; continues underneath*)

BEV: (*Confused*) Stay out of what?

LIZ: (*Moving off*) Damn. The potatoes!

BETTY: Let me—

LIZ: (*Off*) No, no, I'll take care of it.

BEV: Liz, I'm getting the feeling I'm not welcome here.
(SOUND: *Clanks, hiss; off*)

LIZ: (*Coming back on*) Bev, I've had a bad day ... I shouldn't have said anything.

BETTY: (*Changing subject*) Beverly, your gourmet ice cream must be starting to melt.

BEV: Oh, well, I'll put it in the freezer. (*Beat*) Here ... (*Hands LIZ bottle*) I brought us wine.

BETTY: Good. Your sister could use a drink.

KATHY: (*Sotto*) Mom, can I have a few minutes, just Aunt Bev and me?

LIZ: Okay, Kath, I'll stay out of the kitchen.

SCENE TWELVE
(*Kitchen*)

BEV: (*Coming on*) So kiddo, not out with Daddy today?
(SOUND: *Freezer door closes*)

KATHY: The system at his office went down.
(SOUND: *Cupboard door opens and closes*)

BEV: (*Knowing*) Uh huh.

KATHY: It's not fair of Mom, you know. She only gives him one chance a week.

BEV: (*Calling*) Liz, all I see in your cupboard is mugs.

LIZ: (*Off*) Oh lord, the wine glasses are still in the dishwasher.
(SOUND: *Dishwasher door opens*)
(*Coming on*) Hand me a few. I'll give them a rinse.

BEV: What's wrong with the dishwasher?

LIZ: It's broken.
(SOUND: *Taps, running water*)

KATHY: Aunt Bev, how would you define a modern woman?

BEV: Oh, I'm not into definitions. (*Referring to dishwasher*) Liz, want

me to take a look inside?
(SOUND: BEV fiddles with the insides of the dishwasher, speaking with her head inside it)

LIZ: (Annoyed) There's no point fooling with it.

BEV: I bet all this needs is a straightened-out coat hanger.

LIZ: I have one right here.
(SOUND: Clinks and clanks; continues underneath)

BEV: Perfect.

LIZ: (Over the last, insistent) I tried that, Bev.

BEV: (Head still in there) Liz, trust me.

KATHY: (Trying to get in) So … Aunt Bev …

BEV: So, Kath … (Yielding with a sigh) What kind of woman do you have in mind?

KATHY: I guess … women like you.

LIZ: Middle-class white liberal yuppies.

KATHY: White liberal?

BEV: That's a sixties phrase, kiddo.
(SOUND: One big final clink)
(Coming out of the dishwasher) I think I've solved the problem.

LIZ: It means people who think they can solve problems they know nothing about.
(SOUND: Dishwasher door closes)

BEV: Turn it on.
(SOUND: Dial is turned. Dishwasher behaves perfectly)
(Triumphant) There!

LIZ: (Amazed) What did you do?
(SOUND: Dishwasher turned off. Dishwasher door opens)

BEV: I'll show you.

KATHY: (Internal. Public address; over BEV and LIZ) The true modern woman, not like my mother, but exactly like my Aunt Bev, is not hopeless when confronted with a mechanical problem.

BEV: (Underneath Kathy's speech) This hose was completely clogged.

LIZ: I figured that … but I couldn't get at it.

BEV: It takes a bit of flexibility.

KATHY: (Internal. Public address) She exercises regularly so she looks twenty-eight years younger … well, at least eighteen younger than Mom, instead of only eight. And …

BEV: Our kitchen had a machine like this before we remodelled.

LIZ: I sure envy you that kitchen.

BEV: Sam loves cooking in it.

KATHY: (Internal. Public address) Oh, yeah. Early in life she refused to learn to cook or to type, so she cannot be forced into any stereotypical roles such as Mother used to complain about.

BETTY: *(Coming on)* Why is everyone in the kitchen?

BEV: Liz and I are talking, Mother.
(SOUND: A pot clinks)

LIZ: Mother, what are you doing?

BETTY: Turning up the element.

LIZ: *(Irritated)* I just turned it down.

BETTY: But the potatoes have stopped boiling.

LIZ: *(Angry)* For God's sake, I know how to cook potatoes.

BEV: Mother, why don't you go and sit down? We'll bring your wine in a minute.

BETTY: *(Moving off)* As you wish.

KATHY: *(Internal. Public address)* The modern woman can take charge of any situation without sounding crabby like Mom.
(SOUND: Rattle of cutlery drawer)

BEV: Liz, where's your corkscrew?

LIZ: Oh, no …

KATHY: *(Internal. Public address)* And also, unlike my mother, Aunt Bev would never forget to buy important things like corkscrews …

LIZ: Kathy, the Seven Eleven will have one …

KATHY: *(Cool)* I'm busy at the moment, Mom.

LIZ: *(Moving off)* Oh, for the love of heaven.

KATHY: *(Internal. Public address)* The modern woman is the perfect person to make the sixties woman see that it's too late for her to change her life now.

BETTY: *(Slightly off)* Liz, where are you going?

LIZ: Out!
(SOUND: Apartment door closes)

BETTY: *(Slightly off)* Wait for me.
(SOUND: Apartment door closes)
(In hall, off) Liz, you may think you're coping, but it looks to me as if …

BEV: Lord, the door really is thin.

KATHY: Anyway, Aunt Bev, now that we have some peace …

BEV: Kath, to tell you the truth, women's issues don't turn me on.

KATHY: Don't worry … I've got that done … I want you to give me your honest opinion of something entirely different.

BEV: What?

KATHY: In the living room.

SCENE THIRTEEN
(Living room)
(SOUND: Closet door opens, cloth is taken off painting)

KATHY: Here in the closet.

BEV: *(Coming on)* What are you doing?

KATHY: Look, Aunt Bev ... look what Mom has been working on for almost two months.

BEV: *(Astonished)* My lord ...

KATHY: So ... what do you think?

BEV: *(She hates it)* Well, I don't know much about painting.

KATHY: Do you like it?

BEV: *(Beat)* Is that the title on the bottom? *(Giggle)* The bottom edge, I mean?

KATHY: Where?

BEV: "Venus Sucked In" ... oh, I see. Now it makes sense.

KATHY: It does?

BEV: Yes, I think there's a famous painting on this subject.

KATHY: Gran mentioned it ... *Venus Rising*?

BEV: I only remember a Joan Baez song about Madonnas on the half shell ...

KATHY: That was before my time.

BEV: It was before my time too, but your mother was a great fan of Joan Baez. I guess this painting is some kind of parody.

KATHY: You mean it's a joke?

BEV: Your mother may be working out her hostility. The shell must represent old-fashioned male expectations of women.

KATHY: Yeah, but in terms of now ... do you think Mom can make it as an artist or not?

BEV: The subject matter is self-indulgent ... and ... perhaps a bit dated in its aggressive feminist metaphor.

KATHY: You mean it's crap.

BEV: Well ... it might work for today's market if her approach were less literal and a bit more ... playful.

KATHY: It's crap, Aunt Bev.

BEV: Oh. *(Beat)* Anyway, I think we should put it away before she gets back, don't you? *(SOUND: Painting is put back. Closet door closes)*

KATHY: What I think is that you should come straight out and tell Mom that she should throw out her oil paints and go home where she belongs.

BEV: It's a bit late for that, kiddo.

KATHY: No! The divorce isn't final. Legally they're still married.

BEV: But they don't want to be.

KATHY: Only because Mom's being selfish. I mean, Aunt Bev, maybe it's great for you being single, but you don't have a kid.

BEV: Actually, I might soon.

KATHY: Really? You want to have a baby?

BEV: I'm going to have one. *(SOUND: Door opens)*

KATHY: You mean *you're* pregnant?

LIZ: *(Coming on)* You're pregnant?
(SOUND: Door closes)

BEV: *(Sotto)* Oh, lord, where's Mother?

LIZ: Gone, to the store by herself, she wanted more cigs anyway.

BEV: Thank god … with her, I need to announce my wedding plans first.

KATHY: You're getting married?

LIZ: *(Mournfully)* I thought the last thing you ever wanted was to be tied down.

BEV: *(A light tone)* I'm not going to be tied down.

KATHY: *(Overlapping)* She doesn't have to be tied down.

BEV: I can afford a nanny, and Sam's promised to do his share of the parenting.

LIZ: Bev, you've no idea of what you're getting into.

BEV: Oh, Liz, I knew you'd be like this about it.

LIZ: Like what?

BEV: Negative, bitter. Look, it's Sam's idea, and he'll make a wonderful father. He's not like your Dave, you know.

KATHY: What's that supposed to mean?

BEV: Oh, nothing, kiddo.

LIZ: Kath, how about you go see what's keeping Gran?

KATHY: *(Overlapping LIZ)* Dad *is* a good father … he's a good father.

LIZ: Of course he is. Now, Kathy, I want to talk to your aunt alone.

KATHY: I'm not leaving if you're going to say mean things about Dad.

LIZ: Please, Kathy, do as you're told.

KATHY: Okay.

SCENE FOURTEEN
(Hallway)
(SOUND: Door opens and closes)

BEV: *(From other side of door)* Funny how kids are devoted to people who don't care about them, isn't it?

LIZ: *(Under KATHY's speech)* Hush … she might hear you.

KATHY: *(Internal)* Tell her she doesn't know what she's talking about. Dad loves me. You know he does.

LIZ: I find it heartbreaking, and there's nothing I can do about it except try to protect her.

BEV: She's going to see through those computer breakdowns sooner or later.

KATHY: *(Internal)* What's that supposed to mean?

She by Cat Jackson.

Cat Jackson created the above painting in response to *The Birth of Venus*, the painting by Sandro Botticelli (also referred to in this play as *Venus Rising*). Use library resources to find Botticelli's image and investigate what it represents. What do you think the image represents for Jackson? Find out how other artists have parodied or reproduced this image.

BEV: What if she runs into him out with one of his girlfriends sometime? I told you I ran into him last Sunday, didn't I?

KATHY: *(Internal)* No! No! It's not true.

LIZ: Yeah, you told me.

KATHY: *(Internal)* Maybe … it was somebody from work … maybe he was so lonely…

LIZ: *(Overlapping KATHY)* She'd probably find a way to excuse him. She'll probably say I drove him to it.

BEV: Why do you put up with it? If a kid of mine criticized me the way she criticizes you, I certainly wouldn't stand for it.

LIZ: She's been hurt enough already.

KATHY: *(Internal)* I'm not going to cry.

LIZ: Or maybe I'm a coward. Maybe I'm scared she'll say I deserved to be dumped …

KATHY: *(Aloud)* Dad walked out on her … *(Internal)* He dumped *her*?

LIZ: Maybe I'm scared she'll make up a speech about how her mother is such a fool … such a loser … such a statistic!

KATHY: *(Internal)* Oh, Mom …

BEV: *(Overlapping KATHY)* Liz, for pity's sake. You have to stop getting sucked into what other people want from you. You have to learn to make yourself your own priority.

LIZ: My daughter has always been my priority. I'm too old to change now. You can't have a child and still put yourself first, Bev.

BETTY: *(Coming on)* Kathy … what are you doing?

KATHY: Gran …

LIZ: *(Calling from other side of door)* Who's out there? Kathy?

KATHY: *(Sotto)* Gran, pretend we met by the elevator, okay?

BETTY: Why? What's the matter?

KATHY: *(Over her)* Please, Gran … trust me …
(SOUND: Door opens)

LIZ: Kathy, you weren't eavesdropping, were you?

KATHY: No! I was waiting by the elevator … Gran was on it when it came.

BETTY: *(Beat as she decides whether or not to go along)* Here you are. One corkscrew.
(SOUND: Door closes)

SCENE FIFTEEN
(Living room)

BEV: Give it to me, I'll pour.

LIZ: Kath, would you like half and half with soda?

KATHY: No, thanks, Mom.

LIZ: But we have to drink a toast to your Aunt Bev.
(SOUND: *Cork extracted, glasses, wine pouring*)

BEV: (*Upbeat*) Mother, you'll be thrilled to know I've finally said yes to Sam.

BETTY: That's wonderful!

LIZ: Kath, where are you going?

KATHY: To my room.

BETTY: Aren't you even going to congratulate your aunt?

KATHY: Congratulations.

LIZ: Sweetheart, you look upset.

KATHY: I'm fine, Mom. I just have to do that speech.

BEV: I thought you said you had it done?

KATHY: I changed my mind.

LIZ: (*Slightly off*) Okay, Kath. I'll call you when dinner's ready.

KATHY: Yeah, thanks.

BETTY: (*Fading off*) Beverly, tell us your plans. You're not being married in white, are you?

SCENE SIXTEEN
(*Internal and from kitchen*)

KATHY: (*Internal*) Who needs to write a speech about Aunt Bev anyway ... Maybe Mom's idea was better ... yeah ... (*Public address*) In the new millennium we are sure to have a woman prime minister ... What that will mean for women everywhere ... or for our planet ... or for girls growing up ... I don't really know. You take my Aunt Bev. To be honest I don't think she'd be any better than the men.

BEV: (*Slightly off*) Liz, I'm starved. Did you ever put the chicken in the oven?

LIZ: (*Slightly off*) Oh, look, you guys wouldn't like pizza, would you?

BETTY: If it's less trouble.

BEV: (*Slightly off*) I could have stayed home and had pizza.

KATHY: (*Internal. Public address*) Because she only thinks about herself.

LIZ: Okay, okay ...

KATHY: (*Internal. Public address*) Of course, someone like Mom might be different. So what if she can't get around to her painting, or even if she's any good at it ... She really cares about other people ... and that's what would be most important. I mean, what I'm saying is ... that whether a woman prime minister is going to make a difference or not, well, it depends on the woman, that's all.

(*MUSIC: Joan Baez up and out*)

Anne Chislett was born and raised in
St. John's, Newfoundland and Labrador. Her plays have
been performed all over Canada and the United States.
In 1983, she won the Governor General's Award for Drama
for her play *Quiet in the Land*.

I. *Response*

a. Briefly summarize and discuss the plot of this play.

b. Describe the major and minor conflicts the play explores.
How do these conflicts relate to ones with which you are
familiar?

c. How did you feel about the characterization of the
daughter? The other characters? Would you describe any of
them as stereotypes? Explain your answer and the effect of
these characters on an audience.

d. Discuss the meaning and effect of the title and subtitle
with a partner. Now that you have read the play, how suitable
do you think the title is?

2. *Drama* *Present a Scene* Choose one scene from this play and
prepare a presentation of it with two or three other classmates. You could plan your performance as an oral presentation only—since this was originally produced as a radio play—
or you could plan a stage presentation, using visual elements
such as costumes, props, movement, gestures, and facial
expressions. Rehearse
your scene several
times, memorizing
your lines, and
experimenting with
tone, expression,
volume, and pace.

PERFORMANCE TIP You need to know exactly what
your character is like, and how to convey that information
to your audience. What can the audience expect from this
character? How does this character tend to think and act?
What are his/her motivations or feelings?

3. *Oral Language* *Speech* In this play, the main character, Kathy,
is preparing a speech for school about modern women. Given
the same topic, quickly jot down notes for a one-minute
speech. Use those notes to deliver an impromptu, unre-
hearsed speech to a small group. With a partner, discuss the
challenges of public speaking and the skills required to be a
good public speaker.

4. **Writing** *Comedy* Reread the play and reflect on how Chislett has created humour within everyday family situations. Write at least one scene for a situation comedy about your own family or a fictional family; or write another comic scene for Kathy's family. Use the structure and comic techniques of this play as a model.

5. **Language Conventions** *Ellipses and Dashes* Examine the use of *ellipses* (...) and *dashes* (—) in one scene. Discuss how and why they are used, and their effect on the reader or listener. Examine other plays within this unit, noting how frequently dashes and ellipses are used. Consider how you can use this technique within your own scriptwriting to enhance clarity or emphasis, or to mimic normal speech.

Writing has been a way of explaining to myself
the things I do not understand.
—*Rosario Castellanos*

Theme Connections

- *"Groom Service,"* a story about love and relationships, Vol. I, p. 12
- *"Touching Bottom,"* a story about love found and lost, Vol. I, p. 124
- *"Red Bean Ice,"* a story about mother/daughter/granddaughters, Vol. I, p. 164
- *"First Person Demonstrative,"* an anti-love poem, Vol. I, p. 202
- *"A New Perspective,"* an essay about mother/daughter relationships, Vol. II, p. 45

What's your decorating tip for the day? Tom King answers that question tongue in cheek.

Tom King's Traditional Aboriginal Decorating Tips

Radio Comedy Sketch
by Tom King
from *The Dead Dog Café*

JASPER: It's time for King's Traditional Aboriginal Decorating tips with your Aboriginal Decorating expert, Tom King. So, Tom, what's your decorating tip for today?

GRACIE: Used bingo dabbers.

JASPER: What a great idea.

TOM: You want to decorate with used bingo dabbers?

GRACIE: In recent years, many non-Native homes have eschewed the more common uses of paint for interior walls and have gone to the avant garde techniques of sponging and ragging in order to create not only a complex of subtle and complementary colours but also to suggest a sense of depth and age.

JASPER: That sounds like a lot of work.

GRACIE: Indeed it is. Not only is it backbreaking, but you can never be sure that everything will come out even.

JASPER: So used bingo dabbers are the answer?

GRACIE: Exactly. When your bingo dabbers have served their purpose at the bingo hall, bring them home and use them to dab an accent line to complement the treaties.

TOM: Treaties? What treaties?

JASPER: Tom, remember when you showed our listeners how to wallpaper their walls with treaties?

TOM: Oh … yeah.

GRACIE: Treaties as a wall decoration is all well and good, but most treaties lack colour.

TOM: And used bingo dabbers have colour.

GRACIE: They do indeed. I especially like the new hot neon colours.

JASPER: This is great. Most people throw away their used bingo dabbers, so this decorating tip is environmentally sound as well.

GRACIE: Round up a variety of different coloured bingo dabbers and begin dabbing accent patterns on your walls at about the six-foot mark. Make sure to keep your colours co-ordinated, but don't worry about coverage. Being able to see parts of the treaties come through a hot pink dab can be quite effective.

JASPER: Should we just do straight lines or can we be more creative?

GRACIE: Straight lines of dab marks are simple and elegant, but patterns of any kind should be considered if the occasion and the room calls for it.

JASPER: Bingo dabbers ... who would have thought.

GRACIE: As an added bonus, once the dabber is completely used up, it can be set on bookcases or on a fireplace mantel or on an end table and passed off as an objet d'art.

JASPER: What a great tip, Tom. I'm going to start saving my used bingo dabbers right now.

TOM: Well, it was better than decorating with dogs.

Thomas King, born in 1943, has a father of Cherokee descent and a mother of Greek and German descent. King grew up in Northern California, but moved to Canada as an adult. He has written short stories and novels, most notably *Medicine River*. King teaches Native Literature and Creative Writing at the University of Guelph. Many Canadians are familiar with his performance on *The Dead Dog Café* radio show, which he writes for the CBC. The Dead Dog Café is a locale invented by King in an early novel.

I. Response
a. With a partner, assess the effectiveness of this radio comedy sketch.
b. What do you think King means by his last line? Develop two more lines of dialogue by other characters that might explain that line.

c. What do you think King is spoofing? In your opinion, how effective is this spoof?

d. What serious point does this selection make? With a partner, discuss how effectively humour can be used to deliver a serious message.

2. *Making Connections* Compare and contrast this selection with one other selection in this unit that uses humour. Consider content, subject, sources of humour, and techniques. Discuss your comparisons in small groups.

3. *Media* *Humour on Radio* In small groups, discuss radio shows you have enjoyed that were intended to be funny. What techniques did these shows use? What are the advantages or disadvantages of comedy in radio over comedy in other media?

4. *Drama* *Performing Comedy* Work with two other students to prepare a presentation of this sketch. Discuss how these lines should be delivered for comic effect. Rehearse your presentation, experimenting with the delivery of each line—your tone, volume, pace, emphasis, and expression. Record your final, polished performance on tape and play it for another group. Discuss the effectiveness of the presentation and the challenges of delivering a comic sketch.

> PERFORMANCE TIP When a performance involves only your voice, your voice becomes *really* important: certainly you must control your tone, emphasis, inflection, and expression to express emotion appropriately and effectively. However, your pronunciation and articulation are also important, since these allow others to understand your words or your character. Before a performance, you may want to practise some tongue twisters to challenge your pronunciation and articulation.

5. *Focus on Context* Research Tom King's background and writing career. Discuss what motivates him to create comedy sketches such as the one above. How does the content of the selection reflect his background? Visit the *Dead Dog Café's* official Web site and read other scripts for the show.

A writer is a foreign country.

—*Marguerite Duras*

In this innovative and amusing play,
Lindsay Price brings Galileo
to life.

Galileo

The Starry Messenger

A Play in One Act by Lindsay Price

SCENE ONE

*(A lone, blue back light comes up slowly. We can see the outline of
GALILEO but not his face. This is GALILEO in the final days before his
death. He is speaking to a former STUDENT.)*

GALILEO: Stop whispering. I can hear you. Voices ... murmur ....
murmur. I used to walk through the university and the whispers
used to speak to me in loving tones. Tell me about the wonders of
my mind, my experiments, my mistress ... Now they addle in my
ear and I am too weak to brush them aside.

Do you like my prison? Walls are walls, boy. It doesn't matter if
they are here in the villa or in a cell. They keep me in. The
pigeons have always wanted me helpless—always against me,
preventing my success.

Why did you open the window? I can feel the breeze, you fool.
What are you doing? Looking at the stars. The star. We used to be
such friends. That was long ago. Now they are just bitter. "Why
did you desert us Galileo? You left, recanted our existence. We
trusted you and we were betrayed." I can't shut them out. That
was long ago. Close the window! Close it. Don't let them in! I can
hear you ... I can hear you.

*(Lights slowly cross-fade into a wash on GALILEO'S studio. There is a
desk overflowing with papers and books and gadgets. There is a life-sized
pendulum hanging from a frame. There is also a telescope which is hidden
underneath a large cloth. We are now in the year 1609. GALILEO realizes
he is back in his studio in Padua. He moves around the studio, touching
the instruments and enjoying the space. He puts on his jacket and goes to*

his desk to resume writing a letter. He is sitting, writing furiously with his body turned away from the door. He speaks without looking up. This is the first visit of THE STUDENT.)

Wait … Wait … stop fidgeting. I can see you. *(He holds up a hand and gestures THE STUDENT into the room as he continues writing.)* … hold on … one more minute … *(He sneaks a look and watches THE STUDENT cross the room. THE STUDENT moves to touch the pendulum.)* Don't touch that. *(He chuckles and continues writing.)* … Almost there … Galileo … Gal-li-lei. *(Says his last name in syllables as he signs his name with a flourish)*

(He waves the paper in the air to dry the ink and gestures to the pendulum and comes across very sternly.)

If you touch that, it will move. *(Standing, he goes right up into the face of THE STUDENT.)* And the fitting is not so stable. It came crashing down last week on the foot of one of my students. Broke every bone in his foot. *(Turns away and looks up into the heavens)* He'll never walk right again. *(Demonstrating this as he speaks)* Always left, left, left … *(Turns to face STUDENT to see if he got the joke and chuckles)* What's under the cloth? *(Crosses stage and shoos STUDENT away from the pendulum)* I don't divulge every secret to every stranger that walks in. Besides, you haven't paid for your first lesson. Everybody comes here for lessons—why else would you come? *(Turning away from THE STUDENT and holding up the letter he has just finished)*

Here, be useful. Listen to this: *(Clears his throat and speaks in schmoozy tones)* To Belasario Vinta. *(Speaking slowly)* Vinta. Vinta. Belasario? He is the eyes and ears of the Grand Duke of Tuscany. You must know the Medici Family? *(Sizing up STUDENT as if not knowing who Vinta is, is a mark against him)* Hmm. *(Reading through the letter)* Blah, blah, blah … all right now … *(Goes back to speaking in schmoozy tones)*

My thought would truly be to get enough leisure and quiet so that I can complete, before my life ends, the great work … *(Grabs feather and changes the "the" into "three")* three great works that I have in hand, in order that they might be published, perhaps with some credit to me and to *him* who would favour me in these undertakings. Greater leisure than I have here at the University of Padua. So long as I am forced to derive the sustenance of my household from public and private teaching … the rotten little mindless no-neck buggers *(Looks at STUDENT and gives three short laughs)* … the freedom that I have here does not suffice since I am required, at anybody's request, to consume many hours of the day and, often, most of them. This Republic will never offer me such an ideal situation. These things I can only hope to have from a Prince.

(Grabs his carafe and swigs a mouthful. He cradles the carafe as he continues to read.) Of course, I don't want to appear to be asking unreasonable favours without giving something back in return. To obtain a salary from a Republic without rendering public service ... *(He pauses, puts the paper down again to rewrite.)* To obtain a salary from a Republic, however splendid and generous a salary, without rendering public service is not possible since, to draw benefits from the public, it is necessary to satisfy the public and not a particular individual. But I have so many and diverse inventions, only one of which could be enough to take care of me for the rest of my life ... I cannot hope for such benefits from anybody but an absolute ruler. *(Getting bored with reading)* Blah, Blah, Blah, Your humble servant, Galileo Galilei.

What do you think? *(Looks at THE STUDENT who just shrugs his shoulders)* Bah.

(Folds up letter and seals it) I am a brilliant suck-up. Cosimo de Medici used to be one of my students. Now he's the Grand Duke of Tuscany. Everyone talks this way when they want to suck something out of the Grand Duke of Tuscany. *(Looks through his papers)* And if I want to work for the Grand Duke of Tuscany, then I speak in dutiful suck-filled tones. *(Takes both letters and puts them together on the table and sits down on his stool to face THE STUDENT with his arms crossed)* All right, all right, stop fidgeting so. I know who you are. You want to study with me. Want me to teach you everything I know, do you? *(Puffs his chest out proudly)* You've heard stories about me perhaps? *(Deflates at the answer and is a little irritated)* Of course you have, no one comes to study with the great Galileo by chance. *(THE STUDENT says, "My father sent me.")* Yes, well, fathers are always sending their sons somewhere. I got sent to a monastery; you got sent to me. Which one of us is the luckier one, eh? Monasteries are wonderful places to study. It's quiet. No distractions.

(Stands up and walks around the table to stare down at THE STUDENT) But why did your father send you to me? There are many, many other teachers here at the university. Which story dazzled you the most, eh? The Leaning Tower of Pisa? Yes, that's a pretty good story, isn't it? *(To himself)* I almost wish I had come up with that one myself. *(Back to THE STUDENT, picking up two paper balls)* Do you want to climb to the top of the leaning tower of Pisa and be just like me? Throw some different weighted cannonballs off the top to see which gets to the

bottom first? Who is right—Aristotle or me? You're guessing. *(Drops both balls which land at exactly the same time)* All bodies accelerate at the same rate of motion. No playing favourites; you cannot sweet talk her with trips to the countryside or jewelry. Everything gets treated exactly the same. Cannonballs, feathers … it is the wind that bribes the feather away. Feathers bribe very easily. *(Turns to see THE STUDENT writing)* Don't write that down—I haven't accepted you yet.

I'm very expensive and you had better not be stupid. So, you better learn quick. *(Waving the letter)* I don't know how long I'll be here. *(THE STUDENT says he wants to stick it out.)* Determined, eh? Bah. Stupid, more like it. *(THE STUDENT'S face crumples.)* Oh, for heaven's sake. If you can't figure out when I'm serious and when I'm not, we'll never get anywhere. *(Kneels down to be at the level of THE STUDENT)* Look. *(Makes a serious face)* Serious Face. *(Makes a funny face)* Not serious face. Serious Face. Not serious. Which is this? *(Makes a face which is a combination of the two)* You're guessing.

(Counting off the rules on his fingers) Don't look at anything unless I tell you to. Don't touch anything unless I tell you to and don't try to steal anything, or I'll string you up by your thumbs. I can never be sure who is going to try and steal some of my genius away. You can try, of course—they always try—but the thing about genius is that it tends to disappear—poof—the instant it's away from its owner. *(Sarcastic and pompous)* So, are you trustworthy? Can I trust you? You're not going to sell my soul to the rag sheets, are you? Can I fill you with knowledge or will it pour out of you faster than I can pack it in? Will you study day and night? Will you take this journey with me? Once you do, you will never be able to turn back. You will never be able to study with anyone else. I will have corrupted you for life. Can you handle being corrupted for life? Can you touch your tongue to your nose? *(Breaking the mood)* Don't try, you look ridiculous. All right. *(Stands up, gets carafe and takes another swig)*

The first thing you can do is pay me. You've been listening to me for at least five minutes. That qualifies as a first lesson. You want to learn. *(THE STUDENT asks if he can see what's under the cloth.)* First the money, then the cloth. *(Fingers the cloth over the pendulum)* Place it on the table there.

(In response to whether GALILEO wants to count the money) Don't be rude; if it's wrong, you'll pay me double next time. And now … *(Uncovers the pendulum)* It is not a package on a piece of string. It's a pendulum. Don't you know anything? *(Starts the pendulum swinging)* We're going

to have to start at the very beginning, aren't we? *(Watching the swings and thinking of the past, his speech is as soothing as the words)* It's very soothing. It helps me think. Back and forth in equal swings of absolute perfection. Like myself. We've been together for a long time.

(Breaks the mood and is pompous once again. He moves over to the table.) Now, the next thing you can do is take that letter to the Duke's eyes and ears, and that one to my brother there. *(Sits down at the table and begins looking through books)* Go and find my landlady and give them to her. Her son is travelling south tomorrow. I can't get away right now.

(Speaks as he begins to write) Yes, yes, lots of family. It's very mundane; one brother, some sisters, one dead father who I wish was alive and one live mother who I wish was dead. Is your father well? Have you looked at his teeth lately? Oh dear. *(Looks up sharply)* You're not the first son in your family are you? *(The answer is no.)* Count your blessings. You don't have to support one live mother, one brother and some sisters.

(Goes across the stage and takes a letter out of the bag near his cloak. Looks over it by the window. He is talking more to himself than to THE STUDENT.*)*

(He is reading a letter from his sister in which the threat is mentioned.) I on the other hand ... What is the most important ingredient in marriage? *(*STUDENT *says love)* Wrong. It's money. My sister's husband won't leave me alone. "When is the dowry coming, Galileo? Pay up, pay up, pay up!" *(He tears up the letter and goes back to the table.)* Why couldn't my brother be the first son? Why couldn't I have been in his shoes? Then I could go to him and pester him for money whenever I felt like it and refuse to help out the family. Off to Poland, off to Bavaria, off to wherever. Spend every last cent I have to marry an obnoxious braying cow. "Galileo, it's my wedding. I must have the best nuptial banquet." Blah, blah, blah, what a fool.

(Stands up to go to the door and is surprised to see STUDENT *still standing there)*

Are you still here? Go, go, you'll never learn if you sit around all day. *(Shoos* STUDENT *out the door)* How can I teach you anything if you won't go away?

(The lights fade to spot. GALILEO *is seen trying to pray but keeps getting distracted by the whispers and the rumours. He tries to shoo them away*

*from his ears like gnats. He tries to block them out. But then he starts
to listen. His face looks up into the light and the spot fades.)*

SCENE TWO

*(GALILEO goes back to table and picks up two baskets. Inside the larger
basket are lenses. The smaller basket is for the rejects.)*

*(Lights cross-fade back to the wash. GALILEO picks up two lenses.
Holds one up to his eye and holds the other at arm's length.
"No." He brings his outstretched arm in closer. "No." He puts
the two lenses close together. He tosses the two lenses into the reject basket
and picks up two more and starts the process again.)*

*(THE STUDENT wants to know about GALILEO'S life. GALILEO is sort of
telling the story because he likes to talk about himself, but he is cheerfully
talking on autopilot, while he is frantically trying to get the right
combination. He has been up all night.)*

Well, I was born, *(Arm's length)* no, *(Middle length)* no, *(Close-up)* no.

*(Puts the two lenses in the reject basket. Picks up one lens and peers
through it)*

I was going to be a monk, then I wasn't. *(Brings out his handkerchief and
starts to polish the lens)* I was going to be a doctor, then I wasn't. I was
supposed to get a degree, but I didn't. *(Picks up another lens and holds it
at arm's length)* Wait … wait … *(Peers through the lens)* No good.

*(Puts the two lenses in the reject basket and sighs, using one hand
to rub his neck while the other uses the handkerchief to rub his forehead.
He then picks up two more lenses.)*

I should have been an artist. Or a musician. But who needs a degree?
I never did. "No, no, you need a degree." I need your father's money.
(Throws the two lenses into the reject basket in disgust) Bah, these are not
the right thickness; I can't get the right magnification. These are all
wrong. *(Stands and paces. He moves to the pendulum and lets it swing.)* I'm
going to have to get more made. It is so maddening! When you search
for the truth, there is so much guesswork. No, if I wait until tomorrow,
those wretched Dutchmen will get to Venice before I do and they will
get all the credit.

*(Removes his jacket, and sits once again at the table. Takes two lenses
and holds one at his eye and one at arm's length. THE STUDENT
is sitting on the floor, DSR.)*

Are you finished that experiment I gave you? *(Arm's length)* You are not just rolling a ball down a plane, *(Middle length)* you are studying the acceleration of bodies *(Close-up)* and how they change their speed. *(Reject)* You are defying what other scientists have cast in stone. *(Picks up lens and wipes with handkerchief)* The problem is, you are lazy. You sit and listen to professors who give you all the answers and don't make you work. Well, here you have to figure out the answers all by yourself. I have to get rid of all your bad habits somehow ...

*(Drops hands and looks at THE STUDENT who has just said
"I don't understand." GALILEO laughs.)*

There are many things you don't understand. What exactly is it you don't understand today? Slow down, slow down! *(Stands up to talk to STUDENT. GALILEO truly believes that he is not in the wrong.)* It doesn't matter that I never invented this spyglass, far-seeing-whatever-the-Dutch-call-it thing. It matters that I can make it better. If I can make it better, who cares who invented it? Their spyglass has only three times the magnification. You can't even get a clear picture; there's a fringe all around the outside. The image appears upside down. It is a cheap tinker's toy. They should not be allowed to become rich with such an abomination.

Of course they will get rich. *(Stands up and returns to the desk)* They get richer every second they are in Italy and I get poorer. If only I had the time to take this to the Grand Duke of Tuscany. How he would regret not answering my letters. *(Arm's length)* They are going to make a presentation to the Doge in Venice. *(Middle length)* Well, they were, until I stopped them. I have friends in high places, my dear boy. *(Close-up)* It pays to have friends in high places so you can kick the teeth out of your enemies in low places. *(Rejects)*

(Looks up, exasperated at the nagging of THE STUDENT)

I am not cheating. You think in very absolute terms, my friend. Very narrow. I cannot even fit my head between the spokes of your thinking. I do not have a fat head. I know what this instrument can do;

> For the theatre one needs long arms; it is better to have them too long than too short. An artiste with short arms can never, never make a fine gesture.
>
> Sarah Bernhardt

I deserve to get the rewards. *(Arm's length)* You have to create your own opportunity. Well, perhaps *you* don't. *(Changes the lens at his eye)* All *you* have to worry about is that some irate peasants don't deem it fit that you should lose your head. *(Middle length)* Not as big as mine, but I think you would miss it all the same. I wonder how long you will keep your head. *(Rejects both lens and looks at THE STUDENT)* Have you ever had your horoscope done? I had one done for my daughter the day after she was born. Poor child.

Although, if I am right, you could make a fair amount just from being one of my students. You could sell your notes if anyone could read your handwriting.

(Holds up a lense. Notices the dust and starts to polish it) One instrument. That's all I need. Do you know how long I have been trying to find one instrument? Pendulum—no good. Thermoscope—no good. Lodestones—no good. I invented a machine for raising water and irrigating land; even got a patent for it: *(Imitating the language of a commercial)* "Very easy and convenient to use!" You only have to use one hose for spraying twenty buckets of water. I actually gave classes on how to use the blasted thing … but, no good; I only sold one.

(Sorts through the lenses) Military compass—no good. I thought that was going to do it for me. *(Discards a couple without holding them up)* I gave so many away … I had a man making compasses for me—worked him to the bone, but it was still no good. The thermoscope? It measures hot and cold. *(Holds up the lens)* There's a glass bottle about the size of an egg and a long glass neck … wait … almost. Almost.

(Keeps one lens and discards the other) You see, all I have to do is find the right buyers, and I am set for life. *(Picks up a lens. Holds at arm's length)* One instrument. *(Discards one)* This one is so simple. Two lenses in a tube make faraway objects appear as if they were right in front of your nose. *(Picks up another)* I'm sure I would have thought of it myself if I didn't have to spend all this time lecturing and teaching, and being bothered by students. *(Polishes the one he has just picked up)* You don't believe me. That's why I am a genius and you're not. The military alone will pay through the nose for something like this.

(Looks through at arm's length again) No, no, wait. Wait … *(Slowly stands up keeping the arm formation, and moves his arms in an arc)* That's it. The best Venetian glass. Ground. Polished. It matches. *(Looking through the lens)* Magnify. Magnify. Show me your wonders and pour gold through my fingers. This is the beginning.

(Lights fade to blue. GALILEO puts the two baskets on the floor. He then puts on his cape and hat, and exits through the doorway.)

SCENE THREE

(Lights cross-fade to wash)

(GALILEO is drunk. He is singing offstage. As he sings, he repeats one line over a couple of times, as if he is uncertain of the tune. He enters and stands in the doorway, swaying a little.)

"Tantalizing maiden, how shall I woo? ... All my heart is laden for love of you! Oh! I am all on fire with desire ... Tantalizing ... Tantalizing."

That's not right. That is not right. *(Sings the line again)* Where's my lute? *(Enters the space and searches behind the desk)* I know it's around here somewhere. *(Spins around)* Well, hello. You waited! *(Leans on the table)* Thank God you're here. We're celebrating! *(Totters away again, looking for something—he can't remember what)* I'm celebrating. I'm celebrating. You didn't do anything. *(Turns back)* I did it. I got the credit. I presented the spyglass, far-seeing-whatever-the-Dutch-call-it thing to the Doge of Venice. *(Imitates looking out of a telescope)* The top dog. *(Comes up close to the table still looking out of the "telescope")* I can see your nose hairs. Those wretched little Dutchmen didn't know what they were up against. They should know better than to fight a master. *(Arms out wide)*

It was a masterpiece! I am a masterpiece. The humble, middle-aged, dog-eared scientist presenting the lord and master with the sweat of his work. *(Does a sweeping bow)* The work of his life, or a week-and-a-half, depending on how you look at it. I had them in the palm of my hand. *(Shoos THE STUDENT back onto the stool and goes centre stage)* Sit down, sit down. All right? Here I am walking into the room.

(Walks pompously across the stage, stumbles a bit and rights himself. The Venetian court is SL.)

(Deep bow) "Good Morning. Good Morning. Good Morning." *(Looking back over his shoulder to THE STUDENT)* Everyone has their eyes locked on me. I am the centre of attention. *(Turning all the way around to face THE STUDENT)* There is nothing the matter with the way I dress! It's comfortable. Just because I don't trip over a toga every two steps; bah! I would rather go naked ... Now, where was I? Oh yes, the Doge. I am the centre of attention! *(Turns back to the court)*

(Speaking to the Doge, showing him how to use the telescope. They are both at a window looking out into the audience, being very serious.)

"Raise it to one eye and keep the other eye closed. What can you see? What can you see? The campanile and cupola with the façade of the church of Saint Giustina. Yes ... You can see people entering and leaving the church of Saint Giacomo, the gondolas at the Collona at the beginning of the canal of the glassworkers. *(High-voiced courtier)* "I see, I see. Quite remarkable." *(Low-voiced courtier)* "Quite remarkable." *(Looks at* THE STUDENT *and giggles a little. He clears his throat.)*

I have a letter for your honoured sirs. If it is no trouble.

(Gives another deep bow, brings up a portion of his cape to use as a letter. Schmoozingly)

"Galileo Galilei, a humble servant of Your Serene Highness, now appears before you with a new contrivance of glasses drawn from the most recondite speculations of perspective, which render visible objects so close to the eye and represent them so distinctly, that those that are distant—for example, nine miles—appear as though they were only one mile distant.

This instrument is one of the fruits of the science which he has professed for the past seventeen years at the University of Padua, with the hope of carrying on his work in order to present you with greater ones, if it shall please the Good Lord and Your Serene Highness."

(Smiles and bows and falls over. A page has come over to GALILEO.*)*

Yes? The Doge has something to say to me? To me? *(Gives* THE STUDENT *a look, stands up and brushes himself off, and gives another bow)* Oh, my dear Sir, I am glad you appreciate my effort. Yes? *(This is a good thing.)* A raise in my salary? That is wonderful, I do appreciate ... A university position for life? *(Not such a good thing)* A university position for life. And ... *(He is waiting for more and gets nothing. He bows and backs away.)* You are most kind, most kind and generous. Most kind. Thank you for seeing me. You are most kind.

(He gives a raspberry and flips the bird to the Doge. He turns to THE STUDENT *and laughs uproariously.)*

A raise in salary and a university position for life. There it is. *(Removing his cloak and hanging it up)* A raise in my salary and a university position for life. For life. *(With a little giggle)* It's an absolute disaster. How can I keep ahead if I am imprisoned within these walls? What if somebody creates a better instrument while I am chained to the lecturing table? Where does that leave me? All that sucking up for nothing! *(Starting to get riled up)* For life, for life, for life, for life!! ... What a waste of time! *(Crescendo)* If I had known what the outcome was going to be, I would have left it for the wretched Dutchmen! *(THE STUDENT is reproachful, GALILEO turns away from him and crosses right. He gestures to the court.)* Don't look at me like that. Don't look at me like that. Venice is nothing. Venice is not even a stepping stone. *(Looks to the pendulum for support and a new idea)* A different approach. A stronger instrument. Yes, yes, that will work ... Go to the glass blowers, boy; I need more lenses. Do not talk—go! Go now! I can do better.

(Lights fade. GALILEO stands DSC, holding his arms as if he is looking through a telescope. Slowly he raises his arms and looks at the sky. Shaken by what he sees, he runs offstage.)

SCENE FOUR

(Lights cross-fade to a wash as GALILEO re-enters, running.)

(Scattered, shaky, an octave higher than normal. At times he is fighting to maintain composure and failing. There should be nothing controlled in his actions or voice.)

Water, water, I need water. *(Lunging for the carafe)* ... Beer. I need beer.

(GALILEO sits on the floor and drinks long and hard. He should be shaking. He turns the carafe over, trying to get the last drops out, and then hugs the carafe to his chest.)

Water? *(Looking around on the ground)* More beer; why isn't there more beer? *(Leaving the carafe and crawling over to the table)* Paper. Where is paper? No beer, no paper, this studio is a pigsty. Why doesn't anybody keep this place straight? *(Kneeling against the desk he gets a piece of paper and a feather)* Paper, quill, ink, write, write, write. I can't write; my hand won't stop shaking. *(To his hand)* Stop shaking. Beer, I need beer to calm my nerves. *(Looks towards the carafe)* There isn't any more. *(Looking under books)* Wine? Water? Nothing. Sit. Just sit. And don't move. *(He holds himself for a second and bursts out laughing.)* Paper! Hand! Stop shaking!! *(One hand holds the other wrist. GALILEO talks to the hand.)* I command you hand to commit yourself to steadiness. *(Hand speaks back)* "We're too excited, Galileo, we must wave! Bye-Bye." *(Slaps himself)* Get a hold of yourself. Write. The moon.

(Takes a deep breath and begins to write. He speaks and writes while trying to gulp in air. Everything is choppy.)

The moon. Cracks. Flaws. Mountains. Valleys. Crevices, Rough.

(Hears a noise behind him)

Who's there? Who are you? *(Trying to hide what he is writing and finding something to throw at the same time)* Get out! Get out! Get out! You have no business being here and I'll ... *(Recognizes THE STUDENT).* Oh. You. *(Takes a big breath and brings out his handkerchief to wipe his forehead)* What are you doing here? *(Stands and crosses right with the paper in his hands)* Your father, your father. No, don't tell me. I don't want to hear your simpering little problems. *(Shooing motion with his hand while still having his back to THE STUDENT)* I can't talk to you now. I can't possibly talk to you now. *(Stands still)* Why? Why? Why? Why? *(Crosses to stand in front of THE STUDENT)* I've done it. I've done it. Don't you understand? No. You don't. *(Waves the paper in front of THE STUDENT, taunting him)* I'm the only one who knows and I'm not going to tell you, *(Snatches the paper away and turns away to sit on stool)* not for all the ducats in the world. I'm going to show those old Aristotelian scholars who can't stop talking long enough to take their feet out of their mouths. *(Talking with one hand as if it were a puppet)* "I've found you out, you no-neck scholars. I have found you out! The moon is not as you say; it is not smooth, not uniform and precise. It is uneven, rough; there are mountains and valleys. In fact, it looks an awful lot like earth—what do you have to say to that?" *(Using the other hand)* "You were right, Galileo, all along. We were so very wrong." *(Laughing, turning to STUDENT and putting hands over mouth)* I've let it out. Very well, very well, come closer so the whole world won't hear me. *(Gestures to STUDENT to come to CS)*

I've looked up. Into the sky. With the telescope. *(Cuffs THE STUDENT)* No, not the one I gave to the Doge; that was too weak. Pay attention! Where have you been all of these months? What did you think I've been doing—teaching? *(Very conspiratorial)* I have magnified the lens nine times, ten times, twenty times, thirty times. I went up to the roof and I looked up into the sky. *(Getting excited again. Whispering, holding out his sheet)* The moon is not what we think it is. *(Breaking the mood as THE STUDENT spouts dogma)* Yes, yes, yes, the moon is a heavenly body. *(Speaking as a dutiful STUDENT)* The moon is perfect and incorruptible. You know that, because that is what you have been

> Drama is life with the dull bits cut out.
>
> Alfred Hitchcock

told. What you think you see. What you think you know. Who cares about what you know? Who cares about what you can spout? I am giving you something so new. *(Holding out sheet as a gift, which* THE STUDENT *rejects)*

Your head is stuck in your books and your shoes. *(Turns to the window)* The moon, it's so beautiful … it is spotted as the tail of a peacock, is sprinkled with azure eyes, and resembles those glass vases which, while still hot, have been plunged into cold water and have thus acquired a crackled and wavy surface. *(Breaking out of his reverie and goes to his desk to begin writing)* Say, that's rather good. I should write that down. I have to write all of this down. This is better than I expected.

(THE STUDENT starts to talk about Aristotle. GALILEO is starting to get irritated.)

Aristotle says, Aristotle says. The time for Aristotle is past. It is time for scientists to wipe the dust from their eyes and learn something. They haven't learned anything for years. They just keep spouting the ashes of a long-dead man. Aristotle was just a man. He saw with his eyes and he thought he knew what he saw. I have seen more in one night than Aristotle ever saw in his lifetime. He is the dust in our brains; he clouds everything we say and think and do …

(He turns and cuts off when he sees the face of THE STUDENT*. He takes a deep breath. Calmly and rationally, crossing toward* THE STUDENT*)*

The surface of the moon is not smooth. What they told you was wrong. The moon has never been smooth. Aristotle was wrong. All these months you've been experimenting and you didn't doubt me when I said Aristotle was wrong then, did you? How is this different? The principle is the same.

(Irritated) I know what I see, don't I? *(Under control)* I know what I have seen. *(Turning away, goes to table and writes again)* It's absolutely fantastic; I never dreamed … Stop questioning me! I am the master and you are the student. I am right and you are wrong. I know what I am talking about and you never did. *(Gets an idea)* Why don't you look at the moon yourself? Go up to the roof and look with your own two eyes so you can stop with this "Aristotle says." *(Encouraging)* Go ahead. *(Puzzled, stands, his eyes following* THE STUDENT *as he leaves the room)* Where are you going? Come back here! *(Goes to the doorway and shouts after* THE STUDENT*)* Don't you want to see with your own two eyes?

(Lights change)

SCENE FIVE

(GALILEO uncovers the telescope and looks through it when the lights change.
THE STUDENT enters. GALILEO does not leave the telescope.)

You make so much noise when you are trying to lurk. Students, students! This place is like a boarding house sometimes. You have no grace. You should have taken dancing or fencing; something to give you more poise. Light on your feet. Maybe I'll ask Marina to give you some lessons. What would you think of that, eh? Even I would pay to see that. She could give grace to a slop pile. *(Sitting straight to think)* Although, she hasn't helped the girls any ... Virginia trips over her own shadow. They're still young I suppose ...

(Turns and looks at STUDENT. No joking) You have missed three lessons. I still expect to be paid. *(Cutting off THE STUDENT, more calm than irritated, turning back to telescope)* I do not care what you tell your father, I still expect to be paid in full. *(Tired, waving hand)* Yes, Yes, I know I have changed my lecturing schedule. What of it? I have more important things to do.

Three days ago I saw three stars around Jupiter. Two to the east and one to the west. Two days ago, there were three stars to the west. Yesterday it was cloudy and today ... *(Waving hand at STUDENT while still looking through telescope)* Is there some paper over there? Write this down.

(Standing and stretching as he speaks) "On the 10th day of January in this present year, 1610, there were only two stars, both easterly." *(Heading to the pendulum and mumbling to himself)* Now what happened to the third star ... behind Jupiter? Perhaps, perhaps ... *(Looks over at THE STUDENT)* What is the matter? ... You're not writing.

(STUDENT is worried about the local gossip. GALILEO is very calm.)

People always talk. Is that why you have come at such a late hour? What are they saying today?

(Cuts STUDENT off with a snort. Returns to the pendulum)

They may consider me an enemy, but I have no time for childish behaviour. Why should I care about enemies? Why should you? Are you being pelted with eggs in the courtyard because you study with me? The pigeons are restless; rumours flying at top speed around and around the university.

(Takes a big stretch and scratches his chest) What is happening with those stars? They have something specifically to do with Jupiter ... I know that ... *(Sees STUDENT looking at four moon drawings)* Do you like my drawings? *(Grabs one of the drawings)* The full moon was the hardest. With such a small field of view, I could only see a quarter of it at a time. That is something to work on. Something to change. *(Letting the picture drop, trying to add a bit of levity)* I should have been an artist. If only my father had been in your shoes, I could have painted nudes all day long and never finished one painting.

(Laughs and then looks at STUDENT) You take everything so seriously. Which face is this? *(Makes a face)*

All right. If you're not going to help me, perhaps I will help you. It's my generous nature; I give and I give and I give ...

(Wipes his forehead)

Have you ever heard of Copernicus? That is the lesson for today— Copernicus. If you are going to bother me at my studio at this hour, the least you can do is learn something. New lesson.

(Dips the cloth into the carafe. Squeezes some into his mouth and then goes on to wipe the telescope)

Nicholas Copernicus—ah, if only he had lived seventy more years ... what conversations we would have had. I've known about his theories for a long time; well, one theory in particular which is of great interest to me ... no boy, don't take any notes.

(GALILEO stares intently down the wrong end of the telescope, wiping and drying the lens. Not looking at THE STUDENT)

Nicholas Copernicus believed that the earth was not the centre of the universe. He believed that the sun was the centre and the earth revolved around the sun. That everything revolves around the sun ... Mars, Jupiter, Saturn, Venus ... *(GALILEO spits on the lens and wipes the lens clean)*

As you might imagine, this is not a popular philosophy. The church says that the earth is the centre of the universe, therefore the earth *is* the centre of the universe. The church says that the earth does not move, therefore the earth does *not* move. Who is right, eh?

(Galileo looks at THE STUDENT) Close your mouth boy; you'll let the flies in. That's better. *(Returns to the desk to a pile of notes)* So, I've been thinking about Copernicus and those stars I've been recording around

Jupiter. What if those stars are not stars at all? *(Throws notes down)* What if they are moons and they are rotating around Jupiter? What if it were possible for planets to revolve around something that is not the earth? I have seen those stars move with my own eyes. What if the earth is not the centre of the universe? *(Brings hand down to look at fingers)* What if everything we have ever known has been slipping through our fingers? What if we look at our fingers and find out they are not just flesh and bone, but made of something that we have been brought up to reject?

(Moving away from THE STUDENT, *still examining his hand)*

I have lectured that the earth is the centre of the universe. I have lectured that the earth does not move. I have known men who have been burned at the stake for saying otherwise. That will make things difficult, but not impossible.

(Sitting down at desk with the notes)

What did I say before? On the 10th day of January … *(THE STUDENT interrupts.)* I'm making notes. It will be awfully hard to publish a book with incomplete notes. Do you think I'm doing this for my own amusement? What good is discovering something if I don't tell anyone about it? I have a duty as a scientist … I am not a stupid man. I am not going to make mistakes. I am just going to publish my findings in a … you don't understand. I cannot be satisfied with just the moon, because the universe does not consist of the earth and the moon.

(Returns to taking notes)

I must do what I must do. If you do not like it, you are free to leave. *(Slams feather down)* Fine, fine. I should never have invested so much time in the small-minded intellect you possess. *(Turns back on* STUDENT *and waves him away with the back of his hand)* Tell your father that I refuse to teach you anything else. Damn! *(Running to the doorway)* Wait. Wait! Come back! Come back. You still owe me for three classes!

SCENE SIX

(Lights change. GALILEO *picks up some of the balls of paper that are scattered around his desk. He sits on* THE STUDENT'S *stool shooting the paper balls across the stage.)*

"All things are hard: man cannot explain them by word. The eye is not filled with seeing, neither is the ear filled with hearing." *(Shooting the paper ball)* Parabola. *(Picking up another ball)* "What is it that hath been? The same thing that shall be. What is it that hath been done? The same that shall be done." *(Shooting ball)* Parabola. *(Picks up two balls, peeks to see what is written on the paper and re-crumples them)* "Nothing under the sun is new, neither is any man able to say: Behold this is new. For it hath already gone before in the ages that were before us …" *(Shooting a ball)* Parabola. "The perverse are hard to be corrected: and the number of fools is infinite."

(Looks up at THE STUDENT) Well, well, well. *(Bends down to pick up another ball)* You came back. Ah yes, you heard about the book. *(Aiming for THE STUDENT)* Parabola. It's sitting on the table there. I would show it to you if I felt like it, but I don't. *(Shoots it high in the air)* Parabola. That sounds very poetic, doesn't it? Parabola. *(Picks up another and shoots it high in the air)* Science and poetry often go hand in hand. The equal sign in an equation is a metaphor. One thing being equal to another.

(Takes a ball in one hand and pops it to the other) Parabola. *(Showing the piece of paper to THE STUDENT)* I invented the parabola. *(Shifting from hand to hand)* I have invented and discovered. *(From hand to hand)* Invented and discovered. I am surrounded by my inventions. Knee-deep in the mire of discovery, clinging to my days and stinking up my breath. *(Lets the ball go)*

(Picks up a ball and stands) Aristotle says—there's that phrase again— that objects only travel in one direction and when they stop feeling like going in that direction, they drop to the ground. *(Drops the ball)* Boof. If that were true, I could take my brand new book here from the table *(Picks up the book and pretends to throw it across the stage)* and project it across the room and it might go and go and go. *(Watching it go)* The science in this book would take me to the greatest heights. But it's not true. Ah, the truth. You never questioned me on projectiles did you? Objects go in two directions—they go forward and they go down at the same time. My book goes forward into science and is pulled down, down, down, by religion. *(Picking up three paper balls)* No matter how hard I try to throw, it always curves back to earth.

(Shoots a ball) Parabola. Can't get away from science. *(Shoots a ball)* Parabola. I can't leave the church. *(Shoots a ball)* Parabola. Which is more important—science or the church?

(Goes to the pendulum) The pendulum! When I was in school, I invented the pendulum. *(Lets the pendulum go)* If only a pendulum had made me famous. Aristotle never said anything about the pendulum. No one was

ever burned at the stake because of a pendulum. Well, perhaps they were; that would make a good story too. *(Stops movement)* But if I were to take my book and tie it to the end of a rope and let the book go … *(Lets it go)* … It swings from side to side: science, religion, science, religion. But no matter how short the swings get, the rhythm never gives weight to one side or the other. You see? The period of the swings is the same. Science, religion. Science, religion. Each part of the problem receives equal weight. How can I make a proper decision, when everything is weighed so equally? *(Gets two balls and then goes and stands on his chair)* What about the leaning tower of Pisa? I throw science and religion off the top of the tower and *(Drops the paper balls)* they both reach the ground at exactly the same time. *(Gets two more balls and balances them in his palm)* I throw different sizes of ice science and ice religion into water and they both float. They always float! Science, religion. Science, religion. Catholic, scientist. Catholic, scientist. *(Throws them down)* Do I flip a coin? Which am I supposed to choose? Why can't I be both?

(Looks at THE STUDENT and laughs gently at himself. Looks at the studio and the mess he has made. He gives a sigh. As he talks, he picks up the paper balls and puts them into a pile.)

God gave to me the capacity to look up into the sky. The church upholds human reason. I must use my reason to find the truth. What else should I use it for? *(Turns to THE STUDENT)* Why must I let my reason rot just because it goes against the world? Just because I am intelligent, I should waste away? *(THE STUDENT does not answer.)*

Hmmm. *(Looks toward the book)* This will amuse you.

(Going to book and opening to first page, reading in a commanding voice)

"The Starry Messenger. Revealing great unusual and remarkable spectacles, opening these to the consideration of everyman and especially of philosophers and astronomers; as observed by Galileo Galilei, Gentleman of Florence, Professor of Mathematics in the University of Padua, with the aid of a spyglass lately invented by him. In the surface of the moon, in innumerable fixed stars, in nebulae and, above all, in four planets swiftly revolving about Jupiter at differing distances and periods and known to no one before the author recently perceived them and decided they should be named The Medician Stars."

(Looks up) What do you think? I have dedicated the satellites of Jupiter to the Medici family in Florence. The Medicea Sidera. If that

doesn't get me a position in Florence, I don't know what will. *(Closes book and brushes off the cover)* I plan to present the Grand Duke with a personally crafted telescope with the instructions that I will be at his beck and call to teach him how to use it. The damn fool needs me to be there; why can't he see that?

I did not lie. I practically came up with the idea for the instrument. Besides, nobody remembers the wretched little Dutchmen anymore. I have to make the title page impressive. As far as the world is concerned, I did invent it.

(Leans down to stare at THE STUDENT)

Did you know there are seven kinds of torture used by the inquisition, all in the name of truth? The first is the pit—an underground cave twenty feet deep and entirely without light. The second is a cell, so small that a person cannot enter it standing up. The third is the rack, which draws the limbs of the sufferer in opposite directions. The fourth, an iron ring which brings the head, feet, and hands together to form a circle. The fifth is an iron glove which encloses the hand with great pain. The sixth consists of manacles attached to the arms. The seventh, of fetters attached to the feet. This is all, of course, before they march you through the street on an ass, then burn you alive. Or put you in prison for the rest of your life and take away everything you have. *(Walks away to look at telescope)*

This book will change the world. I will be responsible for changing the world. Why would I want to give up an opportunity like that? Besides, I'm running out of time. Sooner or later, someone else will realize and look up into the sky, instead of out at the sea. I will look like a fool if I don't do this now. Galileo knew about this and he let it lie? Galileo knew years ago and he sat on it like a bump on a log, like a frightened old man. I am telling them the truth. Why should they reject the truth? All they have to do is look through the telescope and know that I am right. And the church?

(Hides his shaking hand)

I must tell what I know. This is it. I am tired of being a speck on the wall of this university. A poorly paid, overworked speck of nothing—of dust and dirt—and now I have the power to change the world.

(Regains control and looks at THE STUDENT)

I will publish only a small number of copies. Five hundred or so. In Latin. It's only a book. One book. Why should the church have a problem with one book? I know what I know. I know what I see. I know that I am the one who is right.

SCENE SEVEN

*(Lights change. GALILEO is packing for Florence.
He is covering the telescope with the cloth.)*

Marina, we used to lie on the roof and watch the sky at night. Pointing out the light slashing across the sky. Marvelling at the beauty of the moon. We drank wine, balancing the cup on your swollen belly. Listening to the girls try and sing themselves to sleep, and everything seemed just right. Why do I only miss you sometimes, Marina? Why can't I miss you every hour of my life? I would love to show you these stars, Marina, up close. Through my window, up and far beyond. I know you never liked my works, but still you would love the stars.

*(Noticing STUDENT and continues to look through books,
and tearing and piling papers)*

I didn't hear you come in. You're getting better. My daughters are outside? *(Puts on jacket)* Excellent. Excellent. Yes, I am taking them with me. The boy can stay with Marina for a few more years, but I must see about that convent for the girls. No more dowries; my sisters have cured that in me ... I am not teaching today. I am not teaching again ever. I am done with this university. Bye-bye. My debts are paid; I am a free man, and you are on your own.

(Picks up the carafe)

A toast. We must have a toast to the Chief Mathematician and Philosopher, to the Grand Duke of Tuscany. I am going to Florence! *(Drinks and points to books at the end of the table)* Pass me those books, will you? What? You're shocked? You knew nothing about it? No one knew. I don't open my big mouth all the time. I know, I know; it's not even been a year since the top dog rewarded me with such wonderful prizes. Venice is nothing, not even a stepping stone. Don't look at me like that. Are you going to pass me the books or not? Not. *(Gets them himself)* Fine.

I know people are talking. But people always talk. If it wasn't about me then they would find someone else to talk about. I love being the topic of conversation. *(Speaking loudly)* Besides, the ones with the loudest voices always have the smallest minds. As soon as I'm packed, I will vacate this miserable memory.

(He puts his cape on and looks around.)

I have spent eighteen years here. You gather so many things. I can't take it all with me. I have something for you. I want to leave you something. I know you won't look through the telescope, so see that Marina gets it, will you? She won't look up, but she likes to spy on her neighbours. I want you to have the pendulum. I want you to have it. Use it when you study. It's very soothing.

(Lets the pendulum go)

Can't you even be a little happy for me? I won. No matter what the grumblers might have said, the church did not string me up. The church did not ban my book. Ah, I have only opened the door a crack. There is so much more to say. And now who can stop me with the Duke by my side? *(Goes to the table and picks up a pile of books and the carafe)*

I have enlarged the scope of science a hundred and a thousand times; why should I stop there? I have taken a man's beliefs and made them real. Don't you believe in anything? Wait. You still owe me for a lesson. On the table there. Who will you study with? Hmmm. It will never be the same. You see! I have corrupted you. There is no turning back. This is the beginning.

(The lights fade slowly to back light. GALILEO is returning to his "prison" from the beginning of the play. He removes his cloak and jacket. He fondly caresses the pendulum and stands in the same spot as at the beginning of the play.)

(Lights fade to black)

Lindsay Price is a Canadian playwright and member of the Playwrights Union of Canada. She is involved in Theatrefolk, a stage company in Toronto that specializes in theatre in education. She is currently teaching a playwriting course on the Internet to high school students.

I. *Response*

a. Examine Galileo's first five lines. What do they reveal about his personality? Are these lines effective in capturing the audience's interest? Explain.

b. Imagine that you are Galileo's student. What do you think Galileo would be like as a teacher? Explain.

c. At one point in the play, Galileo says, "Aristotle says, Aristotle says. The time for Aristotle is past ..." Who is Aristotle? Why would Galileo have negative thoughts about Aristotle? If necessary, conduct research to answer these questions fully.

2. *Drama* *Adding Lines* A number of times in the script, the student says something to Galileo but his lines are not presented in the usual script form. Why do you think Price chose to do this? Choose three such incidents and write some lines for the student that would match how Galileo responds. Consider how both characters might move around or gesture during this scene. Present this revised script to a small group and discuss the effectiveness of the added lines.

> PERFORMANCE TIP When performing before an audience, it is important to remain comfortable and balanced while moving and to gesture in a natural way. Your posture is also revealing—are you proudly standing straight, or are you slumped in defeat? Mime several everyday activities to check your movement, posture, and balance. Relaxation exercises will also help you prepare your body for the presentation of a scene.

3. *Research and Inquiry* From this play, what do you learn about Galileo and his accomplishments? Research Galileo further. Does the author, Lindsay Price, exhibit any bias in what she reveals or conceals? Explain. How is this portrayal of Galileo affected by its having been created by a woman living in the twenty-first century?

Theme Connections

- *"When I Heard the Learn'd Astronomer,"* a poem about the study of astronomy not being as meaningful as gazing at the stars, Vol. I, p. 231
- *"Thoughts on Education,"* an essay about the importance of seeking and distributing knowledge, Vol. II, p. 68
- *"Living Like Weasels,"* an essay about living a simple, unexamined life, Vol. II, p. 106
- *"Media Diet: Jane Goodall,"* an interview that explores the life and work of a scientist, Vol. II, p. 139

A monologue gives an actor the chance to deliver thought-provoking or moving lines while enjoying the audience's complete attention. Think of some examples of outstanding monologues you have heard in plays or movies. What made them effective? How did these monologues move or affect you?

What Will Your Verse Be?

Monologue by Tom Schulman
from Touchstone Pictures' Feature *Dead Poets Society*

MR. KEATING: Now, my class, you will learn to think for yourselves again. You will learn to savor words and language. No matter what anybody tells you, words and ideas <u>can</u> change the world. Now, I see that look in Mr. Pitts' eye like... like nineteenth-century literature has nothing to do with going to business school or medical school. Right? Maybe. Mr. Hopkins, you may agree with him, thinking, "Yes. We should simply study our Mr. Pritchard[1] and learn our rhyme and meter and go quietly about the business of achieving other ambitions." I have a secret for you. Huddle up. HUDDLE UP! We don't read and write poetry because it's cute. We read and write poetry because we are members of the human race. And the human race is filled with passion. Now medicine, law, business, engineering, these are noble pursuits, and necessary to sustain life. But poetry, beauty, romance, love...these are what we stay alive for. To quote from Whitman, "O me, O life of the questions of these recurring. Of the endless trains of the faithless of cities filled with the foolish. What good amid these, O me, O life?" Answer: "That you are here. That life exists and identity. That the powerful play goes on and you may contribute a verse. That the powerful play goes on and you may contribute a verse." What will your verse be?

---

[1] **Mr. Pritchard:** The author of the book they are studying.

Tom Schulman is a Hollywood screenwriter who won the Best Original Screenplay Oscar for *Dead Poets Society*. He based the character of Mr. Keating on one of his favourite English professors.

1. *Response*

a. Based on this speech, how would you describe Mr. Keating as a teacher? Do you think he would be a good teacher? Explain.

b. Mr. Keating quotes Walt Whitman. Who is Whitman and why do you think Keating quotes him?

c. Answer Keating's final question: "What will your verse be?"

2. *Drama* *Presenting Monologues*

Prepare a presentation of this monologue or another of your choice. As you plan your performance, remember that monologues consist of one actor communicating strong feelings or ideas to an audience. Ask your audience to record their thoughts on your performance. With your audience, discuss how you might improve your performance.

PERFORMANCE TIP Pronunciation, articulation, and the projection of your voice are all especially important in presenting a monologue. You may find it helpful to think of your voice as something tangible, like a ball, that you are throwing to an audience, using the power of your lungs, diaphragm, and voice. Remember that volume is an important part of projection, but it is just as important to be able to project a whisper as a shout. Practise projecting a whisper across a crowded room.

3. *Focus on Context*

You have just read a monologue that is part of a much larger movie. Discuss how your response to the monologue, in reading it out of context, might vary from your response to it if you watched the whole movie. What advantages and disadvantages are there in reading part of a movie?

4. *Film Study*

Dead Poets Society remains a popular movie many years after its release. Watch Robin Williams delivering this monologue, or watch the whole movie and comment on its popularity. Who is the movie's target audience? How might the target audience respond to this monologue? To the whole movie?

Glossary

In the **active voice**, the subject of a sentence does the action. For example, *The dog ran into the street*. Use the active voice when possible. It uses fewer words and is more precise than the passive voice. See **passive voice**.

An **allegory** is a simple story, such as a fable or parable, whose major purpose is to teach a moral lesson. An allegory can always be read on two levels—one literal, the other symbolic. The underlying meaning can be parallel to, but different from, the surface meaning.

Alliteration is a repetition of the same first sound in a group of words or line of poetry. For example, *The sun sank slowly*.

An **allusion**, in a literary work, is a reference to another literary work, or a person, place, event, or object from history, literature, or mythology. For example, *If you take the last piece of pie, you can expect WW II all over again*.

An **analogy** is the illustration of one idea or concept by using a similar idea or concept. An analogy can be phrased as a simile.

The **antagonist** of a narrative or dramatic work is the primary person in opposition to the hero or **protagonist**.

Apposition is the relation of two parts of a sentence when the one is added as an explanation to the other. For example, in *Mr. Brown, our teacher, is on vacation, Mr. Brown* and *teacher* are in apposition.

An **archetype** is a theme, symbol, character, or setting that can be found throughout literature, folklore, and media so often that it comes to reflect some universal human character or experience. For example, *Robin Hood* is an archetypal hero.

Assonance (also known as *vowel rhyme*) is the repetition of similar or identical vowel sounds within the words of a poem or other writing. For example, *mellow wedding bells*.

Bias is the author's inclination or preference toward one stance that makes it difficult or impossible to judge something fairly. For example, *a Sylvester Stallone fan may be unable to write an objective or balanced review of Stallone's work*.

A **burlesque** is a literary or dramatic composition in which a serious subject is treated ridiculously or with mock seriousness.

A **cacophony** is a harsh or clashing combination of words, often caused deliberately for effect. For example, finger of a *birth-strangled* babe.

A **caesura** is a pause in a line of verse, generally agreeing with a pause required by the sense. For example, *England — how I long for thee!*

Climax See **plot**.

Closure occurs when a story ends without ambiguity. The main crises and/or conflicts are neatly wrapped up, and the reader has a sense that the story is truly finished. In an *open-ended story,* the reader is uncertain about what might happen next; several outcomes are possible.

Codes and **conventions** refer to the different ways in which each media product typically conveys meaning to audiences. For example, we expect certain kinds of movies to open with certain conventions, such as an action movie opening with lots of action, special effects, and maybe a chase scene.

Consonance is the repetition of similar or identical consonants in words whose vowels differ. For example, *gripe, grape, grope.*

Diction refers to the way an author expresses ideas in words. Good diction includes grammatical correctness, skill in the choice of effective words, and a wide vocabulary.

A **dynamic character** is one who undergoes a significant and permanent change in personality or beliefs.

Enjambment occurs when there is no strong punctuation at the end of a line of poetry, allowing a phrase or sentence to carry through that line and into the next without a pause. For example,

> *Let me not to the marriage of true minds*
> *Admit impediments. Love is not love*
> —Shakespeare

A **eulogy** is a tribute to someone who has just died and is often delivered as a speech at a funeral.

A **fact sheet** presents key information about a particular topic, issue, or organization. It provides concise answers to basic questions. Some fact sheets are written in point form, others in full sentences.

Figurative language uses words to paint a picture, draw an interesting comparison, or create a poetic effect. **Literal language** says what it means directly. Language can be figurative or literal.

See the **Film Study Glossary** on page 151 for glossary items related to movies.

Free-verse poetry is written without using regular rhyme or rhythm. Images, spacing, punctuation, and the rhythms of ordinary language are used to create a free-verse poem.

Foreshadowing is a plot technique in which a writer plants clues or subtle indications about events that will happen later in the narrative.

Imagery is the pictures or impressions that writers create in the minds of their readers. To create these pictures, they use descriptive techniques such as figures of speech (simile, metaphor, personification, oxymoron), onomatopoeia, alliteration, and allusions.

Irony occurs when a statement or situation means something different from (or even the opposite of) what is expected. Another type of irony is called **dramatic irony**. It occurs in plays when the audience knows something that the characters do not.

Interjections are words—such as *oh, wow, ha, mmm*—that show emotion, often without any grammatical connection to other parts of the sentence.

Juxtaposition is the intentional placement of dissimilar words or ideas side by side for a particular purpose—to emphasize contrasting ideas, for example.

A **literary essay** presents an interpretation or explores some aspect of one or more works of literature.

Loaded language is language that is intentionally chosen to evoke a strong response in a reader—usually an emotional response. It is also language that is highly connotative, conjuring in the listener much more than its literal meaning.

A **loaded word** is a word intentionally chosen to evoke a strong response in a reader—usually an emotional response.

A **logo** is an identifying symbol used as a trademark in advertising.

Mass media is any method by which a message is communicated to a large audience at the same time—*movies, radio, TV, books, magazines, the Internet*.

A **media text** is any media product—*movie, radio show, CD, TV program,* et cetera—that is selected for critical examination.

A **metaphor** is a comparison of two things that are not alike. The comparison suggests that they do share a common quality: *His words were a knife to my heart.*

An **oxymoron** is a figure of speech that is a combination of contradictory words. One of the most common examples of an oxymoron is *jumbo shrimp.*

Parallelism is the intentional use of identical or similar grammatical structure within one sentence or in two or more sentences. For example, *She likes dancing, singing, and jogging.*

Parallel structure is the repeated use of the same phrase or sentence, or the repeated use of a similar sentence structure. Parallel structure can be used to create balance or place emphasis on certain lines.

In the **passive voice**, the subject of the verb receives the action: *The fire was extinguished.* See **Active Voice**.

The **persona** is the voice or character that represents the narrator in a literary work. A persona is often described as a mask an author deliberately puts on in order to narrate a particular story or poem.

Personification occurs when objects, ideas, or animals are given human qualities: *The sun smiled down on me.*

Plot refers to the events in a story. Plot usually has five elements: exposition, rising action, climax, falling action, and resolution.
- The **exposition** or introduction sets up the story by introducing the main characters, the setting, and the problem to be solved.
- The **rising action** is the main part of the story where the full problem develops. A number of events is involved that will lead to the climax.
- The **climax** is the highest point in the story where something decisive occurs.
- The **falling action** follows the climax. It contains the events that bring the story to its conclusion.
- The **resolution** or denouement is the end of the story and traces the final outcome of the central conflict.

A **point of view** is the vantage point from which the author tells a story. The four most common points of view are *first person* (I, me), *omniscient* (all seeing), *limited omniscient* (all seeing from the viewpoint of a group of characters), and *objective* (he, she, they, it).

A **précis** is a concise summary of a text. It is written in full sentences, but contains only the most important information.

A **process analysis** shows how something is done. It gives information about a process, usually in the same order as the process itself.

A **proverb** is a short saying that expresses a basic truth or useful principle. For example, *Look before you leap.*

Racist language is any language that refers to a particular cultural group or ethnic group in insulting terms, but racism also exists in more subtle forms. To avoid even subtle racism, remember the following:

- Mention a person's race only if it is relevant to the context. If a person's race or ethnic origin is relevant, be specific:
  Irrelevant/Vague: *Dago is African.*
  Relevant/Less Vague: *Dago is proud of her Nigerian heritage.*
- Avoid making generalizations about any racial or cultural group:
  Stereotype: *The Welsh are great singers.*
  Better: *The Welsh have a long tradition of singing.*

Register refers to the level of formality of language. Language can be characterized according to the social context for which it is appropriate. For example, language with a colloquial register might contain slang expressions and unconventional grammar.

Resolution See **plot.**

A **rhetorical question** is one that is asked for effect, and that does not invite a reply. The purpose of a rhetorical question is to introduce a topic or to focus the reader on a concern. For example, *How do I love thee? Let me count the ways*.

Rhythm is the arrangement of beats in a line of poetry. The beat is created by the accented and unaccented syllables in the words used in each line.

A **satire** is a work that criticizes something—for example, *a person, a characteristic, an institution, or a government*—by depicting it in a humorous,
sarcastic, or scornful way.

Sexist language is language that degrades or unnecessarily excludes either women or men. It is best to avoid generalizing about males and females unless the claims are based on scientific facts. To avoid sexist language, remember the following:
- Whenever possible, replace words such as *fireman, policeman,* and *man-made* with non-sexist alternatives such as *firefighter, police officer,* and *fabricated*.
- Avoid using the masculine pronouns *he, him,* or *his* to refer to both men and women.
  Sexist: A doctor must always be polite to his patients.
  Non-sexist: Doctors must always be polite to their patients. **OR**
                A Doctor must always be polite to his/her patients.

A **stereotype** is an oversimplified picture, usually of a group of people, giving them all a set of characteristics, without consideration for individual differences. For example, *the nerd scientist, the rebellious teenager, and the bratty younger brother* are all stereotypes.

Style is the overall texture of a piece of writing; the particular way in which the ideas are expressed. Style is made up of many elements including diction, figurative language, sentences, and tone.

Suspense is a feeling of tension, anxiety, or excitement resulting from uncertainty. An author creates suspense to keep readers interested.

A **symbol** is something that represents something else—for example, *the lion can be a symbol of courage.*

The **symbolic meaning** of a work is developed through the symbols that the author includes.

A **synopsis** provides an overview or summary of a longer work.

A **theme** is a central thesis or idea that is expressed directly or indirectly in a literary work.

The **thesis** of an essay is the main idea or argument that the author is attempting to prove.

Tone is the implied attitude of the writer toward the subject or the audience. Tone differs from mood, which describes the emotional feeling of the work more generally. The tone of a piece of work can be described, for example, as *angry, satiric, joyful,* or *serious*.

Transition words—such as *however, in conclusion,* and *on the other hand*—indicate relationships between ideas. Writers use them to suggest links between sentences or paragraphs.

A **unifying device** connects different parts of a narrative. It can be a metaphor, a symbol, an image, a character, or even an important word or phrase.

Verbals look like verbs but function as other parts of speech. There are three kinds of verbals: infinitives, participles, and gerunds. An infinitive can function as a noun, adjective, or adverb, and takes the form of a verb preceded by "to": *I'll continue to hope for good weather.* A participle functions as an adjective and takes the form of a verb + "ing" (present participle) or "ed" (past participle): *I am hoping for good weather. I hoped for good weather.* A gerund functions as a noun and takes the form of a verb + "ing": *Hoping is something I do all the time.*

Index of Titles and Authors

Acknowledgments

Every reasonable effort has been made to trace ownership of copyrighted material. Information that would enable the publisher to correct any reference or credit in future editions would be appreciated.

12 "What I've Learned from Writing" © Shauna Singh Baldwin. Reprinted by permission of the author. 29 "Art History" by Doreen Jensen from *Give Back: First Nations Perspectives on Cultural Practice: Essays*, Gallerie: Women Artists' Monographs, Issue 11 (Vancouver, BC: Gallerie Publications, 1992). Reprinted with permission of the author. 40 "Making Poetry Pay" from *I Wonder as I Wander* by Langston Hughes. © 1956 by Langston Hughes. Copyright renewed © 1984 by George Houston Bass. Reprinted by permission of Hill and Wang, a division of Farrar, Straus and Giroux, LLC. 45 "A New Perspective" by Janice Fein. Reprinted by permission of *Fresh Ink*, The University of Akron, Ohio. 48 "Only Daughter" by Sandra Cisneros © 1990 by Sandra Cisneros. First published in *Glamour*, November 1990. Reprinted by permission of Susan Bergholz Literary Services, New York. All rights reserved. 52 "My Old Newcastle" by David Adams Richards. Reprinted by permission of the author. 62 "Reviving Fridamania" by Chris Kraul from *The Los Angeles Times*, April 24, 2001. Reprinted by permission of The Los Angeles Times Syndicate. 65 "The Akward Sublime" by Margaret Atwood. © Margaret Atwood. Used by permission of the author. 76 "Rink Rage" by James Deacon from *Maclean's Magazine*, March 26, 2001. Reprinted with permission from *Maclean's Magazine*. 86 "Blue Gold" from *If the Gods Had Meant for Us to Vote They Would Have Given Us Candidates* by Jim Hightower © 2000 by Jim Hightower. Reprinted by permission of HarperCollins Publishers Inc. 101 "Night Spirits" by Candace Savage. First published in *Canadian Geographic* in March/April 2001. Reprinted by permission of the author. 106 "Living Like Weasels" from *Teaching a Stone to Talk: Expeditions and Encounters* by Annie Dillard © 1982 by Annie Dillard. Reprinted by permission of HarperCollins Publishers Inc. 112 "Follows Family Stages a Reunion" by Harry Currie from *The K-W Record*, June 2001. Reprinted with permission of The Record, Waterloo, Ontario. 120 "The Making of *Sense and Sensibility*" Diaries © 1985 by Emma Thompson. All rights reserved. Material reprinted from *The Sense and Sensibility Screenplay & Diaries* by Emma Thompson. Used by permission of Newmarket Press. 125 "Interview With Artist George Littlechild" by Kamala Todd. Reprinted by permission of Kamala Todd and Jeffery Beer. 133 "The Weekly" by Catherine Dubé. Reprinted by permission of the author. 136 "The Accidental Citizen" from *The World We Want: Virtue, and the Good Citizen* by Mark Kingwell © 2000 by Mark Kingwell. Reprinted with permission of Penguin Books Canada Ltd. 139 "Media Diet: Jane Goodall" by Karen Olsen from Sept./Oct. 2000 issue of Utne Reader. Reprinted with permission from Utne Reader. 144 "A Century of Cinema" © 1997 by Susan Sontag. Originally published in *Parnassus: Poetry in Review*. Reprinted with the permission of The Wylie Agency, Inc. 152 "The Movie I'd Like to See" by Geoff Pevere from *The Toronto Star*, August 31, 2001. Reprinted with permission of The Toronto Star Syndicate. 156 "Heroes and Holy Innocents" by Keith Wolfe. Reprinted with permission from *Utne Reader*, August 17, 2001. 163 "Peace a Hard Sell to Skeptical Youth" by David Beers from *The Vancouver Sun*, February 10, 2001. Reprinted by permission of the author. 170 "Translate This!" by Adrian Cooper from *New Internationalist* #333, April 2001. Reprinted by permission of the New Internationalist. 174 "Duel" from *Three Bits of Fry and Laurie* by Stephen Fry and Hugh Laurie. Reprinted by permission of David Higham Associates. 179 "That's Extraordinary!" by Diana Raznovich from *Airborne: Radio Plays by Women*. Reprinted by permission from Blizzard Publishing. 199 "The Dashwoods' Fate Is Decided" by Emma Thompson. Material reprinted from *The Sense and Sensibility Screenplay and Diaries*. Screenplay © The Columbia Pictures Industries Inc. All rights reserved. Used by permission of Newmarket Press. 218 "Introducing Cyrano" from *Cyrano de Bergerac* by Edward Rostand, translated by Lowell Bair, © 1972 by Lowell Bair. Used by permission of Dutton Signet, a division of Penguin Putnam Inc. 224 "Venus Sucked In" by Anne Chislett from *Airborne: Radio Plays by Women*. Reprinted by permission from Blizzard Publishing. 245 "Tom King's Traditional Aboriginal Decorating Tips" © Tom King. Reprinted by permission of the author. 248 "Galileo: The Starry Messenger" by Lindsay Price. Reprinted by permission of the author. 270 "What Will Your Verse Be? excerpts from the script based on Touchstone Pictures' copyrighted feature film *Dead Poets Society* are used by permission from Disney Enterprises, Inc.

Visual Credits
11 C. Brown/Image Bank/Getty Images. 15 Brandtner and Staedeli/Stone/Getty Images. 32 Vickie Jensen. 34 (left) *Mountains and Lake* by Lawren S. Harris (1929)/oil on canvas/ McMichael Canadian Art Collection/Gift of Mr. R.A. Laidlaw/Reproduced with permission of